C000176193

Criminology and Political Theory

Criminology and Political Theory

Anthony Amatrudo

Los Angeles | London | New Delhi
Singapore | Washington DC

© Anthony Amatrudo 2009

First edition published 2009

Apart from any fair dealing for the purposes of research
or private study, or criticism or review, as permitted
under the Copyright, Designs and Patents Act, 1988, this
publication may be reproduced, stored or transmitted in
any form, or by any means, only with the prior permission
in writing of the publishers, or in the case of reprographic
reproduction, in accordance with the terms of licences
issued by the Copyright Licensing Agency. Enquiries
concerning reproduction outside those terms should be
sent to the publishers.

SAGE Publications Ltd
1 Oliver's Yard
55 City Road
London EC1Y 1SP

SAGE Publications Inc.
2455 Teller Road
Thousand Oaks, California 91320

SAGE Publications India Pvt Ltd
B 1/I 1 Mohan Cooperative Industrial Area
Mathura Road
New Delhi 110 044

SAGE Publications Asia-Pacific Pte Ltd
33 Pekin Street #02-01
Far East Square
Singapore 048763

Library of Congress Control Number 2008925136

British Library Cataloguing in Publication data

A catalogue record for this book is available from
the British Library

ISBN 978-1-4129-3049-9
ISBN 978-1-4129-3050-5 (pbk)

Typeset by C&M Digitals (P) Ltd., Chennai, India
Printed in India at Replika Press Pvt Ltd
Printed on paper from sustainable resources

For John Charvet

CONTENTS

ACKNOWLEDGEMENTS

First, I would like to thank Dr Marianna Hordos for many years of friendship, dramas, intellectual sword fencing, laughter and good times in Budapest, London and elsewhere. Prof. Colin Sumner is a great writer, teacher, controversialist, convenor of seminars and raconteur, and he will always rank first in my list of criminological influences. I shall never forget attending a seminar Colin convened on the use of cutlery, and its relevance to the way we ordinarily suppress violence in our daily lives. It ranged effortlessly across academic disciplines, such as Jurisprudence, Political and Social Theory, Anthropology and Ethics – avant-garde, sublime. Prof. Robert Fine, who examined my thesis at the LSE, remains a model of clarity and humane exegesis. Prof. Robert Hancke clarified my thinking on Political Economy and was great company at the CEU. Dr Bjorn Weiler has been a good friend, and occasional critic, for a decade and a half: his concern for history has certainly influenced my approach. I am grateful to Leslie Blake for various formal dinners and cut-and-thrust curries in, or around, Lincoln's Inn. Another lawyer, Matthew Smith, I met when we were both keen rugby-playing students at Cambridge University and today I benefit from his jobbing barrister's take on the law and the criminal justice system. Dr Magnus Ryan, from his ivory tower at All Souls College, has never been anything less than a supportive friend and our wide-ranging conversations, over beers, have certainly influenced the course of my thinking. I enjoyed the nursery food, ale and Bohemian company provided by the Chelsea Arts Club, whenever Dave Ryan signed me in, where the subject of crime always got a good airing. At the University of Sunderland I have the pleasure of teaching some excellent students and benefit from working with some wonderfully supportive colleagues. I am indebted to the Master and Fellows of St Edmund's College, Cambridge for electing me to a visiting research position, which assisted me in the writing of this book. The lavish hospitality and warm collegiality of the Political Science Department at the Central European University in Budapest, while I was a Visiting Fellow there, was an invaluable intellectual fillip. The Wissenschaftszentrum Berlin für Sozialforschung generously allowed me to use their library and facilities. The librarians at the Institute of Criminology in Cambridge, LSE, and the IALS have been enormously helpful to me. Caroline Porter has been a wonderful editor at Sage and I owe her a great deal for so much excellent advice and support. For various kindnesses, inspiration and help, over the years, I have to thank: Prof. Rodney Barker; Prof. Lisa Bernstein; Blackheath Rugby Club; Deborah Bowen; Richard Buckwalter; Jake and Dinos Chapman;

Dr Tom Cockcroft; Lucy Crawford; Vanessa Dietzl; Terence Dowle; Prof. Cecile Fabre; Nicole Fabre; Jan Farndale; Prof. Michael Freeman; Dr Matteo Fumagalli; Dr Loraine Gelsthorpe; Dr Volker Grundies; Ulrike Haas; Claudia Haupt; Dr Keith Hayward; Prof. David Held; Dr Felicia Herrschaft; Tabitha Howard; Valeska Huber; Waldemar Januszczak; Kate Jones; Elene Khatseva; Magdalena Krajewska; Sir Ivan Lawrence QC; Dr Ori Lev; Yana Loukiantseva; Prof. Steven Lukes FBA; Dr Tim Megarry; Rev. Dr Anthony Meredith SJ; Prof. Brendan O'Leary; Mike Presdee; Prof. Fred Rosen; Miss Jamie Rubenstein; Dr Alessandra Sarquis; Monika Schroeder; Barry Sheerman MP; Dr Carsten Sneider; Camilla Soar; Prof. George Steiner FBA; Ligia Teixeira; Dr David Thomas QC; Prof. Steve Uglow; Prof. Andrew von Hirsch and Dr John White. My greatest intellectual debts, however, are to Prof. John Charvet. As a scholar, and as a man, John is without peer in my opinion.

1

THE NATURE OF THE STATE

Political power is, of course, always coercive power backed by the state's machinery for enforcing its laws. But in a constitutional regime political power is also power of equal citizens as a collective body: it is regularly imposed on citizens as individuals, some of whom may not accept the reasons widely believed to justify the general structure of political authority (the constitution); or when they do accept that structure, they may not regard as well grounded many of the laws enacted by the legislature to which they are subject.

John Rawls, 2001[1]

Introduction

The nature of the state is a topic which divides criminologists. There are those who see it as a neutral instrument which upholds civic order or which supports citizens through a system of benefits and support and there are those who see the state as either having interests of its own or advancing the interests of a specific class of persons, in whose interests it governs. The idea of justice as fairness rests upon the idea that the state is a neutral entity and it is fair to say that the liberal tradition within Criminology has tended either to neglect the state or to rely, wholesale, upon liberal political theorists, such as John Rawls and his conception of 'social cooperation among equals for mutual advantage'.[2] The Marxist and Feminist traditions within Criminology have a far richer body of writing about the state and more generally about state control and social regulation. This chapter will set out the main ideas used in contemporary Criminology, either explicitly or implicitly, concerning the nature of the state.

The State

The state is, arguably, the most contested term in political theory and it may refer to a great many different things, such as a philosophical or ideological category, an institution, a territorial power or a functional organising principle. It is a topic covered extensively in the writings of political philosophers since classical times, and certainly Plato, Aquinas, Machiavelli, Hobbes, Locke and Marx are only a few of the writers who have tackled the subject of the state. In Criminology different traditions have grown up which attribute varying motivations to the state. In order to make progress, let us outline four basic and interrelated features of a state. First, the state must have a working political organisational structure. In other words, it must have a set of institutions which allow it to operate, such as the courts, a civil service and a police force. Secondly, for a state to be a working entity it has to persist in time and space, i.e. it must control a set territory and survive changes in its basic organisation, as would be the case if an election altered the government. Thirdly, it must be able to support a single political form of public order and therefore it must have agency. It must be sovereign and be able to claim a monopoly of political authority, law-making and power, and it must be autonomous. Fourthly, but closely linked to the idea of the state as a single political form of public order, it must have the allegiance of its members (citizens, subjects), who are subject to its laws and who have an obligation to obey it. The political theorist John Charvet has noted that: 'For Locke, as well as for Hobbes and Rousseau, entry into political society from the state of nature is possible only if individuals surrender their natural right of private judgement to the public judgement of the community or its agent.'[3]

The two most important features for criminologists are the first and third features. The first feature, that the state is a particular form of political organisation, is the dominant notion at work in contemporary Criminology. It is the view of Karl Marx, who wrote in *The German Ideology* that: 'Through the emancipation of private property from the community, the State has become a separate entity, beside and outside civil society; but it is nothing more than the form of organisation which the bourgeois necessarily adopts both for internal and external purposes, for mutual guarantee of their property and interests.'[4] In contemporary legal theory, Joseph Raz has also argued that the state is a form of political organisation, but he has usefully delineated the state from law and government: 'The state … is the political organisation of a society, its government, the agent through which it acts, and the law, the vehicle through which much of its power is exercised.'[5] Raz has further argued that: 'A state is the political organisation of a society, it is a subsystem of a more comprehensive social system.'[6] This position echoes John Rawls' idea, expressed in *Political Liberalism*, that: 'a society's main political, social, and economic institutions, and how they fit together into one unified system of social cooperation from one generation to the next'.[7] It should be noted here that the political and social basis of the state are not very clearly delineated.[8]

The third feature, that the state is a political form of public order with a monopoly of political authority, law-making and power, was underscored by Thomas Hobbes and John Locke, who defined the state as that form of political power which has the sole right to make laws and to punish those who fail to follow them, and it has obvious connections to the study of crime. Hobbes, in the *Leviathan*, wrote: 'I Authorise and give up my Right of Government myselfe, to this Man, or his Assembly of men, on this condition, that thou give up thy Right to him, and Authority all his Actions in like manner.'[9] Hobbes saw the state as being that thing which preserves men from the state of nature. Hobbes' conception is set out in the *Leviathan*, where he writes: 'The state of nature is simply the condition of men without a sovereign power to compel order. Just as we may never have a perfect vacuum, perhaps we can never have a situation where there are no vestiges of the restraints that sovereignty provides, but inasmuch as sovereignty is absent, to that extent men will begin to exhibit behaviour typical of the state of nature.'[10] In Hobbes, we get the idea that it is not natural for men and women to subordinate themselves for the greater good. Rather, we are presented with a view that social community, and freedom from the state of nature, can only be established through the exercise of political power. Our human society is the outcome of agreements and conventions that men and women make themselves.[11] John Locke, following Hobbes, saw the state as that political institution which maintains order. Locke details his notion of the main function of a state in his description of the Law of Nature: 'For the Law of Nature would, as other Laws that concern men in this world, be in vain, if there were no body that in the state of nature, had a power to execute the Law and thereby preserve the innocent and restrain offenders.'[12] In this passage we note both his understanding that all law requires enforcement and concern for deterrence in punishment.[13] In contemporary liberal political theory, both Charvet and Raz follow the tradition of understanding the state as that thing that maintains law and order and thereby allows persons to live their lives unhindered by the dangers inherent in a state of nature; indeed, it is the standard view.[14] It is important to note that in liberal theory the state is the outcome of a voluntary agreement made by individuals who realise that only a social contract will save them from the dangers of the state of nature. The liberal state is always a protective neutral entity which represents all the people fairly for the common good of all. This conception of a *neutral* state that safeguards its citizens equally from the state of nature is what Marxism and Feminism take issue with.

Marxism and the State

The classic statement within Marxist Criminology on the state, as that thing which frames laws which uphold sectional class interests, was given us by Bill Chambliss when he wrote: '... without doubt the single most important force behind criminal law creation is doubtless the economic interest and political power of those social classes which either (1) own or control the resources of the society, or (2) occupy positions of authority in state bureaucracies'.[15] Marx himself gave two different accounts of the state. The account Marx gives in his Introduction to *Critique of Hegel's Philosophy of Right* is an unfinished work and is a critique of Hegel, rather than a systematic view of his own thinking. The first view Marx outlined for himself was given in the 1848 *The Communist Manifesto*, where he wrote: '...executive of the modern State is but a committee for managing the affairs of the whole bourgeoisie'.[16] In *The Communist Manifesto*, the state simply coordinates the interests of dominant class. We are presented with a straightforward binary opposition between the bourgeoisie and the proletariat. However, Marx also advanced a second view, notably in two other works, the *Class Struggles in France*, written in 1850, and *The Eighteenth Brumaire of Louis Bonaparte*, written in 1852. In these works, he outlines a plurality of classes and details how the state is far more than just a simple coordinator of the interests of the dominant class. Marx also argued, in this second view, that the state itself has some autonomy. This second view of the state has become the dominant view in contemporary Marxist scholarship and Carnoy has written that: 'The State is not regarded simply as an instrument of the ruling class. ... Who rules the State is an important issue, but few, if any, current writers claim that the ruling class controls the State directly.'[17] However, we must not lose sight of the fact that Marx did not furnish a systematic theory of the state and his ideas are often inconsistent or not fully formed, though this is in part due to the fact that he was far more concerned with Political Economy, rather than Political Theory.[18] Marx also tends to underplay the ability of individuals to either act or calculate independently of their economic situation. Because Marx failed to provide a thoroughgoing or clear conception of the state, his followers have had to interpret his writings and this has spawned a variety of latter-day Marxist theories.[19] Nevertheless, the Marxist state is always essentially economic in its character. As Pashukanis said of legal forms, they 'form a united whole with the material relations of which they are the expression'.[20] This position is found in Marx's *Preface to a Critique of Political Economy*:

> My investigations led to the result that legal relations as well as forms of state are to be grasped neither from themselves nor from the so-called general development of the human mind, but rather have their roots in the material conditions of life. ... The sum total of these relations of production constitutes the economic structures of society, the real foundation, on which rises a legal and political superstructure. ... The mode of production of material life conditions the social, political and intellectual life process in general. It is not the consciousness of men that determines their being, but on the contrary, their social being determines their consciousness.[21]

Among contemporary Marxist criminologists Dario Melossi has, perhaps, done most to uncover the original intention of Marx's writing on the state and punishment, though Marx's writings resist a *definitive* definition.[22] Nonetheless, it is possible to argue that there are two main schools within Marxist writing on law, punishment and the state. On the one hand, Melossi and Rusche and Kirchheimer stress the first view given in *The Communist Manifesto* and play up the economic elements in Marx's analysis and the role of state coordination.[23] On the other hand, Hall, Hay, Ignatieff and Sumner tend to favour the second view given in *The Eighteenth Brumaire of Louis Bonaparte* and understand the state as having a deal of autonomy.[24] Hall, Hay, Ignatieff and Sumner all stress the importance of ideology and broader issues of legitimacy. Hay, for example, reasoned that the criminal justice system in eighteenth-century England was essentially ideological in nature, rather than straightforwardly judicial. The proliferation of offences for which people could be executed was, he argued, part of an elaborate system of execution and mercy. The deeper point Hay makes is that state punishment was secondary to its ideological function, which was the preservation of the property rights of a tiny minority of the population. State punishment was actually more concerned with ensuring a compliant citizenry than giving criminals their deserved sentences. Hay wrote: 'Loyalties do not grow simply in complex societies – they are twisted, invoked and often consciously created.'[25]

Gramsci

Of all Marxist theorists, Antonio Gramsci has arguably had the greatest influence upon Criminology, notably through the work of Stuart Hall and Colin Sumner. Gramsci, above all else, wanted to stress human subjectivity in his writing. Gramsci rejected the economic determinism of *The Communist Manifesto* and the *Preface to a Critique of Political Economy* in favour of a type of Marxist theorising which gave primacy to the autonomy of the state and which had an enlarged role for ideology in ordering civil society. Prior to Gramsci, Marxists had, typically, followed Marx and Engel's *German Ideology* in arguing that the capitalist class were, in the same instance, the dominant intellectual class.[26] Gramsci's novelty was to give a much greater weight to the centrality of the ideological superstructures and the autonomy of the state than had Marx, and he advanced a case for the role of consent in running civil society, rather than the brute force of the state. Gramsci maintained that human consciousness is independent and that political life can be separated from the economic base, in which case the masses can be co-opted into the capitalist project through ideological means. He argued that hegemony subtly dominates the culture and thinking of ordinary people and that this is how a capitalist state maintains itself. The hegemony of the capitalist state can maintain dominance without the use of force by moulding the ideas and values of ordinary people, undermining class conflict and providing a backdrop of mutual agreement on those issues which are allowed to be tackled by political action, as happens, Gramsci argues, in capitalist democratic systems.[27]

Gramsci assigned an important role to intellectuals. He understood that no organisation could work properly without intellectuals and no class-based politics could be successful without intellectuals. He therefore stressed the coherence of the intellectuals and the people in developing progressive politics.[28] He saw intellectuals as having an educative function in combating the ideas generated by capitalist hegemonic power, though how the intellectuals obtain the capacity to think outside capitalist hegemony, and to what extent, remains a mystery.

Gramsci's theory of the state is one which is linked to notions of class but his originality is in seeing the superstructure itself rooted in class relations. For Gramsci, therefore, legal and political systems are always 'rooted in class struggle', as Carnoy notes.[29] Gramsci differs from Marx in noting that the state has only a limited engagement with the executive, law and police because he does not see the state as functioning through class rule in the same way that Marx had. Gramsci argued: 'the state is conceived as a continuous process of formation and superseding of unstable equilibria ... between interests of the fundamental group and those of subordinate groups – equilibria in which the interests of the dominant group prevail, but only up to a certain point'.[30] Colin Sumner echoes this reasoning when he writes:

> The criminal justice system is one of the regulatory institutions of modern society charged with the tasks of pacifying, rephrasing, defining, defusing and treating the products of social tension. ... But ruling groups' ideological perception of what is peace, safety, health and order dominate the public articulation of legal and moral censures, and the specification of target populations for those censures. In return, subordinate forces continually contest consciously, or threaten unconsciously, the validity, purpose and morality of hegemonic censures. Such dominance and contestation are vital features of the normal legal procedure and practical pattern of criminal justice systems.[31]

Gramsci saw the state as a 'complex of practical and theoretical activities with which the ruling class not only justifies and maintains its dominance, but manages to win the active consent of those over whom it rules'.[32] This thinking is indebted to Hegel's *The Philosophy of Right*, which saw civil society as the outcome of complex corporatist relationship between groups, such as trades unions. In Hegel, it is civil society which gives rise to the state.[33] Gramsci, like Hegel, tends to identify the state with civil society. Moreover, Gramsci's view that the state is not made up of physical institutions but rather of a dominant set of ideas is also first found in Hegel.[34]

The main elements of Gramsci's analysis of the state are: (1) that the state is not simply a repressive mechanism to do down the working class; (2) that class domination is a very subtle affair; (3) that the state is receptive to ideas and arguments; (4) that Marx had not addressed seriously enough the possibility that the state could be taken by intellectual means rather than by violent revolution; and (5) that control of the state was part of the proletariat's own hegemonic aspiration and it could be advanced through intellectual struggle.[35] However, the attention paid to ideology by Marxists, of the Gramscian-type, has been harshly criticised. The conservative political theorist Michael Oakeshott puts the case well when he writes:

> ...the larger enterprise of exploring the possibility of demonstrative political discourse based upon an 'ideology' composed of categorically informative propositions about human beings and the course of events. It is interesting in itself: but for us its main interest is that the obstructions which frustrated it are, in principle, obstructions which must frustrate every undertaking of this sort. Explanatory 'laws' of social change cannot generate political deliberation capable of reaching 'correct' political decisions, or political discourse capable of proving decisions to be 'correct' or 'incorrect'. The disappointment of the hope of achieving demonstrative political deliberation with the aid of an 'ideology' composed of explanatory 'laws' of social change or development is one of the great traumatic experiences of the early twentieth century.[36]

Althusser and Poulantzas: Structuralism

Structuralism, which is situated within Marxism, runs counter to the work of Gramsci. It stresses the underlying economic structures rather than the agency of individual subjects. Louis Althusser and Nicos Poulantzas are the leading proponents of this approach. They focus upon Marx's *Capital* and emphasise the historico-economic structures which frame the world of ideas, as opposed to the role of human subjectivity. Althusser's rejection of Gramsci is made clear in his most famous work, *For Marx*. Althusser argues: '...ideology is an objective social reality; the ideological struggle is an organic part of class struggle. On the other hand, I criticized the theoretical effects of ideology, which are always a threat or a hindrance to scientific knowledge.'[37] He stresses that the knowledge individuals have is merely 'material activities inserted into material practices governed by material rituals which are themselves defined by the material ideological apparatus from which derive the ideas of the subject'.[38] Later in *For Marx*, he stresses, in a famous passage, that our knowledge of ideology is only a partial knowledge about 'the conditions of its necessity'.[39] In other words, that we understand the state best in terms of the base economic structures that Marx had written about in *Capital*.

Nicos Poulantzas dealt with the question of the state head-on in two books, *Political Power and Social Class* and *State, Power and Socialism*. In *Political Power and Social Class* (1973) he argues for the *relative* autonomy of the state (though, as Milton Fisk has argued: 'This restriction undercuts autonomy and leaves us with an economic reduction ... the state's activity in organising the dominant class for political power is only made to seem autonomous by considering it in isolation from the rigid claim that the state, at least in the last instance, must reproduce the economy.')[40] Poulantzas argued that capitalism shifts the struggle from the economic concerns to the political domain. This, he argues, is part of a process of undermining class struggle through the individuation of persons and 'to mask and obscure class relations (the capitalist State never presents itself as a class State) but also plays an active part in the division and isolation of the popular masses'.[41] Poulantzas has a similar view of the role of law as individualising issues and supporting the reproduction of the capitalist economic system.[42] The capitalist state, through politics and the law, is actively preventing the emergence of class consciousness. In *State Power and Socialism* he maintains that '[t]he State apparatuses organise and unify the dominant power bloc by permanently disorganising – dividing the dominated classes'.[43]

Problems with Marxism

The problem of Marxism is well illustrated by considering the work of Gramsci, Althusser and Poulantzas. There is no agreed position within Marxism. The problems raised in the original Marx have led to a number of theoretical and practical issues, such as the extent to which the economy dictates the form of the state, the role and extent of ideology and the role of law. Marxism is withering as a potent political force and it is now a marginal force in contemporary Criminology. It is not incidental to note that the heyday of Marxist Criminology was in the 1960s, 1970s and 1980s. Yet the Marxist intuitions that the economy, to a greater or lesser extent, dictates the form of the state, that the state seeks to maintain itself and that the state is self-interested all seem plausible ideas. However, the notion that the state organises, or manages, moral panic through its treatment of crime in order to deflect attention away from the central issue of capitalist social and economic relations, and simultaneously thereby increases the power of the state over the citizen, seems increasingly unconvincing as an explanation of how the state works. Yet this is exactly what *Policing the Crisis* (a Gramsci-inspired text) argued when it conceived the treatment of mugging in the London of the 1970s as largely reducible to the state re-legitimating itself through a concentration upon mugging:

> ... a governing class which can assure the people that a political demonstration will end in a mob riot against life and property has a good deal going for it – including popular support for 'tough measures'. Hence the 'criminalisation' of political and economic conflicts is a central aspect of the exercise of social control.[44]

Building upon this analysis, Sumner has stated that: 'The definition of deviance and the organisation of crime control are fundamentally and profoundly, political questions. Deviance, criminality and policing, in the times and societies we know, have never escaped their basic ideological role in the everyday, practical politics of domination by one class, gender and race over others.'[45] Such an analysis seems at best, partial, at worst reductive. Indeed, McLaughlin has suggested that the set of issues that *Policing the Crisis* dealt with were themselves linked to a unique set of socio-political and politico-historical circumstances, rather than being proof of any Gramscian conception of the state and its activities.[46]

The issues thrown up by the concept of collective class politics and the uses and abuses of ideology seem insurmountable. Since Marx died there has been little agreement, among Marxists, as to what the corollary of his writings is. Moreover, in practice, the Marxist state has usually proven despotic, as Leszek Kolakowski, the eminent scholar of Marxism, has argued:

> On the assumption that violence is the midwife of progress, one should naturally expect that the ultimate liberation of humanity would consist in the coercive reduction of individuals to inert tools of the State, thereby robbing them of their personality, and their status as active subjects. This is what in fact all the regimes that base their legitimacy on Marxist ideology try to do; they are incapable in principle, not as a result of temporary deficiencies, of accepting the idea of human rights, for human rights would indeed demolish their very foundation.[47]

—————————————————— **Feminism** ——————————————————

In many ways Feminism might be said to share some features in common with Marxism: (1) an understanding that the world is made up of relations of domination and subjugation; (2) that the state is skewed in favour of particular interests; (3) that it is a basic function of the law that it is used to both confuse and oppress those who threaten its legitimacy and dominant economic mode of production; and (4) that it is a position characterised by internal divisions. By and large, feminist criminologists have neglected the state and concentrated upon more sociological types of issue, such as the development of feminist research methodology, victimisation, and developments in social policy. The state is often implied as the thing that ultimately legitimates relations of patri-archy, through law and the preservation of gendered social practices. Feminism has increasingly stressed the particularities of women's lives. Some feminists have taken over Marxist terminology wholesale (e.g. hegemony, ideology and the mode of production). However, other feminists, such as MacKinnon, reject the old Marxist terminology and argue that it needs to be replaced with a new terminology which better reflects the nature of patriarchy.[48] Dobash and Dobash have similarly argued that 'it is impossible to use the law and legal apparatus to confront patriarchal domination and oppression when the language and proce-dures of these social processes and institutions are saturated with patriarchal beliefs and structures'.[49]

In liberal political theory, feminists have addressed the state, notably the work of Thomas Hobbes. They have critiqued the social contract theory he outlined in *Leviathan*.[50] Coole and Pateman are typical of feminists who have criticised the Hobbesian social contract treatment and its conception of the state.[51] Hobbes had argued that men and women leave the state of nature and contract to live under a sovereign for their own protection and to secure their freedom. Hobbes had argued for the formal equality of men and women and in the text of *Leviathan* there seems to be sexual equality. However, Hobbes also reasoned that there were families in the state of nature where patriarchy exists and Coole has shown how, when considering patriarchal family structures, his 'formal account is at odds with unexpurgated ideological and historical assumptions'.[52]

If we look at *Leviathan*, we get what is technically called a concept of *negative freedom*, i.e. a view of liberty that, in Hobbes' words, consists of 'an absence of external impediments'.[53] However, the feminist political theorist Anne Phillips has made the following point: 'If freedom were simply a matter of non-interference, we might have to say that a slave left alone by a lazy master enjoyed full liberty; or that a wife cherished by her accommodating husband was as free as a bird, even when the laws of her society denied her any independent status. ... Servitude is servitude even when the master is accommodating. The only free people are those who govern themselves.'[54] Phillips' point is that the liberal ideas of freedom and equality do not respect women in practice.

The theorist who has done most to develop this is Carole Pateman, who is reg-ularly cited by criminologists.[55] Pateman's most important works are *The Sexual Contract* (1988) and the essay 'God Hath Ordained to Man a Helper: Hobbes, Patriarchy and Conjugal Rights' (1991), both which detail the liberal social con-tract model, but concentrate upon Hobbes. She is taken with the issue of why women, who are equal in the state of nature according to Hobbes, consent to subordination in civil society. She argues that once the social contract is in place the sovereign enforces all contracts, including the marriage contract. She argues that the marriage contract is the basis of women's subordination.[56] In other words, once the social contract is in place, men come to control women and their sexuality, through the marriage contract and this is what undermines women's freedom. This is done through the concept of the 'property of the person', which posits that we own both our abilities and our freedom and that because of this we can give them up. Indeed, it is what Hobbes argues we do when leaving the state of nature and making the social contract. Richardson argues that Hobbes' concept of the 'property of the person', when understood in relation to marriage, is a mechanism for women to exchange their freedom for subordination in such a way as to emphasise consent.[57] The marriage contract facilitates subordination through contract and though historical change has altered the pattern of sexual contract, it nonetheless has established modes of thought that persist, notably the subordinate role of women. Indeed, Pateman has criticised Rawlsian political methodology for never even considering the issue of how women come to occupy a subordinate position society.[58] Pateman is important because her analysis does not assume the nature or position of women in society. Moreover, she asks important questions about how women became established in a subordinate role in society.

Therefore, although feminist criminologists have tended to undertake research unrelated to issues of the state, the work of feminist theorists, such as Coole and Pateman, nonetheless supports their work. Smith and Natalier have stated:

> How does the law and criminal justice system reflect patriarchal realities? In other words, how do they work to exclude and regulate women? How are they informed by underlying masculine assumptions and prejudices about women? Central to this agenda are themes relating to the regulation of sexuality and the idea of the 'social contract' is really a patriarchal social contract. Such analyses might look at either sexist legal statutes or specific contexts. Rape provides a good example of this. Feminist research on rape demonstrates the patriarchal nature of legal and popular definitions of rape and the ways that these impact upon criminal justice process, such as judicial reasoning or police discretion.[59]

Main Summary Points

- The basic four features of the state are: (1) the state must have a working political organisational structure with functioning courts, a civil service and a police force; (2) to be a working entity the state must have control over territory and be strong enough to survive; (3) the state must be sovereign and be able to claim a monopoly of political authority, law-making and power, and it must be autonomous; and (4) the state must command the allegiance of its members (citizens, subjects), who are subject to its laws and who have an obligation to obey it.

- In liberal theory the state is the outcome of a voluntary agreement made by individuals who realise that only a social contract will save them from the dangers of the state of nature. The liberal state is always a protective neutral entity which represents all the people fairly for the common good of all. This conception of a neutral state that safeguards its citizens equally from the state of nature is what Marxism and Feminism take issue with.
- The Marxist state is always essentially economic in its character.
- The Marxist theorist Antonio Gramsci argued that hegemony of the capitalist state maintains dominance over the people without the use of force by moulding the ideas and values of ordinary people and that this undermines class conflict and provides a backdrop of mutual agreement on those issues which are allowed to be tackled by political action, such as the way society is organised.
- Feminists have argued that the state is often implied as the thing that ultimately legitimates relations of patriarchy, through law and the preservation of gendered social practices.

Questions

1. How are feminist writers developing the idea of the state?
2. What features would a Marxist theory of the state have?
3. Is the state essential to the preservation of our personal freedom and safety?

Suggested Further Reading

Charvet, J. (1995) *The Idea of an Ethical Community*, Ithaca, NY: Cornell University Press.
Hobbes, T. (1991) *Leviathan*, ed. Richard Tuck, Cambridge: Cambridge University Press.
Rawls, J. (2001) *Justice as Fairness: A Restatement*, Cambridge, MA: Harvard University Press.
Raz, J. (1986) *The Morality of Freedom*, Oxford: Clarendon Press.
Richardson, J. (2007) 'Contemporary Feminist Perspectives on Social Contract Theory', *Ratio Juris*, 20 (3): 402–423.

Notes

1. Rawls, J. (2001) *Justice as Fairness: A Restatement*, Cambridge, MA: Harvard University Press. p. 182.
2. Rawls, J. (1973) *A Theory of Justice*, Oxford: Oxford University Press. p. 14.
3. Charvet, J. (1995) *The Idea of an Ethical Community*, Ithaca, NY: Cornell University Press. p. 186.
4. Marx, K. (1978) 'The German Ideology', in R. Tucker (ed.), *The Marx–Engels Reader*, New York: W.W. Norton. p. 187.
5. Raz, J. (1986) *The Morality of Freedom*, Oxford: Clarendon Press. p. 70.
6. Raz, J. (1979) *The Authority of Law*, Oxford: Clarendon Press. p. 100.

7. Rawls, J. (1993) *Political Liberalism*, New York: Columbia University Press. p. 11. See also Rawls, *Theory of Justice*. pp. 7–9.
8. Copp, D. (1995) *Morality, Normativity and Society*, New York: Oxford University Press. Chapter 7.
9. Hobbes, T. (1991) *Leviathan*, ed. Richard Tuck, Cambridge: Cambridge University Press. p. 141.
10. Ibid. p. 42.
11. Ibid. pp. 86–87.
12. Locke, J. (1988) *Two Treatises of Government*, ed. Peter Laslett, Cambridge: Cambridge University Press. s. 7, p. 271.
13. See also: 'Each Transgression may be punished to that degree, and with so much Severity as will suffice to make it an ill bargain to the Offender, give him cause to repent, and terrifie others from doing the like.' Locke, *Two Treatises of Government*. p. 275.
14. Charvet, *The Idea of an Ethical Community*. pp. 153–179; Raz, *The Morality of Freedom*. pp. 70–105.
15. Chambliss, W. J. (1975) 'Toward a Political Economy of Crime', *Theory and Society*, 2 (2): 149–170.
16. Marx, K. (1976b) 'The Communist Manifesto', in *Marx and Engels Collected Works*, London: Lawrence and Wishart. p. 69.
17. Carnoy, M. (1984) *The State and Political Theory*, Princeton, NJ: Princeton University Press. p. 250.
18. Carver, T. (1982) *Marx's Social Theory*, Oxford: Oxford University Press. p. 20. See also Reiner, R. (2002) 'Classical Social Theory and Law', in J. Penner, D. Schiff and R. Nobles (eds), *Jurisprudence*, London: Butterworth. Reiner denies economic ascendancy and attributes a more balanced position to Marx.
19. See Cohen, G. A. (1988) *History, Labour and Freedom*, Oxford: Oxford University Press.
20. Pashukanis, E. B. (1978) *Law and Marxism: A General Theory*, London: Academic Press. p. 184.
21. Marx, K. (1968) *Selected Writings*, London: Lawrence and Wishart. p. 182.
22. Melossi, D. (1980) 'The Penal Question in *Capital*', in T. Platt and P. Takagi (eds), *Punishment and Penal Discipline*, Berkeley, CA: Center for Research on Criminal Justice.
23. Rusche, G. and Kirchheimer, O. (2003) *Punishment and Social Structure*, New Brunswick, NJ: Transaction; Melossi, 'The Penal Question in *Capital*'.
24. Hall, S. (1997) 'Visceral Cultures and Criminal Practices', *Theoretical Criminology*, 1: 453–478; Hay, D. Linebaugh, P. and Thompson, E. P. (1975) *Albion's Fatal Tree: Crime and Society in Eighteenth-Century England*, London: Penguin; Ignatieff, M. (1978) *A Just Measure of Pain: The Penitentiary in the Industrial Revolution*, London: Macmillan; Sumner, C. S. (1983) 'Law, Legitimation and the Advanced Capitalist State: The Jurisprudence and Social Theory of Jürgen Habermas', in D. Sugarman (ed.), *Legality, Ideology and the State*, London: Academic Press.
25. Hay, et al., *Albion's Fatal Tree*. p. 62.
26. Marx, K. (1976a) *The German Ideology*, ed. C. J. Arthur, London: Lawrence and Wishart.
27. Gramsci, A. (1971) *Selections from the Prison Notebooks*, ed. Q. Hoare and G. Nowell-Smith, London: Lawrence and Wishart. p. 244.
28. Gramsci, *Selections from the Prison Notebooks*. p. 334.
29. Carnoy, *The State and Political Theory*. pp. 86–87.
30. Gramsci, *Selections from the Prison Notebooks*. p. 182.
31. Sumner, C. S. (1990) *Censure, Politics and Criminal Justice*, Buckingham: Open University Press. p. 45.

32. Gramsci, *Selections from the Prison Notebooks*. p. 244.
33. Hegel, G. W. F. (1952) *The Philosophy of Right*, ed. and trans. T. M. Knox, Oxford: Oxford University Press. §244, §245, §256.
34. Ibid. §249.
35. Showstack-Sassoon, A. (1987) *Gramsci's Politics*, London: Hutchinson. p. 118.
36. Oakeshott, M. (1991) *Rationalism in Politics*, Indianapolis, IN: Liberty Fund. p. 92.
37. Althusser, L. (1969) *For Marx*, Harmondsworth: Penguin. p. 12.
38. Ibid. p. 170.
39. Ibid. p. 230.
40. Fisk, M. (1989) *The State and Justice: An Essay in Political Theory*, Cambridge: Cambridge University Press. p. 59.
41. Poulantzas, N. (1978) *State Power and Socialism*, London: Verso. p. 66.
42. Ibid. pp. 87, 91.
43. Ibid. p. 140.
44. Hall, S., Critcher, C., Jefferson, T., Clarke, J. and Roberts, B. (1978) *Policing the Crisis*, London: Macmillan. pp. 189–190.
45. Sumner, *Censure, Politics and Criminal Justice*. p. 190.
46. McLaughlin, E. (2007) *The New Policing*, London: Sage. pp. 62–66.
47. Kolakowski, L. (1990) *Modernity on Endless Trial*, Chicago: Chicago University Press. p. 214.
48. Mackinnon, C. (1992) 'Feminism, Marxism, Method and the State: An Agenda for Theory', in M. Humm (ed.), *Feminisms: A Reader*, Hemel Hempstead: Harvester. p. 119; Segal, L. (1991) 'Whose Left? Socialism, Feminism and the Future', in R. Blackburn (ed.), *After the Fall*, London: Verso. p. 280.
49. Dobash, R. E. and Dobash, R. P. (1992) *Women, Violence and Social Change*, London: Routledge. p. 147.
50. Other political social contract models given by Locke, Kant, Rousseau and latterly Rawls have also been tackled by feminist writers.
51. Coole, D. (1994) 'Women, Gender and Contract: Feminist Interpretations', in D. Boucher and P. Kelly (eds), *The Social Contract from Hobbes to Rawls*, London: Routledge. pp. 191–210; Pateman, C. (2002) 'Self-ownership and Property in the Person: Democratization and a Tale of Two Concepts', *Journal of Political Philosophy*, 10: 20–53; Pateman, C. (1991) 'God Hath Ordained to Man a Helper: Hobbes, Patriarchy and Conjugal Rights', in M. L. Stanley and C. Pateman (eds), *Feminist Interpretations and Political Theory*, Cambridge: Polity Press. pp. 53–73.
52. Coole, 'Women, Gender and Contract. p. 193.
53. Hobbes, T. (1994) *Leviathan*, ed. E. Curley, Cambridge, MA: Hackett. p. 79.
54. Phillips, A. (2000) 'Feminism and Republicanism: Is this a Plausible Alliance?', *Journal of Political Philosophy*, 8: 282–283.
55. Smith, P. and Natalier, K. (2005) *Understanding Criminal Justice: Sociological Perspectives*, London: Sage. p. 39.
56. Pateman, C. (1988) *The Sexual Contract*, Cambridge: Polity Press. pp. 77–115.
57. Richardson, J. (2007) 'Contemporary Feminist Perspectives on Social Contract Theory', *Ratio Juris*, 20 (3): 402–423.
58. Pateman, 'Self-ownership and Property in the Person'.
59. Smith and Natalier, *Understanding Criminal Justice*. p. 39.

2

ECONOMICS AND CRIMINAL ACTIVITY

The history of risk distribution shows that, like wealth, risks adhere to the class pattern only inversely; wealth accumulates at the top, risks at the bottom. To that extent, risks seem to strengthen, not to abolish the class society. Poverty attracts an unfortunate abundance of risks. By contrast, the wealthy (in income, power or education) can purchase safety and freedom from risk.

Ulrich Beck, 1992[1]

Introduction

It is taken as read that there is a clear link between crime and the economy. Some scholars have made more of economic factors than others, but nobody rejects the idea that there is some connection between them. If we look over the history of Criminology, we note the moral statisticians such as Quetelet, the Chicago School, strain theory, control theory, and latterly criminologists such as Steve Box, Chris Hale and Jock Young, all focus on the relationship between crime and the economy. Economics itself is a broad subject area, as the leading theorist of an economic approach to law, Judge Richard Posner, has argued.[2] This chapter will concentrate upon the classic positions that criminologists have adopted regarding economics and criminal activity. It also covers the economics of crime and punishment in terms of contemporary Economics.

Quetelet[3]

The Belgium astronomer and mathematician Adolphe Quetelet (1796–1874) looked at the location and instances of crime, and undertook crime mapping for the French government. While employed as a statistician, Quetelet had the task of providing some of the information which the French state required in order to plan and develop a coherent social policy. His work focused upon government statistics and it aimed at scientific rigour. Quetelet was a positivist in that he saw human behaviour as governed by scientifically verifiable laws. His methodology was derived from the natural sciences, in which he had been trained. His observation that crime rates seemed to obey the same 'law-like' regularities that govern the natural world mark him out as a man of his time. Quetelet was engaged in work which had definite economic aspects to it, for example, measuring costs to the state.[4]

The French state under Napoleon wanted to *normalise* the 'dangerous classes' through moral rehabilitation, but this was seen as a failure by both politicians and the people. Theft and public order offences almost doubled between 1813 and 1820. There were huge numbers of poor people (*les misérables*) in the cities, notably Paris, who resorted to crime to make ends meet and who routinely rioted over the dreadful social conditions they had to endure. The initial response to this failure of rehabilitation policy was for the French state to commission a number of detailed studies and to build up a statistical picture of who made up the dangerous classes and why they were committing crimes against their fellow citizens. This apparent failure to *normalise* the dangerous classes through the Napoleonic system led directly to the so-called *scientific* route of managing the dangerous classes through the application of statistical techniques in the fields of crime control and prison policy. This entailed analysing such matters as parish records for births, baptisms, marriages and deaths as well as looking at data on poor relief, taxation, fire and general insurance claims and information concerning public health, especially rates of venereal disease, held at the local, regional and national level. The detailed records of the army on the background and general health of soldiers, along with court records and the files of the gendarmerie, were scrutinised in enormous detail. The population was analysed as never before and particular note was made of mortality, age, occupation, disease and levels of intelligence. For the first time the prisons were analysed by a variety of researchers, including those outside the government service, such as religious groups, who looked not only at prison incarceration rates but also such variables as diet and prison type. In the spirit of the time, no variable was excluded and no question ruled out. Indeed, the question of whether prison was itself a factor in recidivism, since it could lead to the moral degradation of prisoners, was also examined. In 1827 the first ever French national statistical tables on crime, *Le Compte général de l'administration de la justice criminelle en France*, were published. The *Compte* itself was restricted to the analysis of the various courts in the French system, with the addition of information on age, sex, occupation and educational attainment level, although this information was systematically added to in subsequent years. The Compte, as Piers Beirne has argued, was a decisive factor in the development of a positivistic criminology.[5]

This work led Quetelet to construe certain *faits sociaux* (social facts) that pertain to the aggregated nature of human conduct. From this work he derived his *homme moyen* (average man), which illustrated the utility and accuracy of the hypothesised average value over the larger number of empirical observations. The construction of the average man allowed for detailed comparison in predictive statistical work. Quetelet's first sustained work on criminal statistics was in an 1827 essay, which elaborated the relationship between crime and the severity of its punishment.[6]

Quetelet did not naïvely or uncritically go about his work and he was concerned with the limitations of the data he worked with, which was often not standardised or collected in a *scientific* way. He was especially taken with the total population question; put simply, understanding the *actual* number of offences and their ratio *vis-à-vis* the sum of recorded crimes. Quetelet discerned a constant relationship between notified crimes and their prosecution, based on the *Compte* data for 1833–39, and from that analysis and his statistical work, based additionally on a range of other judicial and official data, he inferred a constancy between the total population of crime and recorded crime. Quetelet was stuck by the recurring constancy of the data on crime, from the number of murders per year to the number of property crimes to the numbers of accused failing to appear in court. All of this suggested to Quetelet that, contrary to what had been assumed, and allowing for the vagaries of individual conduct, criminal behaviour, in an aggregate sense, was constant and seemed to obey certain general patterns, or laws.

Quetelet had a definite view of human nature and he assumed that crime was dependent upon an individual's willingness to commit it. Hitherto certain groups, such as the poor, young men, the unemployed and the ill-educated, were said to commit a disproportionate number of crimes. However, Quetelet showed that the correlation did not hold true and that some of the poorest regions of France were the ones with the lowest crime rates. Far more important was the inequality of wealth distributed between persons and the propensity of individuals to commit crime, which was related to issues concerning moral instruction and opportunity. This analysis increasingly pushed Quetelet towards the determination of crime causation, something he had been initially reluctant to study. He came up with a tripartite typology of causation which included *accidental causation, variable causation*, and *constant causation*. Quetelet believed that the last category was the most important factor in determining causation. However, these three categories all relate to Quetelet's conception of the average man, and not to any sociology of causation. Moreover, Quetelet ascribed a fixed level of determination to all three types of causation which, especially when combined with the overwhelming influence of age, sex, occupation and religion, ensured constancy to crime rates.

The *homme moyen* (average man) is also the moderate man who tends to the mean in statistical terms. The average man's moderate life owes more to Aristotle than any notion of a person found in modern philosophical or political thought. Moreover, the notion of the average man, who always chooses the moderate path and who always avoids excess, would appear to be a rare anthropological creature in the era of late capitalism. The average man was also contrasted to other groups, such as gypsies, who, Quetelet argued, had an increased propensity to commit crime (and here Quetelet fails to escape the racism of his age). Quetelet was, from the 1840s onwards, increasingly drawn to biological metaphors, notably around the supposed 'contagion of crime'. He even anticipated Lombroso by factoring in such variables as head measurements in his analysis. Quetelet made explicit reference to the fact that the scientifically measured proportions of the body related to crime rates and that both were social facts. In this way Quetelet was increasingly drawn into using the concept of deviation, though, as Colin Sumner has pointed out, this is a statistical deviation and not the sociological deviation which Durkheim originated and which came to prominence in the twentieth century.[7]

Quetelet went beyond the narrow parameters of statistical analysis in his recommendations for government. He argued that the state should rigorously apply the criminal code and focus police attention towards known criminal minorities, and this included consistent sentencing. He also argued that the state should focus upon the higher moral, intellectual and scientific elements of modern civilisation and promote social stability. He understood that crime was a constant feature of all societies, but he also realised that the state could both exacerbate and ameliorate the conditions which gave rise to it. This social understanding of crime was a major departure from the notions of a freely acting and wicked criminal, which pervaded public discourse in France.

Quetelet was soon overtaken by the giant figures of Durkheim, Marx and Weber, but his contribution is immense nonetheless. His work suggested that crime was the result of social factors, not moral or evil, and in identifying regularities in the statistical record he opened up the possibility of a modern sociological explanation of crime. In these ways his work was progressive. However, Emile Durkheim, who praised Quetelet's focus upon the existence of certain regularities and observable statistical features of the social world, also criticised his use of the average man on the grounds that merely to point to a phenomenon is not to understand that phenomenon. Durkheim specifically cited the phenomenon of suicide, as a case where a given suicide rate does not presuppose that persons, in general, are exposed to the likelihood of committing suicide, and that to argue otherwise is fallacious. Durkheim also took issue with Quetelet's conception of 'normal'. The sociologist Durkheim understood that what was normal always related to a given social institution and a given level of development, whereas Quetelet derived what was normal from the abstraction of statistical analysis and the development of the average man. Quetelet resisted the pathologising of individuals and instead pointed towards the *social* causes of crime. He was the first in a long line of people who understood crime in terms of its economic costs. Crime saps the productive power of the economy, costs the state in terms of policing and prison provision, and undermines social solidarity.

The Chicago School

The Chicago School looked at the relationship between crime and its location. It is an ecological theory which seeks to establish the links between different areas of a city, social disorganisation and criminal activity. Chris Hale has summed up the Chicago School's work by highlighting the underlying economic issues at play: 'Where unemployment is high or economic prospects are poor it will be difficult to muster the necessary resources to combat social disorganization and maintain informal social control. Hence ... deteriorating economic conditions will lead to increasing levels of crime.'[8] Chris Hale is surely right to stress the essentially economic basis of the Chicago School's work.

The first Department of Sociology was established at the University of Chicago in 1892. Chicago had grown spectacularly from being a modest town of under 5,000 people in the 1830s to being a city of over 2 million people before the First World War. By 1930 Chicago's population had exceeded 3 million people. Not only had Chicago grown in scale but it was a very diverse city, even by American standards, and contained a great range of immigrant groups (notably Irish, Italian and Polish populations, as well as Jews from all over Eastern Europe fleeing persecution in Tsarist Russia, notably in Ukraine, and the Austro-Hungarian Empire[9]) as well as an influx of African-Americans who left the southern states, which had been part of the Confederacy, in large numbers from the 1870s onwards. Chicago was also a city characterised by a great deal of deprivation, crime and social disorganisation. Little wonder that the sociologists of the University of Chicago would make their city, and the sociological dynamics of the crime within it, the objects of their study. The Chicagoans would focus upon the concept of social disorganisation, undertake fieldwork and map the city in terms of its development and the distribution of crimes across its geography. The work of sociologists such as Robert Park, Ernest Burgess, Clifford Shaw and Henry McKay, working at the University of Chicago, mainly in the period from the 1920s to the early 1940s, constituted what has become known as the Chicago School, and their work has had an enormous influence upon Criminology, and Social Policy more generally.

The Chicagoans knew of the work of Quetelet, and they certainly used official statistics in their work, but they were influenced far more by the work of the French sociologist Emile Durkheim (1858–1917). Durkheim's work on social solidarity had highlighted the fact that whenever family and community bonds are weak, then crime tends to be higher.[10] Durkheim had conceived two forms of society: one form of society based upon *mechanical solidarity*, which exhibited a strong sense of homogeneity and which was small-scale, possessed repressive laws, was religiously based and had an expanded role for the family and the collective conscience of the community; and another form of society, *organic solidarity*, which was marked by heterogeneity and which was large-scale, had restitutive laws, was secular, tended towards anomie and had an elaborated division of labour.[11] The Chicagoans emphasised the social nature of crime, rather than understanding crime in terms of a person's life history or personal psychology. They saw the Chicago of their time as exhibiting many of the problems typical of a society based upon organic solidarity, with its elaborated division of labour and lack of shared values, compared to simpler societies based upon mechanical solidarity. As sociologists they linked crime to broader social issues, specifically the level of social disorganisation. The Chicagoans analysed the modern city as expanding outwards in concentric circles from an inner-city business district. Next to the inner-city business district is the zone of transition, which is the place in the city where new immigrants, or new arrivals from other parts of America, settle because it is both inexpensive and close to where they work – the inner-city business district. Beyond the zone of transition are more settled and homogeneous working-class communities, middle-class neighbourhoods and, at the outer edge, the richer suburbs. The zone of transition, then, is the poorest area economically. The culture of the zone of transition arose out of its location. It was rundown and poor. The Chicagoans saw a pattern emerging whereby new arrivals to Chicago would initially move in to the zone of transition and then move out to a better neighbourhood in due course, which approximates to the American Dream of self-betterment. However, the pathological nature of the zone of transition was established by the Chicago School. The zone of transition is a place which tends to have all sorts of social problems associated with it in terms of having a poor record in health, housing, education and high crime rates. The zone of transition lacks the proper set of relationships necessary for community life to flourish, due to the fragmented nature of the people who live there. The people who live in the zone of transition have nothing much in common with each other and no shared history or common social values. It is a place where traditional norms and values are lost or forgotten.

The Chicagoans saw the heterogeneous population that lived in the zone of transition as giving rise to an impersonal environment marked by a lack of shared norms about how to live, which in turn facilitated criminal behaviour. It attracted little inward investment and was generally unattractive, possessing few facilities. The Chicagoans saw this as pointing to the fact that delinquency and crime were not located in individuals or racial groups, but rather were understood as the outcomes of the zone of transition itself, which they understood as intrinsically criminogenic. Crime is related to environmental factors that are external to individuals, although the social disorganisation of the zone of transition further allows delinquent behaviour to flourish, as criminal conventions are transmitted by young people to each other through gangs, in lieu of the positive integrative bonds of the more affluent or socially stable neighbourhoods. So whereas, for example, the *shtetl* (the Yiddish word for a Jewish village in Eastern Europe[12]) had been poor, it was nonetheless socially integrated through strong bonds of family, religion, tradition and work. The zone of transition, on the other hand, had few of these bonds of attachment, was socially disorganised and was characterised by high crime rates.

The Chicago School undoubtedly made a huge contribution to the development of sociological and criminological theory as well as to the development of an innovative fieldwork methodology. However, by overwhelmingly concentrating upon the ecology of the city, they also made several errors. In emphasising ecology, they had a tendency in their work to see the relationship between crime and the physical organisation of the city as a *natural* one and they failed to note deeper issues related to class and the distribution of resources. This implied naturalism has been termed the 'ecological fallacy', i.e. the idea that individual criminal behaviour can be entirely explained by environmental, or contextual, factors. The notion that crime and delinquency are themselves socially constructed was missed entirely by the Chicagoans. The fact that both the statistics on crime and the attribution of what counts as criminal or delinquent is largely a matter of convention was never properly acknowledged in the work of the Chicago School. Victims were almost entirely neglected. Moreover, the concentration upon the zone of transition as the criminogenic part of the city tended to overemphasise the criminality of the working class and reinforce negative stereotypes about the poor, immigrants and those living in the most economically deprived areas of the city. Amazingly, the Chicago School undertook no research into organised crime, although Al Capone and his mob were located in Chicago. More worryingly, the work of the Chicago School has fed into long-term political, economic and social policy responses to crime, which have tended, to this day, to ally crime with designated areas. Middle-class crimes, such as mortgage fraud, domestic violence and institutional corruption, still feature less in policing and social policy discussions than social disorganisation. Political discussions about crime are still dominated by talk of social inclusion and designing out crime.[13] Our political deliberations about the nature of contemporary crime still largely flow from an analysis about the nature of the inner city, which the Chicagoans of the 1920s and 1940s would recognise.

Strain Theory

Robert K. Merton's 'strain theory' followed the Chicago School in arguing that the reason for urban crime being concentrated among members of certain groups was 'not because the human beings comprising them are compounded of distinctive biological tendencies but because they are responding normally to the social situation in which they find themselves'.[14] He emphasised the relationship between *culture* and social structure far more than anyone had done previously. Merton's primary aim was to discover how social structures exert a definite pressure on individuals to engage in non-conforming, rather than conforming, conduct. He drew a distinction between culturally defined goals, which he saw as desirable, and the legitimate means of achieving those goals. Whenever goals and means are harmoniously integrated the result is a well-regulated society. 'Strain' is said to occur where there is a disjuncture between culturally defined goals and the institutionalised means of obtaining them. American society, argued Merton, overemphasised the goal of monetary success, relative to other goals. Following Durkheim, he argued that the relationship between culturally defined goals and the legitimate means of achieving them led to anomie because the American economic system had built-in insatiability, in terms of the material aspirations it raised.[15] In other words, anomie occurs within the social structure itself and is, in turn, a measure of the gap between goals and means in society. Strain theory, in this regard, is a theory with definite economic overtones.

Before developing Merton's ideas it is useful to set out his table, which clearly demonstrates his ideas concerning modes of adaptation in relation to the anomie which arises in the social structure. Merton saw individuals as adopting these five strategies in relation to their social and economic circumstances, though he did not properly elaborate why individuals favour one mode of adaptation over another.

Table 2.1   Merton's Typology of Modes of Individual Adaptation

Modes of adaptation	Cultural goals	Institutional means
Conformity	+	+
Innovation	+	–
Ritualism	–	+
Retreatism	–	–
Rebellion	+/–	+/–

(+)   = acceptance
(–)   = rejection
(+/–) = substitution of new values

Conformity
This is what happens in a stable society when all cultural goals and the institutionalised means of achieving them are in harmony.

Innovation
This is what happens when individuals have internalised the cultural goal but lack the institutionalised means of achieving it. This is especially the case in a system which emphasises economically based goals. Innovators are people who substitute their own values in order to achieve their cultural goal.[16]

Ritualism
This is what happens when individuals reduce the scale of their cultural goals in order to make achieving them more realistic. The example Merton gave was of the person who gives up the goal of obtaining a house or new car but who nonetheless goes to work every day and acts out striving for economic success, such as with the lower middle classes.[17]

Retreatism
This is what happens when individuals reject both cultural goals and institutionalised means. It is associated with tramps, alcoholics, drug addicts and psychotics.[18] It is noteworthy that Merton did not see drug addiction and life on the streets as causing anomie, but rather being a result of it.

Rebellion
This is what happens when individuals outside the social structure devise their own social structure and attendant cultural goals and institutionalised means, and it presupposes a rejection of the cultural goals and institutionalised means that apply in a typical liberal society.[19]

Merton did not attempt a general theory of all crime: what his strain theory amounts to is an elaborated theory of anomie, based upon observations drawn from his experience of life in America in the 1930s and 1940s. Durkheim had argued that rapid social change loosens the social bonds that regulate people and that this may lead to the listlessness and dissatisfaction which causes suicide and other social problems, such as crime.[20] Merton followed Durkheim but switched his focus from the moral regulation of individuals to the demoralisation that necessarily follows when individuals seek personal affirmation in material success. Where Durkheim had focused upon rapid social change, Merton focused upon the strains of succeeding in a materialist culture. Merton, unfortunately, follows the Chicago School in as much as his typology of modes of adaptation tends to suggest that crime is associated with poorer people, since they have fewer institutional means to achieve their cultural goals. Merton understands criminality as a response to variable and external structural conditions and in this way he also follows the Chicago School.

Merton's work has had an enormous influence upon generations of policy-makers who took the solution to the problem of crime to be the establishment of anti-poverty programmes and legislation to increase the equality of opportunity, notably in the Kennedy and Johnson administrations in the USA and the Wilson and Callaghan administrations in the UK. His work is still acknowledged by contemporary criminologists, notably, Lea and Young[21] and Messner and Rosenfeld, who have revisited Merton's structural themes. Messner and Rosenfeld have stated that '[a]nomie theory comes closest ... to providing a compelling account of the American crime problem'.[22] However, it is fair to say that Merton has been less influential since the great onslaught represented by the *New Criminology* in the 1970s, which characterised his work as being too wedded to social democratic themes.[23] He has been criticised by feminists, such as Eileen Leonard, who have argued that strain theory is a theory about male crime and neglects female socialisation, which has historically been oriented to the family rather than to the wider material culture.[24] Albert Cohen criticised Merton's approach, which looks at individuals and neglects the wider process of social control and the interactions between control agents, such as the police, and 'deviants'.[25] Sumner argued that Merton was 'taking the cause, motive and effect for granted as scripted moments in the historic defeat of Evil by the forces of Good'.[26] Yet for all the criticisms levelled against Merton's strain theory, the issues thrown up by the role of culture, the need to attain material success and the impact of structural forces upon individuals remain with us as perennial themes in Criminology.

Control Theory

Control theory gives us an explanatory model which places its emphasis upon the 'control' of individuals rather than upon the structural forces which bear upon individuals. The main proponent of control theory is Travis Hirschi, who wrote the classic *Causes of Delinquency* in 1969.[27] The aim of control theory is to show how institutions like the family, school and participation in community activities can prevent criminal behaviour. Again, note should be made of the debt to Emile Durkheim's work, notably in *The Division of Labour in Society* (1933), which stressed the importance of social integration and solidarity to individuals in curtailing criminal behaviour and deviance. Bob Roshier set out Hirschi's four bonds:

> He proposes four bonds: attachment (the extent to which individuals have close emotional ties to other people); commitment (the extent to which they see conventional behaviour, for example at school, as offering immediate or long-term rewards); involvement (the extent to which their time is taken up with conventional activities); belief (the extent to which their beliefs about what is permissible or not coincide with conventional ones).[28]

This four-part scheme was derived from Hirschi's empirical self-report study, and while it aims at scientific neutrality, it actually fails to incorporate an economic aspect. As Chris Hale, when citing Box, has noted:

> ... economic recession and unemployment might be expected to weaken social bonds and hence lead to increased levels of crime. ... Unemployment and increasingly inequality are not likely to improve family relationships. Rather they will produce increased tension, anger and sullenness against society that may be transferred onto the family leading to its breakdown. ... With more unemployment, shorter working hours and more part-time work, people will have less involvement in conventional activity and social bond theory would suggest crime would increase.[29]

Once again, therefore, we note that the real world of economics creates the reality which criminologists observe. It is not possible to do Criminology and ignore the economic context of criminal activity.[30]

The Legacy of Steve Box

The late Steve Box is one of the most important British criminologists of the post-war era. A Marxist himself, he established a structural relationship with capitalist economies and criminality, notably in times of economic recession, using advanced statistical techniques. Box's influence upon British Criminology cannot be underestimated, and after the publication of his *Recession, Crime and Punishment* in 1987 it was increasingly seen as necessary to link any theoretical criminological analysis with both a rigorous basis in the statistical record and an analysis of the economic and political context of crime. In other words, after *Recession, Crime and Punishment*, British Criminology is characterised by the marriage of empirical and theoretical analysis.

In theoretical terms, Box elaborated how crime should be seen as an inevitable consequence of the internal contradictions of any capitalist economy. In *Power, Crime and Mystification* he writes: '...the pursuit of fair profit, the generator of wealth and employment, the backbone on which social welfare is possible – can be viewed ... as the primary ethics for and of an industrial society and conformity to this neutralizes any obedience to the law merely because it happens to be the law'.[31] Box was also one the few criminologists in the 1980s who understood that white-collar crime was also implicated in the relationship between economic downturn. He wrote: '...financial performance was found to be associated with illegal behaviour ... firms in depressed industries as well as relatively poorly performing firms in all industries tend to violate the law to greater degrees'.[32]

However, Box is best known for his work on the relationship between the rate of crime and the level of unemployment, the U–C relationship. Box's analysis in *Recession, Crime and Punishment* reviewed 50 advanced econometric studies, of which 32 were cross-sectional and looked for a connection between the rate of crime and the level of unemployment at different times and in different places, and 18 were traditional time-series studies that sought to measure the rate of crime and the level of unemployment, over a number of years, though only one used victimisation data. He found that 64 per cent of these studies showed a link between the rate of crime and the level of unemployment and the remaining studies did not. This was not considered *strong* evidence that the rate of crime and the level of unemployment are straightforwardly linked, especially since 36 per cent of the studies Box analysed showed no correlation at all.[33] However, Box was alive to the flaws in the way data was collected and he noted the statistically problematic nature of comparing studies which relied on such different bases as officially recorded crime, arrest rates and conviction rates and unemployment, since each of these may give a different overall figure. Nonetheless, he concluded that there was a link between the rate of crime and the level of unemployment, though it was a weak one. (Of course, unemployment is now measured differently from how it was in the 1980s, and criminologists and statisticians are more aware of the complexities of it as a lagging indicator, i.e. they note a lapse between the onset of unemployment and its negative consequences.) Box did note that in one major study he reviewed, young people did not cite unemployment as important in their pattern of offending.[34] More significant though was Box's finding that there was a much stronger link between income inequality and the level of crime.[35]

Chris Hale, who wrote extensively with Steve Box and was his colleague at the University of Kent, is among the group of British criminologists who have carried on Box's analysis of data with an eye on the economic data and political conditions of the day. Hale has been at the forefront of a broader analysis of the labour market by criminologists, who have noted long-run changes in the British economy since 1946. These changes include a diminution of the manufacturing base of the economy and a move towards the service sector, an increased feminisation of the workplace and an increase in part-time, casual and temporary working.[36] Hale notes a dual labour market in operation in England and Wales. There are those workers in the primary economy who are highly skilled, enjoy full employment rights and good levels of remuneration and, on the other hand, there are those workers in the secondary economy who are low skilled, in insecure employment, enjoy few employment rights and receive low levels of remuneration. What Hale notes is a relationship between youth crime and the quality and quantity of work available to young people.[37] Subsequent studies have borne this out.[38] According to Hale:

> Wage inequality in the UK reached record highs for the twentieth century at the beginning of the 1990s. A key factor in this increased inequality was the rapid deterioration in the labour market position of less skilled workers at the bottom end of the wage distribution. The economic model of crime argues that individuals will choose between legal and illegal work on the basis of relative rewards. Many individuals find that, whilst in work, their jobs are insecure, low-paid, and low-skilled. Often they are in part-time or temporary work and they are on the economic and social margins. Many of the theoretical arguments ... for why unemployment and crime might be related apply equally well to low-wage, low-skill employment.[39]

It should be noted that Hale offers both an empirically based critique and a politically and economically savvy account of inequality. Latterly, Hills and Stewart have underscored Hale's analysis that inequality remains endemic to the British economy.[40]

It is important to link the contemporary work of criminologists, such as Steve Box and Chris Hale, with earlier criminological writers, such as Merton. When we do that we note that the economic data does, in fact, support a link between unemployment, relative deprivation, insecure employment and crime. It might be as Reiner has suggested: 'The downplaying of economic "strain" factors in criminal justice policy discourse since the 1970s was due to shifts in dominant political and intellectual perspectives, not evidence that there are no significant correlates.'[41] In other words, strain theory is still a useful and important tool in the criminologist's box.

Rationality and Economics

We can think of crime as a rational, choice and economic modellers as well as criminologists do this. Police departments, local government and the Home Office utilise rational choice theory, particularly when setting out policies on crime prevention. Rational choice theory initially started out in Economics and Political Science departments, but when it is applied to crime it has some interesting conclusions. Jock Young has called it 'administrative criminology'. In other words, he argues that it represents a form of criminology that concerns itself with crime prevention but not the deeper political, social and economic causes of crime.[42] Cultural criminologists, such as Mike Presdee and Jeff Ferrell, have argued for a form of criminological explanation which prioritises the celebratory nature of crime, transgression and the irrational aspects of law-breaking in contrast to the measured, choice-making individual chooser provided by rational choice theory.[43] Rational choice theory always starts from the assumption that people are rational and self-interested. So in the case of criminal activity, it argues that individuals are concerned to maximise their income so may choose work or crime depending on their ability to be successful in the labour market. It argues that individuals also weigh up their chances of getting caught. It is therefore interested in where crime is committed, since location will affect the likelihood of detection. Criminals are said to act as though they are assessing the marginal benefits of committing crime, taking into consideration the possible punishment. We can see immediately that this would appear to be more plausible when applied to premeditated crimes but less plausible when applied to spontaneous crimes.[44]

It is possible to treat crime mathematically and dispense with traditional criminological analysis, as Cooter and Ulen do.[45] For example, taking Cooter and Ulen's equations, if we used x to denote the seriousness of crime and y to denote the likely reward to the criminal, then we could assume that the reward is an increasing function of the seriousness of a crime:

$y = y(x)$

Then if the punishment is f for committing a crime of seriousness x, we could express that as:

$f = f(x)$

If we then expressed the probability p of being punished for committing a serious crime x as the function:

$p = p(x)$

we can then note that the expected punishment equals the product of the amount of punishment and its probability:

$p(x)f(x)$

Finally, we could conclude that rational criminals choose the seriousness of crime x to increase their reward, which is equal to the reward $y(x)$, minus the punishment expected:

$max\ y(x) - p(x)f(x)$

This simple set of equations presents us with a clearly mapped out model of criminal activity. These and other rational choice equations miss out a lot of what criminologists may think is essential to understanding the problems of crime and criminalisation, i.e. culture, class, social structure, gender, age, etc. However, though rational choice theory is not a complete theory of criminality, it nonetheless has been influential in developing a modelling culture among contemporary criminologists, and it has been widely used not only by the police and local and national government agencies but also by town planners and retailers.[46] It is essentially an account focused on the development of practical crime prevention programmes.

Main Summary Points

- Adolphe Quetelet understood crime systematically in terms of its economic costs. He saw that crime saps the productive power of the economy, costs the state in terms of policing and prison provision, and undermines social solidarity.
- The Chicago School showed how high unemployment or times of economic hardship for poorer people make combating social disorganisation and crime more difficult.
- Robert Merton's strain theory emphasises the relationship between *culture* and social structure. He draws a distinction between culturally defined goals, which he saw as desirable, and the legitimate means of achieving those goals. Whenever goals and means are harmoniously integrated the result is a well-regulated

society. 'Strain' is said to occur where there is a disjuncture between culturally defined goals and the institutionalised means of obtaining them. Strain theory, in this regard, is a theory with definite economic overtones.

- Rational choice theory works with the assumption that people are rational and self-interested. Therefore, in the case of criminal activity, it argues that individuals are concerned to maximise their income so may choose work or crime depending on their ability to be successful in the labour market. It argues that individuals rationally work out their chances of getting caught.

Questions

1. Does strain theory still offer the criminologist a way of understanding crime?
2. What connects the work of Quetelet and the work of modern criminologists?
3. Are Hirschi's bonds of attachment tied to the economic conditions alone?

Suggested Further Reading

Cooter, R. and Ulen, T. (2008) *Law and Economics*, London: Pearson.

Hale, C. (1998) 'Crime and the Business Cycle in Post-war Britain Revisited', *British Journal of Criminology*, 38: 681–698.

Messner, S. and Rosenfeld, R. (2001) *Crime and the American Dream*, Belmont, CA: Wadsworth.

Mosselmans, B. (2005) 'Adolphe Quetelet, the Average Man and the Development of Economic Methodology', *European Journal of Economic Thought*, 12 (4): 565–582.

Reiner, R. (2007) 'Political Economy, Crime and Criminal Justice', in M. Maguire et al. (eds), *The Oxford Handbook of Criminology*. Oxford: Oxford University Press.

Notes

1. Beck, U. (1992) *Risk Society: Towards a New Modernity*. London: Sage. p. 35.
2. Posner, R. (1999) *The Problems of Jurisprudence*, Cambridge, MA: Harvard University Press. pp. 353–392.
3. This section largely follows my own analysis in Amatrudo, A. (2009) 'Adolphe Quetelet', in K. Hayward, S. Maruna and J. Mooney (eds), *Key Thinkers in Criminology*, London: Routledge (forthcoming).
4. Reiner, R. (2007) 'Political Economy, Crime and Criminal Justice', in M. Maguire et al. (eds), *The Oxford Handbook of Criminology*, Oxford: Oxford University Press. p. 348.
5. Beirne, P. (1993) 'Adolphe Quetelet and the Origins of Positivist Criminology', *American Journal of Sociology*, 92 (5): 1140–1169.
6. Mosselmans, B. (2005) 'Adolphe Quetelet, the Average Man and the Development of Economic Methodology', *European Journal of Economic Thought*, 12 (4): 565–582.
7. Sumner, C. S. (1994) *The Sociology of Deviance: An Obituary*, Milton Keynes: Open University Press. p. 6.

8. Hale, C. (2005) 'Economic Marginalization and Social Exclusion', in C. Hale et al. (eds), *Criminology*, Oxford: Oxford University Press. p. 328.

9. Amatrudo, A. (1996) 'The Nazi Censure of Art: Aesthetics and the Process of Annihilation', in C. S. Sumner (ed.), *Violence, Culture and Censure*, London: Taylor and Francis. p. 71.

10. Moyer, I. L. (2001) *Criminological Theories: Traditional and Non-traditional Voices and Themes*, London: Sage. pp. 109–117.

11. Durkheim, E. (1933) *The Division of Labour in Society*, New York: The Free Press. pp. 62–86, 377.

12. See Vishniac, R. (1983) *A Vanished World*, New York: Noonday Press.

13. Walklate, S. (2003) *Understanding Criminology: Current Theoretical Debates*, Buckingham: Open University Press. p. 21.

14. Merton, R. K. (1993) 'Social Structure and Anomie', in C. Lemert (ed.), *Social Theory: The Multicultural Readings*, Boulder, CO: Westview Press. p. 250.

15. Walsh, A. (2000) 'Behaviour, Genetics and Anomie/Strain Theory', *Criminology*, 38: 1075–1108.

16. Merton, R. K. (1968) *Social Theory and Social Structure*, New York: The Free Press. pp. 199–200.

17. Ibid. pp. 203–205.

18. Ibid. p. 208.

19. Ibid. p. 209.

20. Durkheim, E. (1970) *Suicide*, London: Routledge. pp. 254–256.

21. Lea, J. and Young, J. (1984) *What Is To Be Done about Law and Order?*, Harmondsworth: Penguin. pp. 215–218.

22. Messner, S. and Rosenfeld, R. (2001) *Crime and the American Dream*, Belmont, CA: Wadsworth. p. 39.

23. Taylor, I., Walton, P. and Young, J. (1973) *The New Criminology*, London: Routledge. p. 101.

24. Leonard, E. (1982) *Women, Crime and Society: A Critique of Criminological Theory*, New York: Longman. p. 57.

25. Cohen, A. (1966) *Deviance and Control*, Englewood Cliffs, NJ: Prentice-Hall. p. 113.

26. Sumner, *The Sociology of Deviance*. p. 78.

27. See Hirschi, T. (1969) *Causes of Delinquency*, Berkeley, CA: University of California Press.

28. Roshier, B. (1989) *Controlling Crime*, Milton Keynes: Open University Press. p. 47.

29. Hale, 'Economic Marginalization and Social Exclusion'. p. 329.

30. Hale, C. (1998) 'Crime and the Business Cycle in Post-war Britain Revisited', *British Journal of Criminology*, 38: 681–698.

31. Box, S. (1983) *Power, Crime and Mystification*, London: Tavistock. p. 57.

32. Box, S. (1987) *Recession, Crime and Punishment*, Basingstoke: Macmillan. p. 99.

33. Ibid. pp. 69–78.

34. Ibid. pp. 93–95. The study in question is Thornberry, T. and Christensen, R. (1984) 'Unemployment and Criminal Involvement', *American Sociological Review*, 49: 398–411.

35. Box, *Recession, Crime and Punishment*. pp. 86–90.

36. Hale, C. (1999) 'The Labour Market and Post-war Crime Trends in England and Wales', in P. Carlen and R. Morgan (eds), *Crime Unlimited*, London: Macmillan; Hale, 'Crime and the Business Cycle'. pp. 681–698.

37. See also Cook, D. (2006) *Crime and Social Justice*, London: Sage. pp. 146–150.

38. Hasluck, C. (1999) 'Employers and the Employment Option of the New Deal for Young Unemployed People: Employment Additionality and its Measurement',

PhD thesis; University of Warwick, Institute of Employment Research; Hill, J. and Wright, G. (2003) 'Youth, Community Safety and the Paradox of Inclusion', *Howard Journal*, 42 (3): 282–297; Webster, C., Simpson, D., MacDonald, R., Abbas, A., Cieslik, M., Shildrick, T. and Simpson, M. (2004) *Poor Transitions: Social Exclusion and Young Adults*, Bristol: Policy Press.

39. Hale, 'Economic Marginalization and Social Exclusion'. p. 335.
40. Hills, J. and Stewart, K. (2005) *A More Equal Society?* Bristol: Policy Press.
41. Reiner, R. (2007) 'Political Economy, Crime and Criminal Justice'. p. 362.
42. See Young, J. (1986) 'The Failure of Criminology: The Need for Radical Realism', in R. Matthews and J. Young (eds), *Confronting Crime*, London: Sage.
43. Presdee, M. (2000) *Cultural Criminology and the Carnival of Crime*, London: Routledge; Ferrell, J. (1997) 'Criminological *Verstehen*: Inside the Immediacy of Crime', *Justice Quarterly*, 14 (1): 3–23.
44. Cooter, R. and Ulen, T. (2008) *Law and Economics*, London: Pearson. pp. 501–503.
45. Ibid. p. 498.
46. Trasler, G. (1993) 'Conscience, Opportunity, Rational Choice and Crime', in R. V. Clarke and M. Felson (eds), *Advances in Criminological Theory*, New Brunswick, NJ: Transaction.

3

RIGHTS AND OBLIGATIONS

Those who consent to the authority of reasonably just governments or respect their laws are subject to their authority and have an obligation to obey their laws.

Joseph Raz, 1988[1]

──────────────── **Introduction** ────────────────

Rights are the things that frame the relationships that exist between the individuals, corporations, such as companies or organisations, and the state. Our modern political lives increasingly focus upon our relationships to the political conduct of government, the activities of the police and the courts and our entitlements to health care. All of these relationships are governed by rights. We use the language of entitlement, which is derived from the concept of rights. Our rights usually imply a duty to the prevailing authority of the state in terms of obeying its laws, technically termed 'obligation'. Obligations are the moral and legal duties that individuals are obliged to undertake in support of the state, and each other. Obligations are often seen as natural in that they follow the pattern of the way we typically view our relations of personal obligation to family and friends.

It is useful to view rights as limits upon the encroachment of the state in the affairs of individuals, and this view has been expressed recently in terms of the debate concerning the length of time suspects can remain in police custody without being charged. In other words, how far can the state encroach on an individual's personal liberty? Rights, therefore, guarantee an agreed level of personal liberty in any given society. The legal theorist H. L. A. Hart argued that rights protect our personal choices and allow persons to be self-realised.[2] More recently, the political theorist John Charvet has written how rights may be understood as the absence of obligation and as a measure of our freedom.[3] Through participation in political society, an individual signals his or her 'acceptance of the system, creating expectations of compliance in his (or her) fellow participants'.[4] Liberal societies may be said to operate with a balance of rights and obligations; and it is fair to say that a lot of practical politics relates to the extension of rights – such as recent moves to allow civil partnerships – and the level of obligation the state demands of individuals, e.g. in relation to military conscription and the level of taxation.

Importantly for criminologists, rights also relate to such issues as the conduct of police activity in relation to citizens, arrest, detention, fair trials and treatment in custody, and a range of other civil liberties issues which include the treatment of prisoners. The discussion of rights has, of course, long been part of legal and political discourse but, increasingly, contemporary criminologists have begun to discuss rights, of different sorts, too. Notably, Stan Cohen, Rod Morgan, Kevin Stenson, Philip Smith, Kristin Natalier and others have begun to make the discussion of rights, and to a lesser extent obligation, part of the *lingua franca* of Criminology. Of these authors, Stan Cohen stands out. He has been responsible for a complete rethink of the concerns of criminological writing, pointing out that the crimes of the state (i.e. crimes which violate human rights) have been almost entirely neglected.[5]

The Basic Arguments: Rights and Obligations

Rights are usually associated with individuals and technically the definition of rights relates to not only to the authority for an individual to act in a given manner but also to the universalised capacity to act, in the same fashion, possessed by all persons, in the same legal system. Put another way, rights are the entitlement to act, or to have others act, in a certain way. Legal rights are always related to judicial principles, laws or rules obtaining in a given legal system. Moral rights relate to the specific roles, or relationships, that exist in a given society, or the promises or expectations that persons may generate outside the statutory legal framework. The classic definition of a moral right, as opposed to a legal one, was given by the political theorist Richard Brandt: 'We can say, roughly, that to have a moral right to something is for someone else to be morally obligated (in the objective sense) to act or refrain from acting in some way in respect to the thing to which I am said to have the right, if I want him to.'[6]

There is general support for rights in political discourse on the progressive left through to the traditional right, though who should possess these rights, and the extent of them, can be more contentious, such as in the case of asylum seekers, people suffering from AIDS, prisoners and the mentally ill. In all of these cases there has been heated political debate, but it is still the case that it is difficult for asylum seekers to obtain work, prisoners and the mentally ill do not enjoy the same ability to vote in elections as the rest of the community and people suffering from AIDS continue to experience discrimination, as in the case of obtaining some forms of insurance. Our legal rights are established in law and are therefore ultimately secured by the courts. These rights are immensely important to the type of society we live in, such as the freedom of speech, the freedom to travel and the freedom to worship. These rights, which we often take for granted, are absent or curtailed in many countries. Burma, for example, prohibits the freedom of speech, China restricts the freedom of worship and Russia curtails freedom of movement. It is easy to see from these examples how, when a right is restricted, the criminal law is, usually, extended. It is a crime, for example, in Russia to move around the country without the necessary official documentation to do so, and many Russians are incarcerated precisely because they left the town or village they live in without the accompanying permissions. We can see that these important legal rights, which are technically called 'positive' rights by political theorists, are vital to the lives that people live and the scope of the criminal law in the lives of men and women. These positive rights are important and are always upheld but may be the site of contestation, as in the issue of rape within marriage. Until 1992 it was not possible for a wife to bring a charge of rape against a husband because under the law, before 1992, the husband had the right to sex with his wife, with or without her consent. Women have had their rights extended. Similarly, the treatment of children and animals has altered as their rights have been extended.

In terms of understanding the idea of *obligation*, the legal theorist H. L. A. Hart made a distinction between *being obliged* to do something, which implies legal coercion (as in the case of taxation or obeying the criminal laws of the land), and *having an obligation*, which only presupposes a moral obligation or duty.[7] Hart's distinction between those obligations which are enforceable through the courts and are obeyed, at least partly, because of the fear of punishment if you do not and those obligations which are obeyed only because the obligation is considered morally right is a useful one. Our obligations to the state are more likely to be backed by force in the last resort. It is useful, though, to see obligations as the reverse side of the coin to rights – one requiring and supporting the other.[8] In terms of political theory, the social contract theories of political philosophers, such as Hobbes, Locke, Rousseau and latterly John Rawls, all suppose a contract between individuals, and between the state and individuals, that secures the authority of state, which in turn secures the safety and well-being of citizens. It is a rather circular justification. Obligation is, in different ways, shown as being essential to the maintenance of the state and the enjoyment of rights. Although the form of the rights and obligation that different theorists outline differ, they all follow this simple binary format. What is certain is that there is no place for criminality in social contract theory. The criminal is the person that violates his or her obligations to the community and/or the state and therefore deserves a forfeiture of their rights.[9]

Hohfeld

The legal theorist, Andrew Halpin, has critically analysed the work of Wesley Hohfeld, the most important theorist of positive rights.[10] Hohfeld considered four types of legal rights: (1) the so-called *liberty rights*, which allow something but do not necessarily oblige the bearer of the right to undertake it, such as the right to ramble or swim in the sea; (2) the so-called *claim-rights*, which entail one person refraining from an action and a relationship of corresponding duties between persons, and this may be the case in terms of assaulting or shouting at each other; (3) there are legal entitlements, or *powers*, such as the right to vote in elections; (4) there are sanctioned *immunities*, which allow certain persons to not be subject to the power of the others, including the state. The example here might be the way we do not expect older people to be part of the workforce after a certain age. However, it can be related to private law where it outlaws the unilateral alteration of a contract.[11] Whether you are critical of Hohfeld, like Halpin, or not, Hohfeld's four-part scheme usefully sets out the issues thrown up by positive rights.

Kant: Duties and Rights and their Relationship with Crime Control

The eighteenth-century German philosopher Immanuel Kant has been enormously influential to both retributive theorists and anti-utilitarian rights theorists. John Rawls, the doyen of liberal theorists, largely took over Kant's ideas in his *A Theory of Justice* (1973), and this entailed adopting Kant's view of rights and the rule of law. In criminological theory, Andrew von Hirsch, the main proponent of Just Desert theory, has acknowledged Kant's influence in his *Past or Future Crimes* (1986). He writes: 'an individual's rights ought not be sacrificed solely to serve another person's interests'. According to von Hirsch, 'Kant ... had a general moral theory, of which this imperative is part, stressing the idea of respecting the value and integrity of persons. ... This theory, with its emphasis on individual rights ... has been so influential in modern ethical thinking.'[12] It is worth setting out Kant's ideas in more detail.

In the *Metaphysical Elements of Justice*, Kant tells us that when a creditor claims the right to demand repayment of a debt, this means that the use of coercion to make anyone do this is compatible with freedom: 'Thus right (or justice) and authorisation to use coercion mean the same thing.'[13] In another passage on property, Kant relates that the notion of an object of property (i.e. legal property) entails a notion of an external obligation on others to refrain from using that object. He claims that such obligations can only be guaranteed through a system of coercive laws. Kant states that 'the condition of being subject to general external (that is, public) legislation that is backed by power is the civil society. Accordingly, a thing can be externally yours or mine only in a civil society.'[14] Kant's view of a legal system is one with a role for rights. He sets out laws that define rights and duties and which, in turn, are backed by the threat of judicial punishment. The legal system is concerned with external duties that can be coerced through a system of negative incentives, punishment. Allen Rosen, when discussing Kant, states: 'We can expect that whenever rights may correspond to duties of justice, there should be narrow, enforceable rights and whatever rights may correspond to ethical duties should be wide, unenforceable rights.'[15] In the *Tugendlehre*, Kant himself wrote: 'To every duty there corresponds one right in the sense of a moral title (*facultas moralis generatim*); but only a particular kind of duty, juridical duty, implies corresponding rights of other people to exercise compulsion (*facultas iuridica*).'[16]

Kant had argued that the laws of a just state are the laws that would be chosen by a rational person to govern all social relationships in a position of initial free choice. Kant is not asking us to believe that there ever was such a position of original choice-making by individuals. Rather, he is asking us to develop a just society by hypothesising a set of laws and social arrangements that a rational and impartial person would choose to adopt if setting up a society from first principles. In Kant's scheme, law is important. Without laws some persons may benefit more than under a system with laws, but this will not be true for all people; and since in Kant's position of original rational choosing nobody could know what person they would occupy, it makes sense that all men and women agree to live under a system of laws which would aim at securing everyone's well-being. This system of laws would bring benefits to all men and women and therefore everyone owes obedience to the law as a debt to all other persons who, by their self-restraint, maintain the laws.[17] If a person chooses not to obey the laws, then he or she has to pay a debt by punishment, in which case it is essential that those persons who break the law are punished otherwise they would obtain an unfair advantage over their fellow citizens. In the Kantian scheme, punishment is important – it is simply paid as a debt to be settled with the law-abiding citizens. However, once it is paid, then there is free and easy access back to the community for the law-breaker, on the same basis as everyone else. This form of punishment is classically termed retributive punishment, and it is only possible in a theory which prioritises law, rights and obligation. Of course, the Kantian system rests upon the certainty of fair laws. Laws must be framed as in the case of an objective rational person choosing them in an impartial setting. If the system of laws does not meet this criterion, then it is not worthy to be the basis of a Kantian scheme. The retributive punishment that Kant advocates is only possible in the context of just laws.

Utilitarianism

Utilitarianism is often criticised for not being able to consider rights thoroughly enough. Bentham famously termed natural rights 'rhetorical nonsense – nonsense on stilts'[18] and along with Marxists (who have often argued that rights-talk is merely code for institutionalising capitalist relations of inequality, and that it is nonsense to apply rights equally to the structurally unequal, notably in the case of property and private ownership) utilitarians are most often cited as being in the anti-rights lobby.[19] Bentham was far more taken with the welfare of men and women than their rights. He wrote: 'There is no right which, when the abolition of it is advantageous to society, should not be abolished.'[20] Contemporary legal theorists, notably Ronald Dworkin in *Taking Rights Seriously*, have noted that since rights are best understood as taking precedence over appeals to utility, this means therefore that utilitarianism cannot always respect rights because their model subordinates rights to broader considerations of overall utility and general welfare.[21] Yet some have argued that rights and welfare are much more intertwined than the simple rhetoric of rights or welfare alone suggests:

> Human well-being depends overwhelmingly on social institutions providing favourable conditions for human enterprise in the broadest sense. ... These all-important conditions are created and maintained principally by enforced social rules. The resulting framework of legal rights and obligations makes normal human functioning possible and abundance achievable. Moreover, to maximise well-being, the framework must secure a realm of equal freedom and personal inviolability to all.[22]

It is usually said to be the case that if we analyse the language of utilitarians, it appears to be against rights – because they are said to be of no utility. John Stuart Mill, writing in the nineteenth century, argued: 'It is proper to forego any advantage which could be desired to my argument from the idea of abstract right, as a thing independent of utility. I regard utility as the ultimate appeal on all ethical questions'.[23] Mill feels that there is nothing in the content of rights which alters the fact that, for him, all political and moral judgements should be understood in relation to the utilitarian notion of increased utility and the measure should be how an action alters that. The problem rights theorists have with this is that if utilitarianism always judges the merit of an action by looking at the consequences it has, then nothing seems to be ruled out as necessarily wrong. In other words, in theory at least, nothing seems to be ruled out. Of course, we are now living in the century following the excesses of the Third Reich, Mao's China, Stalin's USSR and Pol Pot's Cambodia. Though none of these brutal regimes was based on utilitarian principles, our era is one which has an increased role for rights and an increased sensitivity concerning the rights of individuals, over and against the state. We have this concern for rights, partly shaped by the excesses of aspects of twentieth-century history, which would be completely alien to people such as the earliest utilitarian thinkers, like Jeremy Bentham. For Bentham, the important consideration is that of increasing overall welfare.[24] In general terms, rights theorists argue that in certain important cases we should allocate people rights regardless of the utility that has to the majority of people. The utilitarians, on the other hand, are less convinced by this as they believe that any moral rules and arrangements we have seem to be determined solely in terms of the consequences they have. This said, John Stuart Mill did try to theorise rights in his book *Utilitarianism*, written in 1861. In Chapter 5 of that book, entitled 'On the Connection between Justice and Utility', Mill sets out a place for moral rights, though he argues moral rights are derived from utility.[25] For Mill, all rights are judged in terms of the claims they make upon society as a whole, in which case this is what he understands to be utilitarian because the claim is always being made against the general good. It is useful to see what Mill had in mind by looking at a passage from *Utilitarianism* which neatly encapsulates his view of rights and justice:

> While I dispute the pretensions of any theory which sets up an imaginary standard of justice not grounded in utility, I account the justice which is grounded on utility to be the chief part, and incomparably the most binding part, of all morality. Justice is the name of certain classes of moral rules, which concern the essentials of human well-being more nearly, and are therefore of more absolute obligation, than any other rules for the guidance of life, and the notion which we have found to be of the essence of the idea of justice, that of a right residing in an individual, implies and testifies to this more binding obligation. The moral rules which forbid mankind to hurt one another ... are more vital to human well-being than maxims, however important.[26]

This is a clear statement: Mill is simply stating that rights are always or related to the improvement of overall human well-being, i.e. the improvement in general utility.

Human Rights

Human rights increasingly dominant the theoretical discussions of the way we live, legally, morally, politically, socially, and increasingly this is matched by the everyday practice of our lives in relation to the way we relate to each other, to institutions, to the state and to the common law. Human rights are a difficult thing to define, however, technically and in law. At the most basic level they signify a set of rights which relate to persons because they are human, and as such they relate to all persons equally and at all times. No human can be denied these rights – they are fundamental. The problem arises in relation to the expansion of this definition to include such criteria as dignity, health and basic income. In terms of the treatment of human rights in criminological writing, this has been related primarily to the fairness of laws and the treatment of citizens. Policing Studies has been especially taken with human rights, following the Human Rights Act 1998, which altered the way the police go about their business, notably in relation to their investigatory powers and the provision required for suspects in criminal cases.[27]

Human Rights under Attack

Recently there have been increased calls in the UK for greater use of indeterminate, exemplary and preventive sentencing, notably in relation to sexual offences, violent crime, anti-social behaviour and terrorism, since the bombing of the World Trade Center on 11 September 2001. The effect of this has been to loosen the Kantian imperative to treat persons as *ends in themselves* and increasingly to see persons, with regard to criminal sentencing, as a *means to another end*, which has, in turn, undermined the relationship between human rights and criminal justice. A new and censorious language of public safety, risk and security has been developed to trump the language of civil liberties and human rights, with its implicit anti-majoritarian bias and concern for the protection of the individual against the state. This has been reflected recently in the call by the pressure group Migrationwatch to change human rights laws to stop encouraging terrorists.[28] In America, Justice Robert Jackson has argued that a doctrinaire approach to human rights might 'convert the Bill of Rights into a suicide pact'.[29] It is to be noted, at this point, that the European Convention on Human Rights and Fundamental Freedoms, and its five subsequent protocols, enshrine protections which hitherto have been part of the *lingua franca* of western European jurisprudence, notably Article 3, which outlaws torture or inhuman or degrading treatment, Article 5, which ensures liberty and security of the person, except lawful arrest upon reasonable suspicion, Article 6, which secures both a fair trial and special rights for criminal proceedings for individuals, and Article 8, which notes a respect for private life. These four articles may be seen to have been threatened recently, especially in relation to sexual offences, violent crime, anti-social behaviour and terrorism. Moreover, the machinery of government has intervened in this process by broadening the usual investigatory powers of the police and other agencies and by altering the arrangements for criminal trials. This process has been further exacerbated by another set of processes which have sought to realign the relationship between criminal law and sentencing by moving numerous cases normally within the domain of criminal law to civil law, as has happened with anti-social behaviour orders.[30]

Increasingly, the prosecuting authorities have used the issue of *serious* crime to advance a diminution of the usual restraints upon themselves in relation to individual *suspects*. This has been observed in relation to fraud, organised crime, drugs cases, sexual abuse, and terrorism cases. A utilitarian argument has been employed that has argued that *seriousness* is reason enough to overturn the finely balanced protections afforded to suspects. The argument concerning seriousness has become routinely employed by politicians, and it is now the default response in drugs and terrorism cases. In addition to this change in the prosecutory and criminal justice climate, we have witnessed a much more extensive use of surveillance powers, such as eavesdropping devices, internet surveillance, and CCTV, all of which might be said to be in a tense relationship to Article 8. The proponents of wider surveillance have even sought to portray a commitment to human rights as an obstacle to the proper operation of civil society.[31] By stealth, the authorities in the UK, and to a differing extent right across the western world, have extended the admissibility of rules on evidence, though this often conflicts with Article 8, which respects private life, and also with Article 6, which ensures a fair trial.[32] It is difficult to justify the move away from the Anglo-American principle that a defendant does not come to a criminal court to answer for his entire past life,[33] although the English courts have recently upheld the increased use of hearsay evidence in criminal cases (brought about by the Criminal Justice Act 1988 and, even more so, by the Criminal Justice Act 2003).[34]

Even with statutory safeguards, it leaves too much discretion in the hands of the trial judge to influence the final outcome of the case by deciding at a trial-within-a-trial what the jury can hear and what it cannot hear. At common law (and for very good reasons) only the power to include or to exclude confession evidence was so wide-ranging. This power is particularly dangerous in a system (such as the English system) where the judge sits alone, in the absence of the jury, without fellow judges or assessors. Moreover, the same issues of public safety, risk and security have been advanced to obtain longer periods of detention without charge.[35]

The past few years have also witnessed a reversal of the usual burden of proof rules, notably in the case of *Salabiaku* v. *France*,[36] which sent out ripples throughout European legal circles. Legislation too has often had a *reverse burden* flavour to it, notably, in the UK, the Regulation of Investigatory Powers Act 2000. All this has been advanced at a time when the whole presumption of innocence in criminal cases has been increasingly called into question both by politicians and the media. The drift has been away from the language of human rights and towards the language of *risk* and *seriousness*. Accordingly, sentencing tariffs have risen dramatically, terms of imprisonment have lengthened and criminal charges broadened. However, perhaps the most interesting development is concerned with the increased use of the civil law by the adoption of measures to curtail a person's behaviour. In this regard, the ASBO (anti-social behaviour order) in the UK has become notorious, with a breach leading to a possible five-year term of imprisonment. These ASBOs have become notorious because of the fashion in which they have undermined the regular criminal procedures associated with the normal prosecution process.[37] ASBOs are also indicative of another recent development that has undermined the safeguards built into the criminal justice system. They are essentially civil orders, deriving from a civil court, which place restrictions upon a person's actions. In two conjoined cases, the Judicial Committee of the House of Lords held that applications to a Magistrates' Court for an ASBO were civil proceedings in nature, not criminal proceedings.[38] However, the Judicial Committee held that the facts supporting such an application had to be proved to the criminal standard (proof beyond reasonable doubt). Nevertheless, the free reception of hearsay evidence was approved, and has been allowed in English civil cases since 1995.

It may be argued that this in itself is part of another development – the extension of regulatory procedures and processes. These regulatory procedures relate to such diverse issues as financial services, health and safety legislation, and environmental management. What unites these regulatory areas is the status of the defendant. The rights of defendants are not clear; they relate to the basis of the prosecution. This, of course, has major implications for proportionality and desert criteria and, more broadly, for social justice and human rights. Prevention orders have become a much more important element in the criminal justice system than hitherto, and they are now a routine feature of legislation.[39] They have been applied in serious cases, as with sexual offenders, but also routinely in a range of banning orders relating to football hooliganism or other public order cases. It has also become routine to confiscate assets[40] and to register certain classes of offenders for life.[41] Prevention orders have also been used to stop association, as has the Terrorism Bill 2006, which broads the legal notion of 'assistance'.[42]

A case may be advanced that the entire future of the human rights tradition in the UK, and more broadly across Europe, is under threat by numerous encroachments upon the safeguards hitherto built into the criminal justice system.

Rights: Some Limitations in the Criminal Justice System

In an important essay, 'Reaffirming rehabilitation', Francis Cullen and Karen Gilbert stressed the limited role of rights in the criminal justice system in assisting rehabilitation. They wrote:

> The promise of the rights perspective is based on the shaky assumption that more benevolence will occur if the relationship of the state to its deviants is fully adversarial and purged of its paternalistic dimensions. Instead of the government being entrusted to reform its charges through care, now offenders will have the comfort of being equipped with 'rights' – that will serve them well in their battle against the state for a humane and just administered correctional system. The rights perspective is a two-edged sword. While rights ideally bind the state to abide by standards insuring a certain level of due process protection and acceptable penal living conditions, rights also establish the limits of the good that the state can be expected or obligated to provide.[43]

This is point is often neglected. Rights only ever offer a minimal guarantee. They do not aspire to the highest ideals of care possible. Rights may give material improvement to persons in the criminal justice system but they only ever secure minimal conditions and standards; beyond that improvements are not secured by a narrow rights-based agenda alone. Moreover, in the case of prisoners, for example, the rights they enjoy may be inadequate to ensure rehabilitation, and conditions that go beyond the bare provision of what is entailed by individual rights, such as sports facilities or family visits, may be curtailed according to a rights-based argument.

Rights also have the problem associated with them that in order to exercise their rights individuals have to be aware of them in the first place. Rights imply a system of education or awareness-raising. Individuals may not be aware of their rights and so fail to exercise them. In the case of taking legal proceedings to court, it may be that one side is more aware of its rights than the other. Alternatively, there may be an imbalance of power which results in an imbalance in the exercise of rights. Nicola Lacey has noted how, in the case of evidence, the defendant has fewer effective rights over admissibility than the prosecution, and how the court makes presumptions about defendants, which both may run counter to an impartial rights model.[44] We should recall some of the miscarriages of justice that resulted from the treatment of evidence, notably the Maguire Seven case. The defendants were working-class Irishmen and at the height of the IRA bombing campaigns in mainland UK were treated less favourably than English men would have been. Moreover, the Forensic Science Service withheld evidence from the defendants in the case and this resulted in their wrongful conviction, although it was also the main reason for their eventual release. The Maguire Seven case demonstrates how, in a practical way, the institution of rights does not necessarily result in a fair outcome. Rights have their limitations and, as in the case of admissibility of evidence and presumption of character, they fail to always address the great power (and resources) imbalance between defendants and the state prosecution authorities and their agents, such as the police and Forensic Science Service.

Legal procedures and rights do assist in fair prosecutions but, as Sanders and Young have demonstrated, the legal system often fails to operate properly due to a number of systematic issues in the criminal justice system, that are unlikely to ever be completely remedied.[45] Discretion, or at least the decision of whether to take action, operates at all levels within the prosecution process, from the decisions of police officers on the street to the Crown Prosecution Service (e.g. whether to stop and search a 'suspect', deciding whether to arrest someone, deciding upon what charges to bring, deciding on whether or not to grant bail, deciding on the scope of an investigation or the amount of time and funds to allocate to it, decoding whether to prosecute due to costs – the list is seemingly endless). Yet even if procedural systems are well managed and procedural rights respected, this does not result in substantive justice.[46] Moreover, established patterns of bias abound in British society in terms of the differential treatment of certain ethnic minorities and the working class.[47] Rights cannot, by themselves, alter the brute inequalities within society.

Barbara Hudson has argued that rights tend to assume a flat uniformity between persons and their individual experiences and that this indirectly discriminates against bearers of difference, such as women and black people:

> Impartiality and objectivity are primary virtues for this 'justice as fairness'. Philosophical expulsion of difference is reflected in law's model of the abstract subject of law, with all legal subjects constructed as equal in their possession of agency and free will. This assumption of sameness has been the focus of critique by postmodernists, for whom the abstract universal turns out to be the characteristics associated with the white, western citizen of the Enlightenment, and feminists, who point out that the so-called universal norm is in fact predicated on the middle-aged, middle-class male. ... Law based on this logic of identity is castigated for its lack of appreciation of alternative standpoints, and for its failure to recognize that what it presumes to be universal is in fact very partial.[48]

In this passage, Hudson clearly demonstrates the difference between the theoretical aspiration of fairness and the practical reality of everyday lived experience.

Her point does not undermine the case for rights, but merely shows up some of their shortfalls.

Feminist Critique: Carol Gilligan

The point made by Barbara Hudson about difference was originally made by Carol Gilligan in her influential 1982 book *In a Different Voice*.[49] It distinguished between an ethics based on rights, which is understood as masculine, and an ethics of care, which she understood as feminine. Her argument is derived from empirical work undertaken with children. She noted that there appeared to be a systematic difference between boys and girls in their attitudes to the enforcement of the rules of games. Boys, she noted, tend to enforce rules harshly, whereas girls tend to evaluate rule infractions in the context of broader considerations of relationships, and tend to be more empathetic. Gilligan did not find that girls were more lenient than boys in terms of rule infractions, rather that they pay more attention to the impact of enforcing rules maintaining social harmony than to sticking doggedly to hard-and-fast rules.[50] From this research Gilligan developed a gendered typology which noted boys have a rules-based ethical approach, whereas girls have an ethics of care.

By extension, Gilligan argues, in a male-dominated world, where men control the criminal justice system, men have traditionally dominated the rules and ethical standards we all live by, especially in the context of legal rule-setting. This description, which Gilligan offers of the way rules operate in the criminal justice system, has been widely criticised as a parody of the way the law operates in practice and in theory. As Judge Richard Posner has argued:

> ...if we want to emphasize not the epistemological virtues of case-specific legal reasoning but instead sympathy for the underdog (one aspect of the ethics of care), then we have only to list the many male judges who have worn that sympathy on their sleeve. Even the emphasis on maintaining ongoing relationships is not special to feminism; it is the stock in trade of those legal scholars, most of them male, who emphasize the 'relational' aspects of long-term contracts.[51]

Moreover, Gilligan did not properly consider class and ethnicity in her work, which would tend to undermine its validity, as Smith and Natalier have noted.[52] The deeper point against Gilligan's work was made by fellow feminist writers, who have argued that it seems to imply a form of gender stereotyping itself. In any case, the attributes Gilligan ascribes to women – even if we were to accept Gilligan's findings wholesale – are only ever *average* tendencies and do not relate to real women's lives or personal attitudes.[53] And as the feminist writer Catherine MacKinnon has stated, Gilligan seems to offer us an analysis which seems to reinforce notions that women are better suited to caring for children and for a domestic role generally rather than make their contribution to how our society is rule-governed.[54]

Marxist Criticism of Rights-based Approaches

Marxists have been some of the strongest contemporary critics of rights-based arguments and this has brought them into sharp contrast with liberal thinking. It is, perhaps, most useful to note the Marxist objection in relation to Kant and the Kantian scheme of retributive punishment, since our focus is upon law and criminological understanding. Kant had argued that the laws of a just state are the laws that would be chosen by a rational person to govern all social relationships in a position of initial free choice. Marx took issue with this reasoning. First, he objected that before persons could make proper choices they would need information about the human nature and the relationship between men and women that was fair and impartial. Marx argued that this was impossible since ideas come out of the material conditions of life, not the material conditions of life after ideas. In other words, any information that a rational person would have would be based upon a bourgeois science derived from capitalist social relations and that inevitably, using Kantian a methodology, we end up with another bourgeois theory of justice. The classic statement of this was given by Jefferie Murphy in his essay 'Marxism and Retribution'.[55] Murphy elegantly sets out the case against Kant's theory of justice by stating that in a capitalist society not only do persons not enjoy the same level of rights, but also that the abstract character of Kant's writing is implausible as a basis for a theory of justice. It is worth quoting Murphy at length:

> There is something perverse in applying principles that presuppose a sense of community in a society which is structured to destroy genuine community ... the whole allocation of benefits in contemporary society ... presupposes what might be called a 'gentleman's club' picture of the relation between man and society – i.e. men are viewed as being part of a community of shared values and rules. The rules benefit all concerned and, as a kind of debt for the benefits derived, each man owes obedience to the rules. In the absence of such obedience, he deserves punishment in the sense that he owes payment for the benefits. For, as a rational man, he can see that the rules benefit everyone (himself included) and that he would have selected them in the original position of choice. Now this may not be too far off for certain kinds of criminals – e.g. business executives guilty of tax fraud [though even here we might regard their motives of greed to be a function of societal reinforcement]. But to think that it applies to the typical criminal, from the poorer classes, is to live in a world of social and political fantasy. Criminals typically are not members of a shared community of values with their jailers; they suffer from what Marx calls alienation. And they certainly would be hard-pressed to name the benefits for which they are supposed to owe obedience. If justice, as both Kant and Rawls suggest, is based on reciprocity, it is hard to see what those persons are supposed to reciprocate for. Bonger addressed this point ... 'The oppressed resort to means they would otherwise scorn. ... The basis of social feelings is reciprocity. As soon as this is trodden under foot by the ruling class, the social sentiments of the oppressed become weak towards them.' ... It does, then, seem as if there may be some truth in Marx's claim that the retributive theory, though formally correct, is materially inadequate. At root, retributive theory fails to acknowledge that criminality is, to a large extent, a phenomenon of economic

class. To acknowledge this is to challenge the empirical presupposition of the retributive theory – the presupposition that all men, including criminals, are voluntary participants in a reciprocal system of benefits and that the justice of this arrangement can be derived from some eternal and a historical concept of rationality.[56]

Marx had written against the abstract rights advocated by Kant and Hegel in a famous article against capital punishment, published in the *New York Daily Tribune* in 1853. Marx wrote: 'Is it not a delusion to substitute for the individual with his real motives, with multifarious circumstances pressing down upon him, the abstraction of free will.'[57] It is important to note how practical Marx is when compared to the abstract and speculative thinking of Kant and Rawls.

Marx also thought that rights are far too individualistic and even undermine social solidarity. In his essay 'On the Jewish Question' he writes: 'Thus none of the so-called rights of man goes beyond egoistic man, man as he is in civil society, namely an individual withdrawn behind his private interests and whims and separated from the community.'[58] What Marx is drawing attention to is how rights usually protect the self-interested desires of materially acquisitive individuals (consumers in a capitalist economy), as opposed to the rights of citizens *per se*; and they also seem to presuppose a conflict between persons and the society outside them, which constrains their freedom and action. Marx makes this clear in 'On the Jewish Question', where he argues that rights are a 'framework exterior to individuals, a limitation of their original self-sufficiency'.[59]

Main Summary Points

- Rights are usually associated with individuals and technically the definition of rights relates not only to the authority for an individual to act in a given manner but also to the universalised capacity to act, in the same fashion, possessed by all persons, in the same legal system. Rights are the entitlement to act, or to have others act, in a certain way.
- Legal rights are always related to judicial principles, laws or rules obtaining in a given legal system.
- Moral rights relate to the specific roles, or relationships, that exist in a given society, or the promises or expectations which persons may generate outside the statutory legal framework.
- Criminals may be understood as people who violate their obligations to the community and/or the state and therefore deserve a forfeiture of their rights.
- Kant's work on punishment utilises a rights and obligation methodology. Punishment is simply paid as a debt to be settled with the law-abiding citizens. Once it is paid there is free and easy access back to the community for the law-breaker, on the same basis as everyone else. This form of punishment is classically termed retributive punishment, and it is only possible in a theory which prioritises law, rights and obligations.

(Continued)

(Continued)

- Utilitarians are less convinced by this as they believe that any moral rules and arrangements we have seem to be determined solely in terms of the consequences they have.
- Human rights signify a set of rights that relate to the persons because they are human and, as such, they relate to all persons equally and at all times. No human can be denied these rights – they are fundamental.
- Some feminists have noted how rights-talk is skewed to a masculine mindset. Men tend to enforce rules harshly whereas women tend to evaluate rule infractions in the context of broader considerations of relationships, and tend to be more empathetic. Therefore rights tend to ignore empathetic relationships in favour of legal ones.
- Marxists have noted that rights are far too individualistic and even undermine social solidarity.

Questions

1. Are we losing or gaining human rights?
2. What was Marx's main problem with rights?
3. Was Mill right about the relationship of rights to utility?

Suggested Further Reading

Cohen, S. (2007) 'Human Rights and Crimes of the State: The Culture of Denial', *Australian and New Zealand Journal of Criminology*, 26 (2): 97–115. Reprinted in E. McLaughlin et al. (eds), *Criminological Perspectives: Essential Readings*, London: Sage. pp. 542–560.
Coleman, J. (2000) 'Crimes and Transactions', *California Law Review*, 88: 921–930.
Dworkin, R. (1977) *Taking Rights Seriously*, Cambridge, MA: Harvard University Press.
Lyons, D. (1992) 'Bentham, Utilitarianism and Distribution', *Utilitas*, 4 (2): 323–328.
Stenson, K. and Sullivan, R. (2000) *Crime, Risk and Justice*, Cullompton: Willan Publishing.

Notes

1. Raz, J. (1988) *The Morality of Freedom*, Oxford: Clarendon Press. p. 99.
2. Hart, H. L. A. (1982) 'Legal Rights', in H. L. A. Hart, *Essays on Bentham: Jurisprudence and Political Theory*, Oxford: Clarendon Press. pp. 162–193.
3. Charvet, J. (1995) *The Idea of an Ethical Community*, Ithaca, NY: Cornell University Press. p. 179.
4. Brown, A. (1986) *Modern Political Philosophy: Theories of the Just Society*, London: Penguin. p. 191.
5. Cohen, S. (2007) 'Human Rights and Crimes of the State: The Culture of Denial', *Australian and New Zealand Journal of Criminology*, 26 (2): 97–115. Reprinted in

E. McLaughlin et al. (eds), (2002) *Criminological Perspectives: Essential Readings*, London: Sage. pp. 542–560.

6. Brandt, T. (1959) *Ethical Theory*, Englewood Cliffs, NJ: Prentice-Hall. p. 436. See also Brandt's classic article 'The Concepts of Obligation and Duty', *Mind*, 73: 364–393.
7. Hart, 'Legal Rights'.
8. Kramer, M. H. (2001) 'Getting Rights Right', in M. H. Kramer (ed.), *Rights and Wrongs and Responsibilities*, Basingstoke: Palgrave. pp. 28–95.
9. Coleman, J. (2000) 'Crimes and Transactions', *California Law Review*, 88: 921–930.
10. Halpin, A. (1997) *Rights and Law – Analysis and Theory*, Oxford: Hart Publishing. pp. 17–19, 27–59, 264–265.
11. Harel, A. (2005) 'Theories of Rights', in M. P. Golding and W. A. Edmundson (eds), *Philosophy and Legal Theory*, Oxford: Blackwell. pp. 191–206.
12. Von Hirsch, A. (1986) *Past or Future Crimes*, Manchester: Manchester University Press. p. 54.
13. Kant, I. (1965) *The Metaphysical Elements of Justice*, New York and London: Macmillan. p. 37.
14. Ibid. p. 65.
15. Rosen, A. D. (1993) *Kant's Theory of Justice*, Ithaca, NY: Cornell University Press. p. 103.
16. Kant, I. (1964) *The Doctrine of Virtue*, Philadelphia, PA: University of Pennsylvania Press. p. 383.
17. Rosen, *Kant's Theory of Justice*. pp. 60–64.
18. Bentham, J. (1987) 'Anarchical Fallacies: Being an Examination of the Declaration of Rights Issued during the French Revolution', in J. Waldron (ed.), *Nonsense upon Stilts: Bentham, Burke and Marx on the Rights of Man*, London: Methuen. p. 53.
19. Schwarzmantel, J. (1994) *The State in Contemporary Society*, Hemel Hempstead: Harvester. pp. 91–113.
20. Bentham, 'Anarchical Fallacies'. p. 53.
21. Dworkin, R. (1977) *Taking Rights Seriously*, Cambridge, MA: Harvard University Press. p. xi.
22. Lyons, D. (1992) 'Bentham, Utilitarianism and Distribution', *Utilitas*, 4 (2): 324.
23. Mill, J. S. (1962) 'Essay on Liberty', in *Utilitarianism*, ed. M. Warnock, London: Collins. p. 134.
24. See Postema, G. J. (1986) *Bentham and the Common Law Tradition*, Oxford: Oxford University Press.
25. Mill, J. S. (1979) *Utilitarianism*, Indianapolis, IN: Hackett Publishing. pp. 41–63.
26. Ibid. p. 58.
27. Choongh, S. (2002) 'Police Investigative Powers', in M. McConville and G. Wilson (eds), *The Handbook of the Criminal Justice Process*, Oxford: Oxford University Press. pp. 21–42.
28. *The Times*, 9 July 2007.
29. *Terminiello* v. *Chicago* 337 US 1 (1949) – a case of how to interpret Justice Holmes's 'clear and present danger' test for limitations on freedom of expression.
30. Crime and Disorder Act, 1998, Anti Social Behaviour Act, 2003.
31. *Kopp* v. *Switzerland, PG and JH* v. *United Kingdom*, cf. Grant (2005) Crim. LR 955.
32. *Ludi* v. *Switzerland, Khan* v. *UK, PG and JH* v. *UK*; cf. dissenting judgments of Loucaides and of Tulkens and Art. 3 and *A* v. *Home Secretary* (2005) UKHL 71, *Teixeira de Castro* v. *Portugal* 25829/94 (1998) ECHR 52 (9 June 1998).
33. The Criminal Justice Act 2003 allows evidence of previous criminal convictions to be used against a defendant to a far greater extent than the rules of common law relating to 'similar fact evidence'.

34. *R* v. *Al-Khawaja* (2006) 1 All ER 543 (Court of Appeal, Criminal Division) – hearsay evidence of a deceased witness; R v. *Xhabri* (2006) 1 All ER 776 (Court of Appeal Criminal Division) – hearsay evidence of a witness who was nevertheless available for cross-examination.
35. Art. 5 and *Brannigan and McBride* v. *UK, Heaney and McGuinness* v. *Ireland* 2001.
36. *Salabiaku* v. *France* 10519/83 (1988) ECHR 19 (7 October 1988), cf. *Sheldrake, AG's Reference* (2004) UKHL 43.
37. There has been a deal of discussion concerning the whole issue of the status of the criminal sanction cf. *Engel* v. *Netherlands* (1979–80) 1 EHRR 647.
38. *Clingham* v. *Kensington and Chelsea Royal London Borough Council; R. (on the application of McCann)* v. *Manchester Crown Court* (2002) UKHL 39.
39. For example, the Violent Crime Reduction Bill 2005.
40. Cf. *Welch* v. *UK*; Alldridge, P. (2202) 'Smuggling, Confiscation and Forfeiture', *Modern Law Review*, 65: 781–791.
41. *Ibbotson* v. *UK* 40146/98 and *Adamson* v. *UK* 42293/98, which challenged Article 7 and Article 8. See also Serious Organised Crime and Police Act 2005.
42. Clause 5 of the Terrorism Bill 2006.
43. Cullen, F. T. and Gilbert, K. E. (1982) 'Reaffirming Rehabilitation', in A. von Hirsch and A. Ashworth (eds), *Principled Sentencing*, Edinburgh: Edinburgh University Press. p. 33.
44. Lacey, N. (2007) 'Space, Time and Function: Intersecting Principles of Responsibility across the Terrain of Criminal Justice', *Criminal Law and Philosophy*, 1: 233–250.
45. Sanders, A. and Young, R. (2007) 'From Suspect to Trial', in M. Maguire et al. (eds), *The Oxford Handbook of Criminology*, Oxford: Oxford University Press. pp. 953–989.
46. Hudson, B. (2000) 'Punishment, Rights and Difference: Defending Justice in the Risk Society', in K. Stenson and R. Sullivan (eds), *Crime, Risk and Justice*, Cullompton: Willan Publishing. p. 166.
47. Waddington, P., Stenson, K. and Don, D. (2004) 'In Proportion: Race and Police Stop and Search', *British Journal of Criminology*, 44 (6): 889–914.
48. Hudson, 'Punishment, Rights and Difference'. p. 162.
49. Gilligan, C. (1982) *In a Different Voice*, Cambridge, MA: Harvard University Press.
50. Ibid. pp. 209–211.
51. Posner, R. A. (1993) *The Problems of Jurisprudence*, Cambridge, MA: Harvard University Press. p. 407.
52. Smith, P. and Natalier, K. (2005) *Understanding Criminal Justice: Sociological Perspectives*, London: Sage. p. 147.
53. Posner, *The Problems of Jurisprudence*. p. 410.
54. MacKinnon, C. (1987) *Feminism Unmodified: Discourses on Life and Law*, Cambridge, MA: Harvard University Press. p. 39.
55. Murphy, J. E. (1995) 'Marxism and Retribution', in Simmons, A. J., Cohen, M., Cohen, J. and Beitz, C. R. *Punishment: A Philosophy and Public Affairs Reader*. Princeton, NJ: Princeton University Press. pp. 3–29.
56. Murphy, 'Marxism and Retribution'. pp. 25–27.
57. Marx, K. (1853) 'On Capital Punishment', *New York Daily Tribune*, 28 February.
58. Marx, K. (1987) 'On the Jewish Question', in J. Waldron (ed.), *Nonsense upon Stilts: Bentham, Burke and Marx on the Rights of Man*, London: Methuen. p. 147.
59. Ibid. p. 147.

4

POLICE AND POLICING

... the political neutrality or independence of the police cannot withstand serious consideration. It rests on an untenably narrow conception of 'the political', restricting it to partisan conflict. In a broader sense, all relationships, which have a power dimension, are political. Policing is inherently and inescapably political in that sense.

Robert Reiner, 2000[1]

Introduction

For most people the sight of police officers on the streets is the most obvious evidence of the criminal justice system at work in their community. Historically, at least, the police have always been seen as a reassuring presence on the streets. Yet, as McLaughlin has recently noted:

> The police constable [also] occupies a complicated position in Britain's highly strati-fied social structure. He is supposed to be from as well as of the community but there is also a constitutional requirement of police officers to have an arm's length rela-tionship with the community. As an officer of the Crown he is not allowed to engage in politics or over-identify with any particular group or sectional interest.[2]

The police are of us and also not of us: we and they live with that duality. Police officers occupy a complex array of roles and the politics of policing is often an attempt to stress one or other of these roles to the detriment of one or other roles. Should there be more police on the streets? Should police uphold the law in all cases? Should the police have more powers or less powers? Modern polic-ing is about much more than just a reassuring presence on the streets and nei-ther is it reducible to the work of individual police officers. Moreover, modern policing often has a totalising aspect to it. In an important book, *Crime in an Insecure World*, Richard Ericson has stated: '...policing is integral to every insti-tution and relations among institutions, and it has no obvious limits. It entails a perpetual and infinite thirst for knowledge of potential harms as a capacity to overcome uncertainties and underpin security.'[3] Ericson argues that policing in the modern world is all about the management and science of risk and that 'police power is perfected when it results in self-policing among members of the population. The liberal social imaginary of the "house of certainty" is a house of discipline and self-policing.'[4] Ericson's work is indebted to the political theorist Charles Taylor, who emphasises the fact that the sheer complexity of modern societies militates against their governability.[5] Ericson's work attempts to demonstrate how modern policing may have reached the limits of its capacity for public reassurance and crime control. 'The politics of uncertainty, conducted through the sciences of risk and in law, expresses increasing doubt about the capacity of liberal governments to govern the future and provide security. Indeed, in many quarters there is radical doubt, radical uncertainty, suggesting the ungovernability of modern societies.'[6]

It is very interesting to note how Richard Ericson, one of the world's leading criminologists, has both moved away from traditional narratives of policing and towards an analysis deeply indebted to political theory and a broader, and richer, understanding of social processes. The work of McLaughlin and Ericson is a refreshing challenge to more normative understandings of the police, which by comparison seem slightly dated and tinged by positivism, at least to the extent that they see the problems of policing as solvable and straightforward. The older narrative is giving way to the new. For example, Waddington asserts that policing is 'the exercise of the authority of state over the civil population. That authority is based on the monopoly of legitimate coercion – cops usually ask or command people to do something and those people normally comply; but if they do not, then the cops will *force* them into compliance.'[7] McLaughlin's notions of the complexity of 'multi-social' policing and Ericson's ideas about living with uncertainty and risk seem to be truer representations of the world of policing than the simple subject–object relationship offered by Waddingtion.[8]

Building on Ericson and McLaughlin, this chapter will set out three main types of underlying political supposition used to support contemporary writing about the police. These are what I shall term the conservative impulse, the Marxist critique and the community management strategy. Broadly speaking, these underlying suppositions derive from, or were originally developed in, political, as opposed to criminological, theory. This chapter will set out the basis of these three suppositions and link them to forms in existing criminological explanation. What is interesting is how each of these three underlying political suppositions conceives the relationship between the individual and the police and between the individual and the state.

The Conservative Impulse

In the many volumes that have been written by criminologists about policing, little scholarship has been given over to understanding the basic functions of policing in terms of its support in conservative political theory, i.e. in terms of its *raison d'être* for preserving order, maintaining the *status quo* and defending private property, all of which are dealt with extensively by conservative political writers. Rarely is conservative theory set out in contemporary criminological literature in regard to the basic defence of the state either. When criminologists have attempted an understanding of conservative thinking the tendency has usually been to reduce conservatism to a rather naïve and unhelpful set of social attitudes.[9] Not only can it easily be argued that all the basic functions of the police are necessarily conservative, but the political left and right largely agree that they are, and the debate concerns whether this is a good thing in its extent and the rightness of what it preserves. Roger Scruton, a leading conservative philosopher, has argued:

> The law is the will of the state, and the domestic expression of its power. And since state and civil society are interdependent, the legitimate sphere of law will be all that matters to social continuity, all that can be taken as standing in need of state protection. The law must cover all activity through which the bonds of trust and allegiance are cemented or broken. Obvious instances – the upholding of contract, the outlawing of gratuitous violence, the common essence of civil and criminal law – follow from this view.[10]

Conservative political theory upholds the values of traditional forms of social and political organisation. It sees knowledge and wisdom as being passed on through tradition. In doing this, it acknowledges that any society is more than the sum of its parts, and that issues of justice always have an intergenerational aspect. Society is understood by conservatives as functioning through a delicate mechanism of mutual adjustments which arises out of practical lived experience. In such a way, it is argued, individuals come to see the way things are done and understood. It is a tacit and intuited understanding of how society should be, which always looks backwards in time for its justification and its arguments are always historically situated. Conservative political theory posits that any understanding of how individuals ought to operate in society is learned through the day-to-day practice of living within a particular society and is always informed by historical practice.[11] Tradition and traditional ways of doing things are esteemed, as are the structures which maintain existing forms of civic life. The conception that there is value in tradition necessarily privileges a particular historical perspective, i.e. continuity is prized over change.[12]

A classical legacy

The state, in conservative thought, is the ultimate facilitator of civic order. The state's institutions are understood as allowing the functioning of civil society through the establishment of order, legal codes and a minimal level of welfare. The most important function of any conservative state is the resolution of conflict and this necessitates that the state always has sovereignty over all citizens and associations, though this sovereignty can only be secured by proper (i.e. authentic) political representation and an independent legal system and a legitimate policing function.[13] An example of this is given by the conservative political theorist, Leo Strauss, who derived his ideas from his reading of how the Greek *polis* functioned.[14] In his book, *Natural Right and History*, he argued: 'The best regime will then be a republic in which landed gentry, which is at the same time the urban patriciate, well-bred and public spirited, obeying laws and completing them, ruling and being ruled in turn predominates and gives society its character.'[15] In advocating this, Strauss follows the Greek philosopher Plato, in upholding a moral hierarchy built on natural law and which establishes the primacy, and co-identity, of philosophical knowledge and political order.[16] The notion that a stratified society is the proper natural outcome of human history as well as the underpinning of political life is not only a political dogma but also a moral evaluation. This form of reasoning Strauss derived from Plato, but it may also be found in the work of the Roman statesman, lawyer and political theorist, Cicero, and the thirteenth-century Christian theologian and philosopher, St Thomas Aquinas.[17] Persons are not equal in conservative thought though they enjoy a technical equality before the law.[18] An ordered political society under law and policed through consent is the precondition of civic life and private property. What Rowe has argued about Plato's *Republic* might too be said of all conservative ideas concerning the role of law, and law enforcement, in the affairs of men and women:

> What Plato wants is ultimately the improvement of humanity at large; and the majority of us will require more than exhortation to push us in the right direction. The tools which lie to hand are the laws and institutions of society, by which – to a degree – our behaviour is normally controlled. Plato's political proposals consist essentially in the extension and transformation of those laws and institutions for the effective production of virtue.[19]

The defence of private property is essential to contemporary conservative political theory but its origin is in the classical period. As Cicero had argued in *De Officiis* (*On Duties*):

> ...although it was by nature's guidance that men were drawn together in communities [*congrebantur homines*], it was in the hope of safeguarding their possessions [*rerum suarum*] that they sought protection of cities [*urbium*][20] ... the chief purpose in the establishment of states and constitutional orders [*res publicae civitatesque constitutae*] was that individual property rights might be secured [*sua tenerentur*] ... it is the peculiar function of state and city [*civitatis atque urbis*] to guarantee to every man the free and undisturbed control of his own particular property [*suae rei*].[21]

Here Cicero is giving a justification for *tutela*, which means guardianship or trust. *Tutela* is best understood as an aspect of Roman Law that, in its original formulation, is concerned with the relationship between individuals, private property and the state and which sought to defend property, especially family property. Moreover, Cicero advocates the use, if necessary, of state sanctioned violence to defend public order and private property, though he is generally antithetical to the use of force.[22]

The Romans had an elaborated conception of private property which covered its acquisition, transmission and defence in law. The role of the state was to defend private property by upholding the laws which protected it. Cicero, as a practising lawyer, made sure that the defence of private property was at the heart of his political theory.

Private property

Roger Scruton has argued that:

> The first thing to be said is that ownership is the primary relation through which man and nature come together. It is therefore the first stage in the socializing of objects, and the condition of all institutions. It is not necessarily a product of greed or exploitation but it is necessarily a part of the process whereby man frees himself from the power of things, transforming resistant nature into compliant image. Through property man imbues his world with will, and begins to discover himself as a social being.[23]

This rather Hegelian view sees private property as the basis of all social relations, the site of self-realisation and the justification for the state, i.e. as the ultimate protector of private property and social relations. In defending private property the conservative does not so much defend wealth accumulation but the self-realisation of the individual and civil society, both of which are assured by it in turn. The state alone can defend this conception through civil and criminal legal codes, though the law is itself secured by our own personal relation to it under a system of private property. The state and the law are things that individuals can have a direct relationship with through political life. The state on this view is a personality, a corporate personality in the terms set out in conservative thought by von Gierke and Maitland.[24] It follows from this that the most basic function of the police is to uphold the prevailing system of private property relations and, in so doing, uphold the state.

Hobbes

This form of conservative reasoning found its pre-eminent expression in the work of the seventeenth-century English political philosopher Thomas Hobbes, though it should be noted that Leo Strauss always understood Hobbes as a liberal contract theorist.[25] Modern conservative theorists, such as Hannah Arendt,[26] have always looked to Hobbes' work as a starting point for their own ideas. In Hobbes, the basic problem for individuals is how they are to be preserved from the state of nature, the war of all against all. Hobbes argued that this is achieved only by a strong sovereign (from which we may infer a state) which individuals both give rise to through deliberation and, in turn, are protected by. The sovereign (state) severely punishes all those who disobey the law and if the sovereign is successful, then no individual will feel threatened, as would be the case in the state of nature. The sovereign's function is to facilitate law-abiding behaviour and civil order. Hobbes suggests in *Leviathan* that there is a vertical relationship between the ruler and the people.[27] This has been termed a 'foundational' relationship, though that is misleading because what is really being suggested is that there is a contract between an existing society and the ruler who is outside it.[28] The hypothetical nature of the original contract supports and justifies a rule of law which is already in place. What the conservative derives from this is the political rationale that one consents to be ruled. Roger Scruton has written how '[f]ree and open contract presupposes a sufficient order, not because it would otherwise be impossible to enforce contracts [although that is true], but because without social order the very notion of an individual *committing* himself, through a promise, would not arise'.[29]

Hegel

Following Hobbes, the German philosopher Georg Wilhelm Frederick Hegel, writing in the early part of the nineteenth century, addressed the issue of wrong, which includes crime.[30] Crime is seen as an offence against the particular and general will. As with Hobbes, the issue of contract arises, but in Hegel it is more concerned with the way a person becomes individualised in society through private property. Contract is the realisation of personality in the sense that through contract and private property a person's rights become known and acknowledged by others. The criminal is the person who, through theft, denies the rights of another. Criminal punishment is therefore that which annuls crime, restores right and re-establishes the proper civic order. Again, as with Hobbes, the conservative defence of private property and civic order is to the fore. The law and its enforcement not only protect the individual but also underpin the whole idea of Man, as an abstract and universal idea. Hegel goes beyond the implied need for a force to uphold private property and civic order and gives an elaborated explanation of legal codes, courts and society's necessary policing function.[31] In Hegel, the system of law is matched to a notion of its enforcement. Hegel did not believe human societies could ever be self-regulating and saw an elaborated role for the public authority (police) in intervening in and regulating the relationships of citizens. Indeed, the public authority may even intervene in the lives of citizens even when individuals are not breaking the law if that prevents persons from imposing harm on others.[32] This is akin to the notion of the police as agents of social discipline that, among others, Lucia Zedner, following Choongh, has set out.[33]

It is relatively easy to infer that the issue of policing in conservative theory is a straightforward issue of upholding law and order, the existing authority and the institution of private property, and that it is a view which is largely uncritical of the *status quo*. However, it would be wrong to underplay the importance of the conservative impulse as a constituent in *any* rationale for policing. The idea that contract, order and private property should be upheld would appear to be universal features of all forms of modern liberal jurisprudence and political theory. The remaining issues are not so much with the notions that conservative thought works as with their extent (in theory and practice) and how critically, or otherwise, the basis of authority is determined. What is certain about the conservative impulse is that it has a benign conception of the state and the public authorities. It is this basic feature of the conservative impulse that is disputed in the Marxist critique.

The Marxist Critique

The Marxist critique is associated with a progressive political analysis. It has a view of policing which always asks questions of authority and existing sources of legitimacy and whereas the conservative impulse looks benignly upon the state as the upholder of law and order, authority and the institution of private property, the Marxist critique is sceptical of these. It is far more concerned with the rightness of how things ought to be rather than how they are and accordingly it sees no point in defending the *status quo* when it is determined as an illegitimate basis for addressing profound issues of justice or when the *status quo* itself is the outcome of a prior unfair settlement. The Marxist critique has been especially popular in England, where it has been developed by both theorists and empirical researchers, notably in relation to the policing of race, especially 'mugging', and industrial relations disputes, such as the 1984–85 Miner's Strike, which brought the organised working class into direct conflict with the Thatcher government and the police.[34] This may be, in part, because of the type of policing employed in England. As Reiner has pointed out, in contrast to most other nations: 'A characteristic of the English police tradition is the attempted unification in the same organisation of the "high policing" function of regulating explicit political dissidence with the "low policing" task of routine law enforcement and street-level order maintenance.'[35] In England, it is therefore easier to detect a basic continuity between what Reiner terms the high and low functions of policing and essentially this is what the Marxist critique does in upholding the self-interested nature of the capitalist state.

Marx is a towering figure and his writings have informed the work of numerous criminologists and social scientists, notably since the 1960s. Indeed, his influence has been so immense that many aspects of his political and economic analysis have found their way into a great deal of contemporary criminological scholarship that would not term itself Marxist, or Marxian. This is because many of his ideas have become orthodoxy, such as the notion that the 'capitalist' state is fundamentally skewed, in an unfair way, towards those groups, and their values, that already enjoy economic and political power. Marx's own voluminous writings are open to a wide variety of interpretations but this section will concentrate upon Marxist treatments of the state, its values, and its defence, all of which underscore policing policy. Marx himself wrote almost nothing about policing, and so those who follow in his footsteps have had to infer a position, based upon his general politico-economic position. He certainly saw criminals in a negative light. He thought people who broke the law should be punished.[36]

Marxist analysis, in all its forms, shares several of the key theoretical elements used in conservative thought, especially a concern for history and for the self-realisation of persons, though the understanding of them is radically different from the analysis offered by modern conservative thinkers, such as Leo Strauss or Roger Scruton. However, unlike in conservative thought, history, as related by Marx and his followers, is concerned with a dogmatic account of economic development, related to historical materialism, and the present alienation of persons.

The laws of the capitalist state are maintained by its agents, the police. The coercive power of the capitalist state is seen as its most important function because only through this coercive power can unfair property relations be protected and existing class divisions be maintained.[37] The state is seen not to serve all but to serve only the sectional interests of the capitalist class. It should be noted that Marxist analysis is rooted in a materialist philosophical scheme which has a far more elaborated conception of the economy than in conservative thought. As David Garland has stated when discussing Marxism:

> ...'economy' – that sphere of activity which produces the material necessities of life – will always be the key locus of power in any society. Those groups which dominate in this realm will thus be able to impose their power – and the distinctive social relations which this economic power requires – on to the other spheres of social life. Consequently, the institutions of law, politics, morality, philosophy, religion and so on will tend to be forcibly adapted to fit the conditions of economic life, and will come to take on forms and values which are in keeping with the dominant mode of production.[38]

The big assumption here is that the dominant economic class, the capitalist class, will go on to maintain its economic dominance through the domination of non-economic arenas in the superstructure, such as law, culture, politics and education. Moreover, it will achieve this straightforwardly due to the overwhelming determining power of the economic base.[39] Since all things in the world are derived from the economic base, the police may be said to straightforwardly function as part of the apparatus that maintains the capitalist class in its structurally dominant position.[40]

Marxist Criminology

In Criminology, Marxism had enjoyed some limited support in the early part of the twentieth century, especially with William Bonger,[41] but it was the 1970s that witnessed a resurgence of interest in Marxism from mainstream theorists like Bill Chambliss, Bob Fine, Colin Sumner and Ian Taylor.[42] The 1970s witnessed an unprecedented level of Marxist scholarship in social and political history, much of which focused on law and punishment, and which had an impact in sociological and criminological circles at the time.[43] It is also worth noting the work of Stuart Hall's Centre for Contemporary Cultural Studies at Birmingham University in the 1970s, which drew heavily upon the continental Marxist tradition. It emphasised Marxist thinkers, especially Antonio Gramsci, and utilised the concept of hegemony. In the *German Ideology*, Marx had argued that the ideas of the ruling class were always the ruling ideas of the day and Gramsci developed his ideas in relation to a form of Marxist scholarship, indebted to Lenin, which rejected economic determinism and tried to understand the processes of capitalist ideological domination. Gramsci had been concerned with how the 'ruling class not only justifies and maintains its dominance, but manages to win the active consent of those over whom it rules'.[44] Later Marxist thinkers, using the concept of hegemony, sought to address the issues of how consensus is maintained in an unequal class society and how people become alienated from their true interests. Consequently, they tend to focus upon issues of culture, including the media. This emphasis upon the work of Gramsci is particularly pronounced in Criminology with Sumner's classic *Reading Ideologies*.[45] The publication of *The New Criminology* in 1973 witnessed a movement away from both 'orthodox' Criminology and Sociology.[46] It also broke with the 'orthodox' Marxist tradition of the time, which had aligned criminals with the lumpenproletariat and those persons sapping the revolutionary spirit from the working class. *The New Criminology* was prefigured in its revision of the way Marxist criminologists understood criminals by earlier work in political theory, notably by Draper and Hirst.[47] Before the 1970s, Marxism had given little attention to criminals. Marxism had always had a very moral tone in relation to crime and *The New Criminology*, in Sumner's words, made 'the central accusation ... that the creative, human, element in deviant behaviour had been neglected at the expense of economic determinism'.[48] This shift of focus within Marxist scholarship ushered in a new way to understand criminality and there was an explosion of work which emphasised the role of policing in repressing the working class. It also always had an eye on politicising the working class through its writings on the unfairness of policing and the oppressive nature of capitalist social relations: it is a shibboleth of Marxism that one cannot disentangle political action and scholarship, and that the one should seek to reinforce the other.[49]

This renewed interest in the work of Gramsci and the idea of hegemony at Birmingham found a ready reception in the sociological and criminological analysis of the time in Britain. Phil Cohen wrote *Policing and the Working Class City* from a Marxist perspective which is indebted to Gramsci.[50] Cohen argued that the British police force were part of a wider educational state system. The police were said to be arbiters of deviance and administrators of a juridical ideology of crime. In other words, the police have both expressive and repressive functions, derived from their place in the overall structure of the capitalist state.[51] The police are the organisation which has the task of 'imposing the elements of a properly capitalist urban discipline in the name of public propriety'.[52] In the same collection, Bob Fine summed up the issue thus: 'It is only when we view the connection between the form and the content of bourgeois law that its class character becomes apparent.'[53] This form of Marxist analysis sees the police as maintaining an unfair system of law and property relations. They are nothing less than agents of *capitalist* social control. The movement away from understanding criminals in terms of Marx and Engels' *The German Ideology*, i.e. emphasising the non-revolutionary aspects of the lumpenproletariat (which contains the criminal classes) and towards an understanding of law and policing in terms of their hegemonic aspects, was transformative for Marxist criminological analysis. It allowed Marxist criminologists to ask broader questions relating to the structure of society and to contextualise, rather than merely censure, criminal activity and policing.

The Marxist critique is now an established theoretical stance within Criminology. Its emphasis on structural and economic inequality and the role of policing in maintaining it has spawned some of the most influential work in Criminology over the past 30 years. It has also had a huge effect upon policing practice and the way we understand policing.[54] However, to assent to its overall conclusions about crime and policing, and not merely to note some of the points that it makes, requires one to believe in a Marxist analysis of the economy and nature of social structures which many believe to have been largely discredited. Therefore just as some elements of the conservative impulse have become orthodoxy, such as the belief that private property needs to be defended, the Marxist critique has given us new orthodoxies, such as the notion that policing, at least in part, is about maintaining the *status quo*. It should be noted that elements of the Marxist critique have entered Feminist analysis and, latterly, Green Criminology. However, in the past 20 years a far more pragmatic notion has taken hold of Criminology, that of devising an effective *community management strategy* for the irreducible policing issues that are thrown up by all modern societies.

Community Management Strategy

The community management strategy is not a straightforward focus upon real-world policing issues so much as an analysis informed by the implementation of communitarian ideas, within policy and criminological analysis. New forms of policing, including the use of wardens and PCSOs (Police Community Support Officers) who work with local people, may be seen as 'part of a wider move to engage ordinary people in running their own communities. This evolving process is predicated upon an active citizenry – it may be possible to manage and police public space without the active support of ordinary people but it is unlikely to be successful. The idea underpinning these developments in the management of public space is partnership.'[55] The concern for community relates, approximately to the post-*After Virtue*[56] concern, by political theorists, to frame 'the common good'.[57] It was a critique of the limited government liberalism that marked the Thatcher and Reagan era, which had tended to downplay the role of community contexts and stress the culpability of individuals in the criminalisation process. It focused upon the notion that communities have common social purposes and it displayed optimism about the ability of the police, working in collaboration with citizens, to have an impact upon crime levels – something

Bill Clinton made much of in his administration. However, some writers have claimed that it is unrealistic to ever assume high degrees of social and political homogeneity in terms of the values espoused in complex contemporary societies.[58] Communitarianism typically eschews grand narratives, like those found in Marxism, in favour of understanding the dynamics of specific communities and it focuses upon developments in practical policing which have an incremental impact upon crime levels. Alasdair MacIntyre has outlined exactly what Communitarianism aims to do when he writes in terms of 'an account of the good which is at once local and particular – located in and partially defined by the characteristics of the *polis* – and yet cosmic and universal'.[59] The communitarian account emphasises a community management strategy based on a partnership between community and police that relies on the public not only to report crime but also to work with the police to develop a 'sense of community' and thereby undermine crime formation.[60] It is based on a high sense of community engagement. Moreover, police success is evaluated in terms of its ability to respond to community values and priorities and not simply in terms of its ability to control crime. However, as McLaughlin has argued: 'Community policing approaches are [also] inherently undemocratic because the police define the parameters of the debate for other agencies and the community is conceptualised as just another resource to be used in the officially defined fight against crime.'[61]

It has also stressed the role of social control in late modernity as part of the policy package aimed at promoting the common good. As David Garland has noted:

> ...the development of late modernity reduced the extent and effectiveness of 'spontaneous' social control – which is to say, the learned, un-reflexive, habitual practices of mutual supervision, scolding, sanctioning, and shaming carried out, as a matter of course, by community members. The current wave of crime prevention behaviour tries to revive these dying habits, and more importantly, to supplement them with new crime control practices that are more deliberate, more focused, and more reflexive.[62]

Unlike the conservative impulse, or the Marxist critique, its main concern is with the day-to-day management of criminal activity and police effectiveness, gauged in terms of the common good. It also underscores the need for citizens to act with a high degree of social responsibility.[63] The notions that strong communities are the best basis for tackling social alienation and crime, and that the state should promote communal life, have infused policy discussions on both sides of the Atlantic for over two decades now. However, some criminologists, notably Gordon Hughes, have mistakenly taken the communitarian concern with past ways of organising communities, along with its positive view of social control, to be evidence of neo-conservatism. This is profoundly mistaken as neo-conservativism derives its inspiration from past ways of organising societies, whereas communitarians seek to develop new forms of social organisation.[64] Rather, Selznick makes the better point that, in practice, communitarian ideas are usually blended with existing liberal values, in which case they 'treasure liberal values and institutions, but also take seriously the promise of community and the perils of ignoring the need for community'.[65] The overall aim that Selznick has in mind is the development of a political and social environment better able to address the profound issues affecting crime formation. However, David Downes has argued that the inability to properly fund the police and other agencies has often led to increased levels of juvenile crime and school exclusions.[66]

In Britain it has sometimes been allied with the 'new realism' in the Labour Party, beginning with Neil Kinnock and developing under Tony Blair.[67] The community management strategy, in policy terms, is built upon a collaborative approach to policing, which is reflected in legislation such as the Police and Magistrates' Courts Act 1994 and the Police Act 1996, both of which focus upon police authorities as part of the managerial accountability process. The political point here is that in using the term 'accountability', those who advocate the community management strategy are focusing upon the notion of the police as performing a public service for the common good. The spread of communitarian ideas coincided with a convergence in policy thinking between many in the senior ranks of the police and those at the top of the governing Labour Party, as Barry Sheerman MP has pointed out.[68] Nevertheless, this 'new realism' had support right across political parties in Britain. Who now could talk about policing without reference to communities and their values? Police and citizen are increasingly focused upon the same ends and engaged in similar practical defences of communal life.[69] The Crime and Disorder Act 1998 was allied to the Crime and Disorder Strategy, which set out local priorities, targets and performance measures. The task of crime fighting went local under the Blair government and the Crime and Disorder Act 1998 gave responsibility for crime and disorder to the local authorities, who were expected to work in collaboration with the police.[70] The Crime and Disorder Act 1998 emphasised the participation of communities and took seriously the issues faced by women and ethnic minorities, among others. The intellectual shift away from understanding policing as separate from the local community and towards a more collaborative and communitarian understanding of the relationship between citizens and police officers has established a more fluid relationship between the police and the policed. Moreover, as Bayley has noted,[71] the values and practices of the police in a communitarian model of policing always relate directly to the context of the given community, and the Crime and Disorder Act 1998 emphasised this in the British example. Beneath the Crime and Disorder Act 1998 lies a much deeper reorientation of the democratic principles that inform policing away from crime control alone to the broader embrace of community problems.[72] Following the Crime and Disorder Act 1998, the whole thrust of policing became premised upon community partnership and engagement. The necessity of an active citizenry has altered the face of policing practice a great deal. Indeed, as Zedner has pointed out: 'Private citizens also fulfil important policing duties as special constables, neighbourhood watch coordinators, members of citizen's patrols, and as participants in community-based crime prevention programmes.'[73] However, Reiner has made the counter point: 'The police are becoming part of a more varied assortment of bodies with policing functions, and a more diffuse array of policing processes, within and between nation-states. Police officers can no longer be totems symbolizing a cohesive social order which no longer exists.'[74]

The community management strategy seeks to develop a positive relationship between the public and the police in order to tackle crime and build strong communities. However, political theorists, such as Gutmann and Wallach, have pointed to the dangers of its implicit majoritarianism, especially in a multicultural context.[75] It is easy to see that policing priorities and social values are contested and, by extension, to understand how certain groups, in the minority, could feel themselves excluded from the basis of policing in the community in which they live. Political liberals, notably Ronald Dworkin,[76] have attacked the communitarians' lack of any serious consideration of rights, especially for minorities. The leading political theorist John Charvet has made the point that 'communitarians affirm one general principle: each is to follow the norms of his society'.[77] Charvet's work underscores the might of the majority view and the inability of individuals to resist the general view of the community. The community management strategy is undoubtedly right to link effective policing with the development of partnerships between the community and the police, and yet a narrow appeal to 'community' settles nothing in a modern multicultural society. No modern multicultural society can ignore the development of shared values if it is to successfully organise itself. The problem for contemporary policing is that to be engaged in both crime-fighting functions and the development of positive community values, which foster the common good, is to be continually involved in a discussion about which of these two elements is the more important.

Jean Charles de Menezes: Assumptions behind a Blunder

We have seen how political theorists have tried to develop practical models of the world and how those models have, in turn, impacted upon policing theory and practice. However, the world, unlike the models, is a messy place where things do not always follow the paths predicted by theorists. Yet sometimes this messiness can result in light being thrown on the assumptions about the nature of policing that are ordinarily hidden from our view. On 22 July 2005 Jean Charles de Menezes, an innocent working man, was killed by police officers in Stockwell underground station. The police officers were involved in counter-terrorism work. The killing was a horrendous error and at one level could be treated as a regrettable operational blunder. However, at the time of the killing, the nation, especially in London, was at a heightened state of alert after a series of terrorist outrages and Jean Charles de Menezes was mistaken for a terrorist suspect. He apparently looked like a Muslim from the Middle East, though he was actually Brazilian.[78] As McLaughlin has noted:

> The clinical nature of the SAS-style killing and the police rationalization of the need to 'test' the new counter-terrorism protocol touched a raw nerve. ... Human rights groups warned that providing the police with SAS-style 'licence to kill' was adding to the climate of public fear rather than providing public reassurance.[79]

The de Menezes killing threw the relationship between the police and government and the news media under the spotlight.[80] It also highlighted, and accentuated, the distance of senior police personnel, who had become prominent public figures, from the general public, whom they serve.[81] Moreover, it demonstrated how the twenty-first century is one where policing is prioritised as the site of arguments over human rights, democratic values and the nature of cosmopolitan citizenship.[82] As Sivanandan has argued, after the bombings of 7 July 2005 the civil liberties of non-white citizens were compromised and the promise of multiculturalism gave way to the alienation and victimisation of large numbers of non-white British citizens.[83]

So what does the work of McLaughlin and Sivanandan teach us about the conservative impulse, the Marxist critique and the community management strategy? In terms of conservative political thought there is support, as we have seen, in Cicero for state sanctioned violence to maintain public order. After terrorist outrages this may be legitimate. In Hegel, the conservative can find support for the regulation of citizens because there is a limit to the ability of citizens to regulate themselves. A conservative position therefore could give support to the police tactics employed against terrorism, which resulted in the de Menezes killing. Marxists could feel vindicated that the killing demonstrates how a coercive capitalist state functions and how the operational deployment of police officers to Stockwell was evidence of both the state's monopoly of power and its willingness to use force. However, the community management strategy is challenged most by the de Menezes killing because the whole notion of defending a community was thrown wide open. What community? Whose values? The questions are not simple ones in a world-city like London. The de Menezes killing also highlighted the criticisms made about the police setting agendas. The managerialism of the police was exposed, with senior police officers seemingly unaware of life on the streets but rather concerned with their own policy directives and procedures. New Scotland Yard seemed removed from the practical community life it policed. Most of all, the criticisms made by Gutmann and Wallach about the neglect of minority points of view in a communitarian scheme seemed to ring true. After the terrorist outrages the police force did not consider the fact that racial profiling meant that not all citizens were policed equally. Jean Charles de Menezes looked Islamic (though actually Brazilian) and this highlighted for many Londoners that they too were potential victims of mistaken identity; that they were not equal citizens. A practical policing issue was really, at heart, a political consideration.

Main Summary Points

- Conservatives believe that an ordered political society, under law, which is policed through consent, is the precondition of civic life and private property. Accordingly, the most basic function of the police is to uphold the prevailing system of private property relations and, in so doing, uphold the state.
- The Marxist view of policing is sceptical about state authority and other existing sources of legitimacy, such as private property. Marxists see the capitalist state as fundamentally skewed, in an unfair way, towards those groups, and their values, that already enjoy economic and political power.
- Bob Fine has expressed a Marxist view of law: 'It is only when we view the connection between the form and the content of bourgeois law that its class character becomes apparent.' Marxist criminologists have stressed the class nature of policing.
- The Communitarian account of policing emphasises a community management strategy based on a partnership between community and police. It relies on the public to report crime and it measures police success in terms of its ability to respond to community values and priorities.

Questions

1. What are the agreed functions of the police?
2. Should the police be more concerned with crime control or community values?
3. What can we learn about policing from the political theorists of the past?

Suggested Further Reading

Ericson, R. (2007) *Crime in an Insecure World,* London: Polity Press.
Garland, D. (2001) *The Culture of Control,* Oxford: Oxford University Press.
McLaughlin, E. (2007) *The New Policing,* London: Sage.
Scruton, R. (1984) *The Meaning of Conservatism* (2nd edition), Basingstoke and London: Macmillan.
Zedner, L. (2004) *Criminal Justice,* Oxford: Oxford University Press.

Notes

1. Reiner, R. (2000) *The Politics of the Police* (3rd edition), Oxford: Oxford University Press. p. 8.
2. McLaughlin, E. (2007) *The New Policing,* London: Sage. p. 37.
3. Ericson, R. (2007) *Crime in an Insecure World,* London: Polity Press. pp. 28–29.
4. Ibid. p. 29.
5. Taylor, C. (2004) *Modern Social Imaginaries,* Durham NC: Duke University Press.

6. Ericson, *Crime in an Insecure World*. p. 21.
7. Waddington, P. A. J. (2006) *Policing Citizens*, Oxford: Routledge. p. 30.
8. McLaughlin, *The New Policing*. p. 169; Ericson, *Crime in an Insecure World*. pp. 204–219.
9. Waddington, *Policing Citizens*. pp. 101, 116.
10. Scruton, R. (1984) *The Meaning of Conservatism* (2nd edition), Basingstoke and London: Macmillan. p. 75.
11. Scruton, R. (1991) *Conservative Texts*, New York: St Martin's Press. pp. 5–7.
12. Scruton, *Meaning of Conservatism*. pp. 40–45.
13. Scruton, *Conservative Texts*. pp. 13–18.
14. Strauss, L. (1953) *Natural Right and History*, Chicago: University of Chicago Press. p. 92.
15. Ibid. p. 142.
16. Plato (1974) *The Republic*, London: Penguin. 368a–434c; Plato (1970) *Laws*, London: Penguin. 625e–713a.
17. Strauss, *Natural Right and History*. p. 135.
18. Scruton, *Conservative Texts*. p. 24.
19. Rowe, C. J. (1984) *Plato*, Brighton: Harvester. p. 125.
20. Cicero (1913b) *On Duties* (*De Officiis*), Loeb Classical Library. Cambridge, MA: Harvard University Press. 2, 73.
21. Ibid. 2, 78.
22. Cicero (1913a) *Laws* (*De Legibus*), Loeb Classical Library. Cambridge, MA: Harvard University Press. 3, 11.
23. Scruton, *Meaning of Conservatism*. p. 99.
24. See Gierke, O. von (1934) *Natural Law and the Theory of Society*, ed. E. Baker, Cambridge: Cambridge University Press. pp. 1–40; and Maitland, F. W. (1911) 'Moral Personality and Legal Personality', in H. A. L. Fisher (ed.), *The Collected Papers of Frederick William Maitland*, Volume 3, Cambridge: Cambridge University Press. pp. 304–320.
25. Strauss, L. (1936) *The Political Philosophy of Hobbes: Its Basis and Its Genesis*, Oxford: Oxford University Press. pp. 159–160, 165; Strauss, L. (1950) 'On the Spirit of Hobbes' Political Philosophy', *Revue Internationale de Philosophie*, 4 (14): 30–50.
26. See Arendt, H. (1963) *On Revolution*, New York: Viking Press.
27. Hobbes, T. (1991) *Leviathan*, ed. Richard Tuck, Cambridge: Cambridge University Press.
28. Dubeiel, H. (1997) 'Hannah Arendt and the Theory of Democracy: A Critical Reconstruction', in Kielmansegg, P. G., Mewes, H. and Glaser-Schmidt, E., *Hannah Arendt and Leo Strauss: German Emigres and American Political Thought after World War Two*, Cambridge: Cambridge University Press. pp. 11–28.
29. Scruton, *Meaning of Conservatism*. p. 30.
30. See Hegel, G. W. F. (1967) *The Philosophy of Right*, trans. T. M. Knox, London: Oxford University Press; Tunnick, M. (1992a) *Hegel's Political Philosophy: Interpreting the Practice of Legal Punishment*. Princeton, NJ: Princeton University Press; Tunnick, M. (1992b) *Punishment Theory and Practice*, Berkeley, CA: University of California Press.
31. Hegel, *Philosophy of Right*. §228.
32. Ibid. §240.
33. Zedner, L. (2004) *Criminal Justice*, Oxford: Oxford University Press. pp. 133–136; Choongh, S. (1997) *Policing as Social Control*, Oxford: Clarendon Press. p. 41.
34. See Hall, S., Critcher, C., Jefferson, T., Claske, J. and Roberts, B. (1978) *Policing the Crisis*. London: Macmillan; and Fine, B. and Millar, R. (eds) (1985) *Policing the Miners' Strike*, London: Lawrence and Wishart.

35. Reiner, *The Politics of the Police.* p. 8.
36. Marx, K. and Engels, F. (1974) *The German Ideology*, ed. C. L. Arthur, London: Lawrence and Wishart; Marx, K. (1973) *The Eighteenth Brumaire of Louis Bonaparte*, trans. B. Fowkes, in *Surveys from Exile*, Harmondsworth: Penguin.
37. Coleman, J. (1990) *Against the State*, London: Penguin. pp. 140–141.
38. Garland, D. (1994) *Punishment and Modern Society: A Study in Social Theory*, Oxford: Clarendon Press. p. 85.
39. Ibid. p. 87.
40. Smith, P. and Natalier, K. (2005) *Understanding Criminal Justice*, London: Sage. p. 103.
41. Bonger, W. (1916) *Criminality and Economic Conditions*, London: Heinemann. pp. 402–405, 667–672.
42. Chambliss, W. (1975) 'Towards a Political Economy of Crime', *Theory and Society*, 2: 149–170; Fine, B. (1979) *Capitalism and the Rule of Law: From Deviancy Theory to Marxism*, London: Hutchinson; Sumner, C. S. (1979) *Reading Ideologies*, London: Academic Press; Taylor, I. R., Walton, P. and Young, J. (1973) *The New Criminology*, London: Routledge.
43. Hay, D., Linebaugh, P. and Thompson, E. P. (1975) *Albion's Fatal Tree*, London: Allen Lane; Thompson, E. P. (1975) *Whigs and Hunters: The Origin of the Black Act*, London: Allen Lane.
44. Gramsci, A. (1971) *Selections from the Prison Notebooks of Antonio Gramsci*, ed. Q. Hoare and G. Nowell-Smith, London: Lawrence and Wishart. p. 244.
45. Sumner, *Reading Ideologies.*
46. Taylor et al. *The New Criminology.*
47. Draper, H. (1972) 'The Concept of the "Lumpenproletariat" in Marx and Engels', *Economy and Society*, 6 (12): 2285–2312; Hirst P. Q. (1972) 'Marx and Engels on Law, Crime and Morality', *Economy and Society*, 1 (1): 28–56.
48. Sumner, C. S. (1994) *The Sociology of Deviance: An Obituary*, Milton Keynes: Open University Press. p. 279.
49. Sumner, *Reading Ideologies.*
50. Cohen, P. (1979) 'Policing and the Working Class City', in B. Fine et al. (eds), *Capitalism and the Rule of Law: From Deviancy Theory to Marxism*, London: Hutchinson. p. 136.
51. Ibid. pp. 128–129.
52. Ibid. p. 136.
53. Fine, B. (1979) 'Law and Class', in B. Fine et al. (eds), *Capitalism and the Rule of Law: From Deviancy Theory to Marxism*, London: Hutchinson. p. 45.
54. Reiner, *The Politics of the Police.* pp. 8, 167–198.
55. Amatrudo, A. (2004) 'Crime in the Country', *Criminal Justice Management*, May: 62.
56. MacIntyre, A. (1981) *After Virtue: A Study in Moral Theory*, London: Duckworth.
57. Kymlicka, W. (1989) *Liberalism, Community and Culture*, Oxford: Clarendon Press. pp. 76–79.
58. Phillips, D. L. (1993) *Looking Backward: A Critical Appraisal of Communitarian Thought*, Princeton, NJ: Princeton University Press. p. 156.
59. MacIntyre, *After Virtue.* p. 112.
60. McMillan, D. and Chavis, D. (1986) 'Sense of Community: A Definition and Theory', *Journal of Community Psychology*, 83: 6–23.
61. McLaughlin, *The New Policing.* p. 83.
62. Garland, D. (2001) *The Culture of Control*, Oxford: Oxford University Press. p. 159.
63. Etzioni, A. (1989) 'Towards an I and We Paradigm', *Contemporary Sociology*, 18: 171–177; Ericson, R. (1994) *The Spirit of Community: The Reinvention of American Society*, New York: Touchstone Books.

64. Hughes, G. (2007) *The Politics of Crime and Community*, Basingstoke: Palgrave Macmillan. p. 190; Hughes, G. (1996) 'Communitarianism and Law and Order', *Critical Social Policy*, 16 (4): 17–41.
65. Selznick, P. (1994) 'Foundations of Communitarian Liberalism', *The Responsive Community*, 4: 16–28.
66. Downes, D. (1998) 'Toughing It Out: From Labour Opposition to Labour Government', *Policy Studies*, 19 (3–4): 191–198.
67. Reiner, *The Politics of the Police*. p. 207.
68. Sheerman, B. (1991) 'What Labour Wants', *Policing*, 7 (3): 194–203.
69. Garland, D. (1996) 'The Limits of the Sovereign State: Strategies of Crime Control', *British Journal of Criminology*, 36: 445–471.
70. Newburn, T. (2002) 'Community Safety and Policing: Some Implications of the Crime and Disorder Act 1998', in G. Hughes, E. McLaughlin and J. Muncie (eds), *Crime Prevention and Community Safety: New Directions*, London: Sage. p. 109.
71. Bayley, D. (1988) 'Community Policing: A Report from the Devil's Advocate', in J. R. Greene and S. D. Mastrofski (eds), *Community Policing: Rhetoric or Reality?*, New York: Praeger, pp. 225–238.
72. Eck, J. and Rosenbaum, D. (1994) 'The New Police Order: Effectiveness, Equity and Efficiency', in D. Rosenbaum (ed.), *The Challenge of Community Policing*, Thousand Oaks, CA: Sage. pp. 3–26.
73. Zedner, *Criminal Justice*. p. 126.
74. Reiner, *The Politics of the Police*. p. 217.
75. Gutmann, A. (1985) 'Communitarian Critics of Liberalism', *Philosophy and Public Affairs*, 14: 308–327; Wallach, J. (1987) 'Liberal Communitarianism and the Tasks of Political Theory', *Political Theory*, 15: 581–611.
76. Dworkin, R. (1979) *Taking Rights Seriously*, London: Duckworth.
77. Charvet, J. (1995) *The Idea of an Ethical Community*, Ithaca, NY and London: Cornell University Press. p. 4.
78. Sivanandan, A. (2006) 'Race, Terror and Civil Society', *Race and Class*, 47 (3): 2.
79. McLaughlin, *The New Policing*. p. 169; Ericson, *Crime in an Insecure World*. p. 206.
80. McLaughlin, *The New Policing*. p. 169; Ericson, *Crime in an Insecure World*. pp. 207–212.
81. McLaughlin, *The New Policing*. p. 169; Ericson, *Crime in an Insecure World*. pp. 217–220.
82. McLaughlin, *The New Policing*. p. 169; Ericson, *Crime in an Insecure World*. p. 220.
83. Sivanandan, 'Race, Terror and Civil Society'. pp. 1–8.

5

THE AIMS OF PUNISHMENT

He asked a very simple question: 'Why, and by what right, do some people lock up, torment, exile, flog, and kill others, while they are themselves just like those they torment, flog and kill?' And in answer he got deliberations as to whether human beings had free will or not; whether or not signs of criminality could be detected by measuring the skull; what part heredity played in crime; whether immorality could be inherited; and what madness is, what degeneration is, and what temperament is, how climate, food, ignorance, imitativeness, hypnotism, or passion affect crime; what society is, what its duties are – and so on ..., but there was no answer on the chief point: 'By what right do some people punish others?'

L. Tolstoy, *Resurrection*[1]

Introduction

The issues thrown up by punishment are some of the oldest issues in political theory. It was dealt with extensively by Plato.[2] The problem was perhaps best framed by the politically and morally concerned nineteenth-century author, Count Lev Nikolaevich Tolstoy, in his 1899 novel *Resurrection*, quoted above.

In this quote, we can see that punishment is nothing less than the exercise of power over a person, or persons. Through punishment a community labels a person, or persons, 'criminal', and allows for coercive measures to be instituted. Punishment allows for a society to express its opinion as to what is, and what is not, acceptable behaviour.[3] The rule of law ensures that such decisions about punishment are always related back to agreed codes and standards in an open setting; and so the rule of law is itself subject to political consideration, not least, in the choice of rationales employed when sentencing criminals. A given judicial structure will always reflect its political context. The punishment of persons, and the sentencing rationales which inform that, are always political products.

A community imposes punishment (coercion) on persons who fail to abide by the morally constructed bonds of cooperation that assist the proper functioning of society. Punishment may be understood as simply the necessary coercion required to protect people and property from any person who rejects the commonly agreed morally constructed bonds of cooperation that assist the proper functioning of society. Crime may be understood, in political terms, as a rebellion against the rules which allow society to function by allowing persons to live freely and cooperatively and to own private property. Punishment is moral because it not only serves to uphold the morally constructed bonds of cooperation that assist the proper functioning of society, but also because it treats the criminal as a moral person, and so it also has an educative function in that it serves to inform the criminal what he did was wrong.[4] Durkheim offers an analysis, which is indebted to medieval Christian thinkers such as Augustine and Thomas Aquinas, that views punishment as a mechanism through which a social order based on commonly held views enforces a criminal law, which is religiously informed in its content, in order to preserve the 'collective conscience'.[5] Durkheim's position on punishment, in his own terms, seems to relate more readily to mechanical than to organic society, and is not generally advocated by contemporary theorists because of its avowedly religious overtones and notions of consensus, although Lacey has shown how punishment theory still operates with the background idea of notions of reinforcing both commitment to the law and the reinforcement of social solidarity.[6] In this regard the Durkheimian insight still forms a part of our political and sociological understanding of how a given community regulates itself. Durkheim does not offer us a full-blown political or sociological theory of punishment, but rather an insight into how punishment functions, a point elaborated by Garland.[7]

This chapter will show how different approaches to punishment, in the form of rationales to sentencing, reflect differing political conceptions of the world and the place of criminal law within it.

Backward-looking and Forward-looking Justifications for Punishment

A classic way of thinking about punishment is to employ the distinction of forward-looking and backward-looking justifications for punishment. Backward-looking justifications are said to be retributive and are best exemplified by Kant and Hegel.[8] Andrew von Hirsch, the leading contemporary retributivist, is a neo-Kantian theorist of punishment, who employs a desert-based model, Just Deserts, which is based on considerations that are backward-looking. In the Just Deserts model, the actual crime and its seriousness are the overriding considerations for sentencers and not issues relating to the consequences following the crime, such as the rehabilitation of the criminal.[9] Forward-looking justifications are said to be utilitarian or consequentialist, and typically also give more weight to future states, such as deterring others from committing crime and the rehabilitation of offenders.[10] Those advocating mixed models, such as Michael Tonry,[11] use both sets of considerations.

The Backward-looking Approach

The advocates of backward-looking considerations maintain that the most important issue in punishment is the crime itself, which always predates any punishment. This view is termed retributivist and it holds that it is proper to punish to the extent that the criminal deserves it. It is a necessarily moral view and in the Kantian and Hegelian schemes it entails the idea that criminals bring the punishment on themselves.[12] In other words, the maxim the criminals are said to act upon is a universal maxim and so they will their own punishment, i.e. in violating the freedom of others they accept that others will violate theiss. A crude version of this view is given in the *lex talionis* formulation, which states that a criminal ought to receive punishment that is the same as that which he inflicted on others.[13] This view is dealt with by Lacey,[14] but it is easily criticised on the grounds that it only works in one case, i.e. where a single murder has been committed.[15] The *lex talionis* is far too crude to use in modern societies, and it only serves to highlight the more complex backward-looking notions of desert and the fairness of punishments.[16] In their modern form, backward-looking theories employ a notion of desert which seeks to justify punishment in terms of the moral appropriateness of punishment. In this case the degree of punishment is always taken to be proportionate to the wrongdoing done.

Retribution and desert: the contemporary position

The term 'retribution' is often misunderstood as entailing severe or excessive punishment. This is not the case and the word itself derives from the Latin *retribuere*, which means to 'repay' or 'give back'. In simple terms, retribution sees punishment as the proper response to the criminal's behaviour. In other words, it seeks to give the criminal that which he deserves.[17] The contemporary re-emergence of retributivist thought goes back to the 1960s and 1970s. Robert Martinson undertook a series of studies in the 1970s, which concluded that the American criminal justice system, with its rehabilitative emphasis upon reform, was no better than that of any other type of criminal justice system when it came to rehabilitation. Indeed, it was not rehabilitating.[18] This research had a great impact on public opinion and gained political support in Congress and the Senate. In this way, it assisted the resurgence of interest in retributive ideas, by giving it empirical support. There was perceived to be a crisis in the underlying rationale for punishment, rehabilitation. Writers such as Fogel, Frankel, Kellogg, Morris and von Hirsch became disillusioned with the state of the American criminal justice system, notably in regard to its treatment of offenders.[19] These writers contributed most to the formation of Just Deserts theory. They came to see the lack of a properly worked out philosophical or moral justification for the then sentencing regime in the USA as leading to great inequity in the criminal justice system, with indeterminate sentencing and widespread use of a discretion, notably in parole cases, operating against the backdrop of a criminal justice system, supposedly focused on the rehabilitation of offenders. The leading advocate of this group was Andrew von Hirsch, and it was he who wrote *Doing Justice: The Choice of Punishments* in 1976, which argued for a system grounded in theory. The main practical ideas behind Just Deserts were the development of a presumptive sentencing structure that might shape and also constrain judicial practice and ensure fair and proportionate punishment based on the severity of offences and the culpability of offenders. It advocated the increased use of fines and community-based sanctions, with imprisonment reserved only for the most serious offenders.

The upsurge in interest concerning retributivist ideas in the 1960s and 1970s was followed by a plethora of writing on the subject, much of which was influenced by Kantian ideas. The *raison d'être* for Just Deserts is avowedly neo-Kantian. This neo-Kantian thinking stressed the criminal's moral desert in the distribution of punishments and this ran counter to the then prevailing notion that rehabilitation or deterrence were the primary concerns in sentencing. The notion that the criminal is a free, autonomous and moral agent whose punishment is deserved is seen especially in Kant's *Groundwork of the Metaphysics of Morals*, where the idea that it would be wrong not to punish the criminal is presented. In *The Metaphysics of Morals*, Kant advances the notion of a rebounding maxim in terms of the criminal bringing the punishment on himself through his own actions.[20] Moreover, following Kant, recent retributive thought seeks to emphasise the 'fairness' of punishments in terms of the relationship between the offender and the punishment rather than between the punishment and its consequence for society. The correspondence in terms of fairness is always between the gravity of a given offence and the required level of punishment deserved. In such a fashion the criminals are given their just deserts and the criminal justice system is forced to concentrate on issues of culpability, rather than wider social considerations. Kant's injunction that we should treat people as ends in themselves rather than as means to some other end is at the heart of his conception of respect for persons. This concern for persons is at the heart of the Just Deserts approach.

Frederic Kellogg and Andrew von Hirsch started to develop a critique of consequentialist thinking in the criminal justice system, especially utilitarian treatments of sentencing. In doing so they relied on a justice as fairness approach and were indebted to the work of both the political theorist John Rawls and the philosopher W. D. Ross.[21] The need to resolve the issue of a lack of moral consensus in society led some philosophers and political theorists, notably John Rawls, to develop a theory based on some ideally objective deliberative context. This approach led Rawls to posit that nobody in an 'original position' would favour 'unfairness', since they would not know what place they would occupy in society. The deeper point for desert theorists is a determination to ensure that all persons are treated equally, the point being that desert-based theories are more likely to ensure equal treatment since offenders are sentenced in accordance with their own actions alone and broader social criteria are not of great importance in determining the tariff. The main unfairness von Hirsch detected in utilitarian systems of punishment was the realisation that it could never be correct to place the punishment of any one person in any calculation which weighed the incidence of a single given punishment against the potential costs and benefits for unknown others.[22] Kellogg and von Hirsch centred their work on three central issues: (1) devising a measure to rank the seriousness of offences; (2) devising a measure of criminal sanctions; and (3) the determination of a consistent match between criminal offences and sanctions. Following Kant, both Kellogg and von Hirsch view civil society as the outcome of an agreement to live under a common authority, a primary feature of which is a consistent system of legal punishment. In this model, punishment is something designed both to secure civil society and to ensure external freedom. Just Deserts is a political theory of the individual and his or her relationship to the state.

Much of Just Deserts doctrine seems to cohere with our moral intuitions that there must be a clear relationship between some past act of offending and the person punished, and that any punishment should be proportionate to the guilt of the offender. It upholds that only the guilty should be punished. Just Deserts suggests a humane and rational mechanism for deciding who to punish, and how much to punish them. Unlike orthodox utilitarian justifications of punishment, which maintain that punishment is to be justified in terms of the consequences it has, such as deterrence, rehabilitation, incapacitation and the satisfaction of grievances, the Just Deserts model is tied to the concept of desert. This is the fundamental issue – is punishment to be advocated on desert criteria or the consequences that it has? The utilitarian account locates value in situations or states of affairs, and not in individual moral agents. Utilitarianism, therefore, fails to uphold the proper value of persons. Just Deserts doctrine came about largely as a corrective to the excesses of utilitarian ideas in the criminal justice system, especially in response to indeterminate sentencing and the fact that rehabilitative models did not seem to be rehabilitating. It gained widespread public support because it appeared to place the culpability of individuals above the ends of public policy at a time when people became more wary of the state and more focused upon the politics of the personal. Just Deserts came out of a broader, more political, concern for social justice. It raised important questions regarding public policy and the decline of utilitarian justifications for punishment by challenging the then dominant notion of rehabilitation.[23] In the USA, the idea that penal policy should alter people's characters, attitudes and behaviour seemed reasonable, but when allied to an increase in therapeutic intervention in the twentieth century its shortcomings were exposed. Around this time Noam Chomsky set out a critique of public policies based on human malleability, especially in relation to obtaining consent for government action.[24] Furthermore, it was felt reasonable to allow judges and other officials in the criminal justice system to have widespread discretion. While the therapeutic strategy was in the ascendant, questions about crime definition and guilt were largely overlooked. It was not until the 1960s that academics, lawyers, civil rights activists and the mass of ordinary people started to ask questions about who were the subjects of all this therapy and why were people being given indeterminate sentences. Eventually, the rehabilitative mechanisms of the state came to be seen as part of a political policy of socially controlling the poor and the weak. The voices raised against rehabilitation grew louder, notably after the Civil Rights Movement, as people became wary of explanations of crime that failed to take on board its political dimension. The Watergate scandal and the excesses of the Nixon administration led to widespread public cynicism about the notion of an enabling state and the role of the state in assisting persons through penal measures such as rehabilitation. Likewise, widespread 'discretion' in sentencing was seen as arbitrary and something to be rid of. Just Deserts argued that the function of the criminal justice system was to punish culpable behaviour and that the severity of sanctions should be proportionate to the degree of culpability. In other words, the consequentialist calculus employed by those who advocated rehabilitation was rejected in favour of desert criteria. This was not new but in the post-Kennedy and Johnson era it chimed with an egalitarian ethos that wanted discretionary power curtailed and which demanded that rules apply equally to all persons, and that all people should be treated equally.

The distinctiveness of Just Deserts theory lies in the way it stresses the criminal's moral desert in the distribution of punishments and the way it conceives the criminal justice system as concentrating on issues of culpability and proportionality, rather than wider social considerations, notably in relation to criminal sentencing. It takes its inspiration from older versions of retributive writing, in particular the writings of Kant, and to political theorists such as Rawls, but it is essentially a practical approach which is underpinned by a commitment to a modern liberal political framework, as has been noted by Lacey.[25] Kantianism always assumes that the autonomy of moral life is the basis on which to found a political theory. Just Deserts theorists, especially von Hirsch, have made the case that sanctions must be both definite and apply equally to all persons; it is a liberal theory in that regard. In focusing on the role of desert the opposition to utilitarianism is clear. Utilitarianism sees desert as only, at best, an indirect means to achieve some future value. Desert theories are tied to claims about personal responsibility. A person must deserve something, in this case a punishment, which is contingent on a minimal level of voluntarism, in terms of any criminal act committed. This backward-looking element is vital for in placing the emphasis on what has been done, rather than on something which will be done, it is clear that the desert basis must be enacted before a person can properly deserve. Punishment and desert must relate to the individual's action and not some wider social goal or outcome. Desert is also a social concept because it is based on certain judgements about a person's blameworthiness, which are socially and politically constructed. The Just Deserts doctrine is a bold attempt to place the issues of desert, proportionality and justice, in the broadest sense, at the heart of sentencing theory and practice. The focus on the proper basis for treating individual persons is a useful antidote to theories whose foundation is the neglect of the individual in the pursuit of the greater utility, or some other measure, for the many.

The Forward-looking Approach: Bentham and Consequentialist Theory

Bentham's position

The most important political theorist to write on punishment from a forward-looking perspective is Jeremy Bentham, although Bentham was less concerned with the purpose of punishment than with the overall functioning of society, in terms of optimising utility. He thought of punishment as only one of the tools in the hands of the 'legislator', whose end is 'to augment the total happiness of the community; and therefore, in the first place, to exclude, as far as may be, everything that tends to subtract from happiness: in other words to exclude from mischief'.[26] Bentham viewed crime in the broader context of overall society and delineated between those situations in which punishment should be used and those when it should not.[27] He saw that the *mischief* of crime conflicted with happiness but also that the *mischief* of punishment may do so as well. Any punishment which serves to deter the criminal from repeating his crime is called, by Bentham, a 'particular prevention'. This may be achieved in three main ways: incapacitation, reformation and intimidation. Bentham's main writings relate to general prevention, in which case the prevention of crime by the example of the punishment suffered by criminals is seen as the aim of punishment, and its primary justification.

Bentham understood that punishment is only one of the measures that may be used against crime. However, given the general preventive end of punishment, it ought not to be used where it is (a) groundless, (b) inefficacious, (c) unprofitable, and (d) needless.[28] It has to be noted in the promotion of overall societal utility and not in giving the criminal that which he deserves. Bentham's general justification for punishment is not focused upon the criminal so much as the political justification to the general population, whose interest is simply in the best ordering of society.[29] This general approach to issues of punishment delineates utilitarian treatments of punishment from other theories of punishment. Utilitarians are committed to doing whatever, in any given situation, is likely to promote the happiness of the greatest number and, if it is not possible to promote happiness, then to that which will cause least unhappiness. In terms of punishment, the notion is that the sentencer will only punish when, and only when, and in such a fashion and to the extent that there is likely to be less *mischief* than if he or she did not punish at all.

Bentham's utilitarian moral justification for the practice of punishment is often couched in terms of deterrent and reformatory terms. Bentham's utilitarian theory of morality ruled out retributivism a priori. Moreover, Bentham and other utilitarians cannot see rational justification for inflicting suffering for its own sake, even though they accept the principle that criminal desert gives us the right to punish, as Flew noted in his classic essay.[30] The purpose of punishment, in Bentham, is only considered in its immediate use to the community, and this use is thought to be best served by deterring and/or reforming criminals. Deterrence is best understood as an account of the justification of punishment that looks to the future and the consequences which flow from criminal punishment. It may be juxtaposed with the retributivist position, which looks to the past for its justification of punishment. Deterrence, unlike reform or prevention, finds no justification for action in a past offence and its arguments depend entirely upon the consequences of punishment. The view that punishment is justified by the value of its consequences alone is compatible with an ethical theory, which allows meaning to be attached to moral judgements. Deterrence holds that the infliction of suffering is of no value or that it is of negative value and that it must therefore be justified by further considerations. Bentham states:

> General prevention ought to be the chief end of punishment as it is its real justification. If we could consider an offence that has been committed as an isolated fact, the like of which would never recur, punishment would be useless. It would only be adding one evil to another. But when we consider that an unpunished crime leaves the path of crime open, not only to the same delinquent but also to all those who may have the same motives and opportunities for entering upon it we perceive that punishment inflicted on the individual becomes a source of security to all.[31]

Yet Bentham further notes: 'All punishment is mischief; all punishment itself an evil. Upon the principle of utility, if it ought at all to be admitted, it ought only to be admitted in as far as it promises to exclude some greater evil.'[32]

Bentham's argument is that punishment is only a technique of social control that operates to reform the criminal, to prevent him or her from committing crime or it is to deter others from similar offences. However, elsewhere Bentham argues that if the damage to the offender outweighs the expected advantage to society, it loses its justification, for then it produces more *mischief* than it prevents. The calculus would also have to take into account the strength of the deterring effects upon others. So it seems that the strongest utilitarian case for punishment is that it serves to deter potential offenders by inflicting punishment on actual ones.

Deterrence

Deterrence theory builds on the understanding that people are rational beings who adjust their conduct in terms of the calculations they make as to the consequences of their behaviour, in this case with regard to the criminal law. This calculus, originated in its modern form by Bentham, has had wide appeal in economic circles where sentencing tariffs might be said to mirror an economic pricing model. The classic illustration of this is given by Posner, though, as is common with this rationale, it has the effect of reducing crime to deliberative action.[33] The practical empirical issues seem insurmountable as Ashworth, reviewing the research evidence, has noted in relation to determining whether deterrence might be said to work in practice.[34] Perhaps, the most notable use of deterrence theory relates to the work of H. L. A. Hart, who advocated a mixed model of sentencing which used deterrence as the general justifying aim of punishment while ensuring desert criteria were used for the distribution of punishments.[35] Hart's view has been popular in public policy circles because it seems to cohere to our common-sense notions of what a criminal sentence should seek to achieve. The 2001 Halliday Report suggested that deterring persistent offenders should be the main focus of sentencing practice, and argued for more mandatory and minimum sentences to achieve this, within the overall framework of desert.[36] Yet, as Lacey has shown, the problems associated with mixing sentencing criteria, however appealing, result in a less than satisfactory philosophical outcome.[37]

Though Bentham gave us the modern form of deterrence theory it has an ancestry going back to references in both the Bible and the Koran, and was historically the dominant rationale employed by most jurisdictions, until comparatively recently.[38] One detects the underlying political premise of general deterrence to be the greater good for the greater number but it is compromised by what is technically referred to as the certainty and severity of punishments – in other words, the possibility of being caught. Therefore, whenever the risk of being caught is low, one would expect a countervailing tendency for high levels of severity. The classic example of this tendency was the so-called 'Bloody Code' of the eighteenth century, when detection rates were very low but where petty criminals could be executed for minor acts of theft.[39] It can be argued that this tendency may still be detected in the contemporary world, with large fines for smoking or fare-dodging on public transport, as Zedner has argued, or the three strikes and out model.[40]

Perhaps the strongest arguments against deterrence relate to (1) its institution in practice; (2) the possible human rights issues associated with using either utilitarian calculation or a simple rational choice economic model; and (3) the model it has of human agency. On the first point, Andrew von Hirsch has shown how deterrence needs to be understood in terms not only of its initial deterrent effects, but also of what he terms 'marginal deterrence' effects.[41] In other words, von Hirsch demonstrates that initial deterrence provides the theoretical justification for deterrence as a sentencing policy, and that it is the marginal effects that provide the justification in terms of the amount of punishment or the form it takes. In a famous 1999 study, von Hirsch et al. found a weak link between the certainty of punishment and offending rates, but they also found that the link was even weaker with regard to severity of punishment and offending, and that it was highly contextually dependent in any case.[42] Therefore, deterrence does not seem to be wholly convincing as a sentencing regime. On the second point, Lacey has argued (I think convincingly) that deterrence is open to the Kantian critique:

It is thus open to the objection generally aimed at utilitarian principles, that they treat individuals as 'means to end' rather than 'ends in themselves'. ... The state's role in punishing, on the general deterrence theory, is to reduce certain unwanted and economically reducible forms of behaviour: individuals may be sacrificed to this dominant purpose.[43]

On the third point, deterrence seems to be on shaky ground with regards to the model of human agency it employs. It can be argued that people do not always make rational choices as to their actions or assess risk in the way deterrence theory suggests. Less still might a rational choice model, whether classically utilitarian or economically determined, be employed by drug users, young people or vandals. It might well be the case that punishment itself causes crime as it brings with it, among other things, stigma from others, complications in the employment market and the disruption of normal life, to say nothing of the role of prison conditioning upon people.[44] Indeed, as cultural criminologists have noted, punishment may itself become a desired outcome for aspiring young criminals, who may see it as affirming a criminal identity or understand a completely different meaning to the punishment than that desired by the deterrence model – making a mockery of the theory of deterrence altogether.[45]

Rehabilitation

Rehabilitative approaches, like other utilitarian treatments, exist to preserve the political and moral basis of society, though they may also have individuals as their focus. They also appear to be capable of empirical validation, as the myriad of studies carried out by criminologists and government agencies around the world attest. Yet, as Lacey and numerous others have argued, there is still no agreement on whether rehabilitative approaches actually work.[46] The history of rehabilitation, since its heyday in the nineteenth century, is marked by a focus upon individual social pathology and an interventionist social welfare policy, both of which came under attack from political and legal theorists after the Second World War, although most notably after the 1960s. Rehabilitation may be contrasted with deterrence, which sees persons as rational calculating actors, because it sees individuals as in need of help, support or treatment. It is therefore dependent upon an infrastructure of professionals, such as social workers, court officers and therapists, to advise on the form of the rehabilitation to be specified. All such professionals work within a framework that operates with a typology of offenders, which may rank persons in terms of their capacity for rehabilitation.[47] Of course, this may be problematic for in leaving the determination of sentence to a group of persons without clearly defined or agreed criteria one may well be treating persons as bundles of problems rather than individuals with rights and self-determination, to say nothing of the possibility for class, racial, gender and other bias. This stated, it would seem churlish not to view rehabilitation as a positive aspect of the criminal justice system, facilitating persons to make a move back into a properly socialised life; and whatever short-comings might be noted it would seem to be the mark of a properly functioning polity that it seeks to integrate persons.

But before we decide that rehabilitation is a humane and generously motivated system it should be noted that many of its claims are dubious, not least its inherent positivistic notion that causes of offending may be detected and that persons can respond *positively* to rehabilitative measures, when the economic conditions in which they exist may be either unaltered or made worse by the criminalisation process itself, for example by being disadvantaged in the job or housing market. Indeed, the rehabilitation process may be aimed wrongly at addressing a systemic issue when the criminal action that gave rise to the rehabilitation process may well be random and/or opportunistic or part of a short-lived episode, as in the case of teenage delinquency, or even being female and subject to patriarchal *assistance* or moral concern.[48] Or that crime may be the result of profound structural political and economic forces and not the result of a pathological tendency; and the whole of Critical Criminology posits as much.[49]

It is easy to see that rehabilitation has considerable political support both at a national and a local level as well as within the criminal justice system, including the Civil Service. Rehabilitation is also, through the state, a considerable employer of professional staff focused on rehabilitation and, moreover, of academics and statisticians who audit the success, or otherwise of rehabilitation.[50] Yet, rehabilitation is an amorphous thing covering an enormous range of persons, crimes and motivations – so how can success ever be a simple affair? Leaving aside the issues that re-offending rates necessarily only relate to those caught, prosecuted and processed by the criminal justice system and that the soundness of statistical data on rehabilitation rates may be doubted, there is the issue of the massive disparity between persons, similarly situated, in terms of the treatment or 'sentence' they receive under a regime of rehabilitation.[51]

The decisions persons make about the validity, or otherwise, of a rehabilitative regime are to a large extent based upon the emphasis they give to consistency, which implies the penal concept of proportionality, which, in turn, is a strong indication about their political conception of their ideal society, and about the role of censure in affirming societal consensus and its importance in it. Rehabilitation divides people along political lines. There are those who trust in the fair functioning of the criminal justice system and the potential of criminals to change, and there are those who do not. Typically, people see the potential benefits to individuals and the wider society as well as the potential pitfalls in a rehabilitative regime, and that is probably how it should be. A system of rehabilitation remains both a mark of a humane criminal justice system and a regime in need of expert management to contain the gross disparities of consistency and proportionality it may contain within it. What the existence of a rehabilitative regime cannot be is an indicator of 'a more human penal system' by itself.[52]

Incapacitation

Incapacitation is typically very popular with the political right and many who champion victims in the criminal justice system.[53] Zimring and Hawkins (1991) have noted that incapacitation appears to have dominance by default in the criminal justice system, notably in the USA. This is partly due to less scrutiny on it as a rationale *vis-à-vis* other consequentialist approaches, such as rehabilitation and deterrence. It is also responsible for the explosion of prison building – a prison building programme focused upon protecting good citizens from the criminal intentions of bad men and women. However, unlike both rehabilitation or deterrence theory, it is not dependent upon a specific view of how persons act so much as a straightforward assessment of restraining criminals in custody in order to prevent them re-offending, at least for the period of incarceration. It may be accepted for serious crimes, such as murder or rape, but the argument begins in relation to how advocates of incapacitation assess risk in offenders where similar objections to it may be raised, as with deterrence, i.e. that it may grossly over-punish individuals for some desired future free from criminal harm.[54] It is in the risk assessment and prediction game, in which case the level of risk assessed will always be weighed against the norms of a given society, which may fluctuate wildly.

Moreover, the rights of individuals are compromised by incapacitation in terms of the prediction of future risk, which may be wrong, and there remains the major criticism directed at utilitarian treatments generally, i.e. that it weighs the interests of one against those of the many. The political philosopher Ted Honderich, writing on the conflict between desert and risk assessment under a system of incapacitation, has shown how attention to risk factors can, in itself, result in higher tariffs than those typically deserved.[55] One can see how attractive incapacitation is to politicians and sentencers because it offers certainty that no criminal will offend during the period of his incarceration.[56] The attraction of incapacitation is simply that it removes convicted persons from public space, unlike community-based measures. The problems, aside from the cost of incapacitation in terms of capital and running costs, and the disruption to family and work life likely to result from imprisonment, relate to the efficacy of breaching proportionality considerations and the trust one places in prediction. Ashworth has pithily noted that where 'there is a conflict between the rights of two people (albeit that one of them is merely a potential or predicted victim), it is the right of the convicted offender that should yield ... it is questionable whether it justifies the prolongation of incarceration in a prison, as distinct from some less harsh environment.'[57]

Censure and penal communication

Censure may be conceived as an ideological form, as in the work of Colin Sumner,[58] but typically censure is said to be part of the response made by any given political community in expressing proportionate disapproval of injustice and crime. In this way, censure allows persons collectively to determine what is blameworthy. It therefore has political and deliberative aspects. It is an element in the Just Deserts doctrine, and in what may be termed 'penal communication',[59] that demands that we all assess, and reassess, our ethical choices. Censure may offer grounds for justifying a non-utilitarian account of proportionality consistent with a consequentialist general justifying aim. The censuring of crime is something often taken for granted even where punishment is allocated in terms of crime prevention. The sanction of censure is directly related to how blameworthy, or otherwise, the crime is. If proportionality is not adhered to, then criminals are treated unfairly, as von Hirsch has indicated.[60]

It could be said that punishment's other defining characteristic, that of censure, is justified as the expression of a morality that holds persons responsible for their actions. It is this condemnatory element that explains why punishment should be proportionately allocated and why different crimes are blameworthy. Punishment expresses censure or blame and the pre-eminent theorist of censure remains Joel Feinberg. His classic 1970 book, *Doing and Deserving*, spawned increased interest in expressive theories of punishment. In 1974, the philosopher Peter Strawson wrote his groundbreaking book *Freedom and Resentment*, which elaborated a straightforward account of human action. It determined that our capacity to respond to wrongdoing by censure is simply part of the broader morality that holds persons responsible for their conduct. Moreover, Strawson argued that the capacity to respond to wrongdoing is essential to our life as moral beings. If one did not confront the criminal with censure, that would be the same as treating him as if he were not responsible and without a moral compass. If we apply Strawson's ideas to punishment, we are also assuming that criminal behaviour is *usually* wrong. This would seem a reasonable thing to do in our relationship to the criminal law. It is the case that crime affects others negatively and it may be freerider activity, in the sense that the *thief* does not earn his wage.

It is a generally held assumption that we share certain moral standards and a capacity to respond to criminal action in terms of the blameworthiness. Primoratz argues that censure can be seen as intrinsic to the process of preventing crime.[61] It provides a disincentive against criminal behaviour. In expressing disapproval or censure of this form of behaviour, it follows that the criminal sanction has two main features: first, imposing painful consequences and, secondly, public censuring. The blame visited by the penalty should therefore reflect just how blameworthy and serious criminal behaviour is deemed to be. The importance of censure in Just Deserts theory cannot be understated. At its most basic level a censure theory will hold that punishment, in the form of hard treatment, is justified because it is the appropriate mode of censure for certain crimes. However, criminal law addresses not only the moral accountability of individuals, as Strawson details, but also third parties.[62] The fact that third parties are addressed matters, for in this case the censure ought to be understood as proportionate to the punishment. Andrew von Hirsch has noted:

The normative message expressed in penal statutes is not reducible, as penal utilitarians might suppose, to a mere inducement to compliance – one utilized because the citizenry could be more responsive to moral appeals than bare threats. If persons are called upon to desist because the conduct is wrong, there ought to be good reasons for supposing that it is wrong; and the message expressed through the penalty about the degree of wrongfulness ought to reflect how reprehensible the conduct indeed is.[63]

Moreover, since the censure and the hard treatment are intertwined, any increase, or decrease, in the severity ranking of a given punishment will alter how much censure is expressed and will, therefore, have to be justified by reference to the seriousness of the crime. Alternatively, any increase, or decrease, in the censure will require reference to the severity ranking of a given punishment. Of course, any alteration to the rank ordering of offences is a political activity, as is arguing for the *status quo*.

Restorative justice

Unlike the other aims of punishment outlined, restorative justice (RJ) has a different focus altogether. It makes the mending of social relationships and the acknowledgment of the harm done (to victims, offenders and the community) the main issues under consideration. It has as its central tenet the aim of making the community come together by recognising harm in a way which looks to a better future state. However, in giving primacy to the harm done the issue of offender culpability may be compromised.[64] It has an expanded role for the victim in its workings, which is a major difference from other treatments of punishment that tend to ignore victims in the pursuit of 'impartial justice' and concentrate upon the offender. The impact of victims in the sentencing process has long been noted by academics as a positive development.[65] Restorative justice is not, however, a unified theory as much as a general approach which is critical of conventional justifications of punishment, notably retribution.[66] It has never been applied wholesale in modern western criminal justice systems but it has had considerable impact, particularly in the youth justice arena, where it has enjoyed some success. The model being employed in RJ is the social reintegration of persons, especially youth offenders, and John Braithwaite has set out the principles of this in his *Crime, Shame and Reintegration*.[67] This, though, may be witness to the fact that RJ has never seriously challenged the current legal arrangements for criminal justice in the generality of cases. It is merely used for certain cases deemed to be particularly suitable to it, and where the level of seriousness is minimal. RJ is a highly political position for it is often the case in RJ that the state, or the law, should not automatically dictate punishments from a list of tariffs. It sees a determination of sentence coming out of a process entered into by several parties, including victims and offenders themselves. These parties will agree an outcome on punishment but the main issue is the process whereby decisions are made with the maximum amount of participation in order to facilitate social reintegration.

RJ does have several drawbacks. It works best with crimes that involve single victims. In cases where there are numerous victims, especially when they do not agree on their response to the crime, or where there the crime is against a corporate body, such as a company, the whole enterprise of RJ is compromised. The sentence tariff too leaves open a raft of problems. For example, what does it mean for a criminal to make amends for their crime? If a criminal's making amends is determined, then the issue of consistent sentencing, the primary function of the judge, still remains. The mediation sessions that RJ advocates doubtless have great success when the level of seriousness is fairly low, but how can the tortured man be expected to react to his torturer in a reasonable way? And if the tortured man had to suggest a punishment, what would it be?[68] The history of the legal process is one of removing emotion from the courtroom in an effort to concentrate upon the 'facts' of the case. RJ opens up the possibility of irrationality, raw emotion and compromise being introduced into the treatment of criminals, as opposed to reasoned argument concerning the facts of the case. Moreover, the public nature of crime is overlooked entirely in a process which prioritises the immediate parties of a crime and which also might be said to 'privatise' the situation.[69] A process which may even make victims feel worse, as Braithwaite, the leading exponent of RJ, concedes.[70] To conclude, RJ is undoubtedly motivated by the highest ideals of social integration. It offers, arguably, a more personal and humane treatment for victims of crime and it allows communities to express an opinion about crime, but it is, of its nature, a less formal and a more organic process than that advocated by other justifications for punishment; and that is its strength as well as its weakness.

Practical Considerations

The entire reason for having aims of punishment is so that judicial punishment is undertaken in accordance with the highest ideals drawn from our legal, political and social theories of ethics and moral conduct. When our legal system advances aims of punishment, it is moving beyond raw vengeance and linking the treatment of criminals to wider considerations: it is upholding the fact that criminals have human rights too. This means that when we look at the aims of punishment we see far more than a list of tariffs for various offences. Rather, we witness a tangible expression of the highest ideals a society wishes to uphold.

It is important to see the policy context of sentencing and to be aware that, in practice, a criminal sentence will include elements drawn from differing theoretical bases, within any given tariff. In practice, the policy and practice of criminal sentencing relates to a hierarchy of elements within a sentence: so that a judge may pass a sentence which includes elements of censure, deterrence and incapacitation, for example. At differing times the stress put on any element will alter with the sentiment of the nation, as expressed in law, at the time. For example, where there is a popular view that there are too many persons in prison we can expect less emphasis upon incapacitation. We should always be aware that the laws of the land are derived from Parliament and therefore the form of the laws, specifically the rationales being advanced in sentencing, bear the mark of political fashion, to some extent. At times prison is favoured and at other times community sentences; sometimes strict proportionality is overridden in favour of restorative justice. Judges can only pass sentences in accordance with the existing law and in line with existing judicial practice. The sentencing of the courts must always reflect the rationales of laws passed in Parliament. However, the Criminal Justice Act 2003 did address this issue by setting out five key purposes of sentencing: (1) punishment; (2) crime reduction; (3) rehabilitation; (4) protection of the public; and (5) the making of reparation by offenders (which may be RJ). The Criminal Justice Act 2003 also had regard to the level of seriousness of an offence. However, proportionality, in other words, the proper relationship between the offence and the severity of its punishment, was the key principle advanced. No punishment should be unduly harsh of lenient.

In conclusion, it is necessary to understand the proper theoretical basis of punishment and of criminal sentencing, and to understand how these considerations operate in the real world. A modest understanding of legal history will show how the aims of punishment always closely match what are believed to be the highest ideals drawn from the legal, political, and social theories of ethics and moral conduct of the day. The alterations we find in the practice of judicial sentencing are always related to far deeper issues found in political and legal reasoning. The aims of punishment that a society chooses say as much about that society's view of itself as of the individual instance of punishment.

Main Summary Points

- Punishment labels a person, or persons, 'criminal', and allows for coercive measures to be instituted. Punishment allows for a society to express its opinion as to what is, and what is not, acceptable behaviour.
- Backward-looking considerations maintain that the most important issue in punishment is the crime itself, which predates any punishment. This view is termed retributivist and it maintains that it is proper to punish to the extent that the criminal deserves it.
- Desert theory seeks to justify punishment in terms of the moral appropriateness of punishment, in which case the degree of punishment is always taken to be proportionate to the wrongdoing done. This theory is especially associated with Andrew von Hirsch. It sees culpability and proportionality as more important than wider social considerations.
- Utilitarian theorists look at the consequences of punishment and therefore seek to use punishment as a means of reforming the criminal, to prevent him or her from committing crime in the future or to deter others from committing similar offences.

- Punishment censures criminals and thereby allows persons collectively to determine what is blameworthy. The sanction of censure is always directly related to how blameworthy, or otherwise, the crime is.
- Restorative justice makes the mending of social relationships and the acknowledgement of the harm done to victims, offenders and the community the main issues under consideration. It uses meetings and conferences in its decision-making as it sees the involvement of many people as leading to the social reintegration of criminals and victims.

Questions

1. Why does Bentham advocate forward-looking justifications for punishment?
2. Is retribution a sufficient reason for punishment?
3. How is restorative justice a punishment at all?

Suggested Further Reading

Lacey, N. (1988) *State Punishment: Political Principles and Community Values*, London: Routledge.
McConville, S. (ed.) (2003) *The Use of Punishment*, Cullompton: Willian Publishing.
Tonry, M. (2004) *Punishment and Politics*, Cullompton: Willan Publishing.
von Hirsch, A. (1993) *Censure and Sanctions*, Oxford: Clarendon Press.
Zedner, L. (2004) *Criminal Justice*, Oxford: Oxford University Press.

Notes

1. Plato (1960) *Gorgias*, London: Penguin. p. 525; Plato (1970) *Laws*, London: Penguin. 5. pp. 735–736, 11. p. 934; Plato (1991) *Protagoras*, Oxford: Clarendon Press, p. 324.
2. Tolstoy, L. N. (2005) *Resurrection*, Kila, MT: Kessinger Publishing, pp. 358–359; also cited by Duff, R. (1986) *Trials and Punishments*, Cambridge: Cambridge University Press. p. 187; Matravers, M.D. (1994) *Justice and Punishment: The Rational for Coercion*, Ph.D. thesis. LSE. p. 8.
3. Garland, D. (1994) *Punishment and Modern Society: A Study in Social Theory*, Oxford: Oxford University Press. p. 46.
4. See Hampton's classic article on this: Hampton, J. (1984) 'The Moral Education Theory of Punishment', *Philosophy and Public Affairs*, 13 (3): 208–238.
5. 'It is necessary, then, that the collective conscience be affirmed forcibly at the very moment when it is contradicted, and the only means of affirming it is to express the unanimous version which can consist only in a suffering inflected upon the agent.' Durkheim, E. (1947) *The Division of Labour in Society*, trans. George Simpson, Glencoe, IL: The Free Press. p. 108; Augustine, St (1998) *City of God*, Cambridge: Cambridge University Press. 19.16; Aquinas, T. (1993) *Summa Theologiae*, Notre Dame, IN: University of Notre Dame Press. 2–2. Q 33 A7.

6. Lacey, N. (1988) *State Punishment: Political Principles and Community Values*, London: Routledge. pp. 91–92; Zedner, L. (2004) *Criminal Justice*, Oxford: Oxford University Press. pp. 76–77.
7. Garland, *Punishment and Modern Society*. pp. 23–46.
8. Kant, I. (1964b) *Groundwork to the Metaphysics of Morals*, New York: Harper & Row; Hegel, G. W. F. (1967) *Philosophy of Right*, ed. and trans. T. M. Knox, London: Oxford University Press. §86A.
9. von Hirsch, A. (1993) *Censure and Sanctions*, Oxford: Clarendon Press.
10. Bentham, J. (1982) *Introduction to the Principles of Morals and Legislation*, London: Methuen. See Chapter 13.
11. Tonry, M. (1996) *Sentencing Matters*, New York: Oxford University Press.
12. Kant, I. (1991) *The Metaphysics of Morals*, Cambridge: Cambridge University Press. p. 169; Fleischacker, S. (1992) 'Kant's Theory of Punishment', in H. William (ed.), *Essays on Kant's Political Philosophy*, Cardiff: University of Wales Press. pp. 191–212; Hegel, *Hegel's Philosophy of Right*. §86A.
13. See Exodus 21: 23–25. However, the *lex talionis* is not the only position in the Old Testament. See, for example, Proverbs 13: 24 and 19: 18; Malachi 3: 2–3; Job 5: 17–18.
14. Lacey, *State Punishment*. pp. 17–18.
15. Kleinig, J. (1973) *Punishment and Desert*. The Hague: Martinus Nijhoff. pp. 120–121.
16. Durkheim, *Division of Labour in Society*. pp. 79–80; Rawls, J. (1973) *A Theory of Justice*, Oxford: Oxford University Press; Rawls, J. (1958) 'Justice as Fairness', *Philosophical Review*, 67: 164–194.
17. Walker, N. (1991) *Why Punish?* Oxford: Oxford University Press. p. 67.
18. His 1974 research and other findings may be found in Lipton, D., Martinson, R. and Wilks, J. (1975) *The Effectiveness of Correctional Treatment*, New York: Praeger.
19. Fogel, D. (1975) *We Are Living Proof: The Justice Model for Corrections*, Cincinnati, OH: W. H. Anderson and Co; Frankel, M. E. (1973) *Criminal Sentences: Law without Order*, New York: Hill & Wang; Kellogg, F. (1977) 'From Retribution to Desert', *Criminology*, 15: 179–192; von Hirsch, A. (1976) *Doing Justice: The Choice of Punishments*, New York: Hill & Wang.
20. Kant, *Metaphysics of Morals*. p. 169. See also Pincoffs' classic contemporary statement of this. Pincoffs, E. A. (1966) *The Rationale of Legal Punishment*, Atlantic Highlands, NJ: Humanities Press. pp. 8–9.
21. Rawls, J. (1955) 'Two Concepts of Rules', *The Philosophical Review*, 64 (1): 3–32; Rawls, J. (1973) 'Justice as Fairness', pp. 164–194; Rawls, *Theory of Justice*; Ross, W. D. (1965) *The Right and the Good*, Oxford: Clarendon Press.
22. von Hirsch, A. (1985) *Past or Future Crimes: Deservedness and Dangerousness in the Sentencing of Criminals*, Manchester: Manchester University Press. p. 54.
23. Gottfredson, M. (1979) 'Treatment Destruction Techniques', *Journal of Research in Crime and Delinquency*, 16 (1): 39; Lerman, P. (1975) *Community Treatment and Social Control*, Chicago: University of Chicago Press. p. 80.
24. Chomsky, N. (1975) *Reflections on Language*, New York: Pantheon Books. p. 132.
25. Lacey, N., in McConville, S. (ed.) (2003) *The Use of Punishment*, Cullompton: Willan Publishing. p. 181.
26. Bentham, *Introduction to the Principles of Morals and Legislation*. p. 158.
27. Ibid. pp. 158–164.
28. Ibid. p. 159.
29. Halpin, A. (1997) *Rights and Law: Analysis and Theory*, Oxford: Hart Publishing. pp. 227–232.
30. Flew, A. (1954) 'The Justification of Punishment', *Philosophy*, 29: 291–307.

31. Bentham, J. (1838–43) *Principles of Penal Law*, in *The Works of Jeremy Bentham*, Vol. 1, ed. J. Bowring, Edinburgh: W. Tait. p. 383.
32. Bentham, J. (1948) *Introduction to the Principles of Morals and Legislation*, ed. J. H. Burns and H. L. A. Hart. London: Methuen. p. 281.
33. Posner, R. (1985) 'An Economic Theory of Criminal Law', *Columbia Law Review*, 85: 1193–1231; O' Malley, P. (2004) 'Globalising Risk? Distinguishing Styles of Neoliberal Criminal Justice in Australia and the USA', in T. Newburn and R. Sparks (eds), *Criminal Justice and Political Cultures: National and International Dimensions of Crime Control*, Cullompton: Willian Publishing. p. 34.
34. Ashworth, A. (1992) *Sentencing and Criminal Justice*, London: Weidenfeld and Nicolson. pp. 60–62.
35. Hart, H. L. A. (1992) *Punishment and Responsibility*, Oxford: Oxford University Press. pp. 1–28.
36. Halliday, J. (2001) *Making Punishments Work: Report of a Review of the Sentencing Framework* (Halliday Report), London: Home Office.
37. Lacey, *State Punishment*. pp. 47–54.
38. Beattie, J. A. (1990) *Judicial Punishment in England*, London: Faber & Faber. pp. 36–49; Hood, R. (1989) *The Death Penalty: A World-wide Perspective*, Oxford: Clarendon Press. p. 120.
39. Hay, D. (1975) 'Property, Authority and the Criminal Law', in D. Hay et al. (eds), *Albion's Fatal Tree: Crime and Society in Eighteenth-century England*, London: Penguin. pp. 17–63.
40. Zedner, *Criminal Justice*. p. 91.
41. von Hirsch, A. et al. (1999) *Criminal Deterrence and Sentence Severity: An Analysis of Recent Research*, Oxford: Hart Publishing. p. 5; von Hirsch, *Censure and Sanctions*. p. 41.
42. von Hirsch, et al., *Criminal Deterrence and Sentence Severity*. p. 5.
43. Lacey, *State Punishment*. p. 29.
44. Woolf, H. (1991) *Prison Disturbances, April 1990: A Report of Inquiry*, London: HMSO. Paras 12.228 and 12.229.
45. Presdee, M. (2000) *Cultural Criminology and the Carnival of Crime*, London: Routledge; Hayward, K. J. (2002) 'The Vilification and Pleasures of Youthful Transgression', in J. Muncie, G. Hughes and E. McLaughlin (eds), *Youth Justice: Critical Readings*, London: Sage. pp. 80–93; Brotherton, D. and Barrios, L. (2004) *The Almighty Latin King and Queen Nation*, New York: Columbia University Press.
46. Lacey, *State Punishment*. pp. 30–31. See also Allen, F. A. (1981) *The Decline of the Rehabilitative Ideal: Penal Policy and Social Purpose*, New Haven, CT: Yale University Press.
47. Ashworth, *Sentencing and Criminal Justice*. p. 64.
48. Zedner, *Criminal Justice*. pp. 96–97; Chesney-Lind, M. (1997) *The Female Offender: Girls, Women and Crime*, Thousand Oaks, CA: Sage.
49. Sumner, C. S. (2004) 'The Social Nature of Crime and Deviance', in C. S. Sumner (ed.), *Blackwell Companion to Criminology*, Oxford: Blackwell. pp. 1–31.
50. Hughes, G. (2002) 'Plotting the Rise of Community Safety: Critical Reflections on Research, Theory and Politics', in G. Hughes and A. Edwards (eds), *Crime Control and Community: The New Politics of Public Safety*, Cullompton: Willan Publishing; Stenson, K. (2002) 'Crime Control, Social Policy and Liberalism', in G. Lewis et al. (eds), *Rethinking Social Policy*, London: Sage.
51. Hall, N. G. C. (1995) 'Sexual Offender Recidivism Revisited: A Meta-analysis of Recent Treatment Studies', *Journal of Consulting and Clinical Psychology*, 63: 802–809; Pearson, F. S. and Lipton, D. S. (1999) 'A Meta-analytic Review of the Effectiveness of Corrections-based Treatments for Drug Abuse', *Prison Journal*, 79: 384–410.

52. von Hirsch, A. and Maher, L. (1998) 'Should Penal Rehabilitationism be Revived?', in von Hirsch, A. and Ashworth, A. (eds), *Principled Sentencing: Readings on Theory and Policy*. Oxford: Hart Publishing. p. 32.
53. Ashworth, A. (1993) 'Victim Impact Statements and Sentencing', *Criminal Law Review*, 498–509.
54. Bottoms, A. E. and Brownsword, R. (1982) 'The Dangerousness Debate after the Floud Report', *British Journal of Criminology*, 22: 229–254.
55. Honderich, T. (1982) 'On Justifying Protective Punishment', *British Journal of Criminology*, 22: 268–275; Honderich, T. (1988) *The Consequences of Determinism: A Theory of Determinism*, Oxford: Clarendon Press. pp. 193–223.
56. Tonry, M. (2004) *Punishment and Politics*, Cullompton: Willan Publishing. p. 65.
57. Ashworth, *Sentencing and Criminal Justice*. p. 66.
58. Sumner, C. S. (1994) *The Sociology of Deviance: An Obituary*, Milton Keynes: Open University Press. pp. 297–300.
59. Duff, R. A. (2001) *Punishment, Communication and Community*, Oxford: Oxford University Press.
60. von Hirsch, *Past or Future Crimes*. pp. 34–36.
61. Primoratz, I. (1989) 'Punishment as Language,' *Philosophy*, 64: 187–205.
62. Strawson, P. F. (1974) *Freedom and Resentment*, London: Methuen. pp. 1–25.
63. von Hirsch, *Censure and Sanctions*. p. 11.
64. Ashworth, A. (1985) 'Punishment and Compensation: Victims, Offenders and the State', *Oxford Journal of Legal Studies*, 6: 86–122.
65. Ashworth, 'Victim Impact Statements and Sentencing'. pp. 498–509.
66. Marshall, T. (1999) *Restorative Justice: An Overview*. London: Home Office.
67. Braithwaite, J. (1989) *Crime, Shame and Reintegration*, Cambridge: Cambridge University Press.
68. Ashworth, A. (2000a) 'Victim's Rights, Defendant's Rights and Criminal Procedure', in A. Crawford and J. Goodey (eds), *Integrating a Victim Perspective within Criminal Justice*. Aldershot: Ashgate. p. 186.
69. Zedner, *Criminal Justice*. p. 105.
70. Braithwaite, J. (1999) 'Restorative Justice: Assessing Optimistic and Pessimistic Accounts', in M. Tonry (ed.), *Crime and Justice: A Review of Research*, Chicago: Chicago University Press. p. 22.

6

THE CONCEPT OF CENSURE

Our feelings consist in desires, which we take to be justified, that the person of whom we disapprove should at least suffer ssome discomfiture. He should in some degree have distress for the wrong he has done, if perhaps only the distress of knowing that he has the disapproval of others, a disapproval which is not self-concerned or idiosyncratic but is based on moral convictions or principles. What we want is at least that what he has done should be brought home to him. In other cases, perhaps such as has been imagined, our desires in disapproving of a man are stronger, and do issue in resolutions to act and of course in actions itself.

Ted Honderich, 1988, pp. 65–66.

Introduction

Nicola Lacey has argued that when it comes to criminal responsibility it is useful to delineate two things: the fact of the social meaning expressed in a criminal conviction and the discourse about fault, culpability and condemnation.[1] Lacey's point elegantly encapsulates the way in which we condemn (i.e. censure) criminals. It necessarily involves us in a process that attributes blame, in terms of the wrongness of an offence, and involves normative judgements which relate to a given jurisdiction or society. In other words, crime may be wrong but 'wrong' is not a simple concept and is always to be understood historically, morally and socially, and as part of a normative model of criminal law. The ideological treatment is an overtly political treatment of censure and the normative treatment is similarly political, in as much as it does not contest the historical, moral and social constitution of any given censure in using the term in a largely unproblematic fashion. This chapter will set out these two archetypal treatments of censure employed in Criminology by concentrating upon the work of Colin Sumner and Andrew von Hirsch, interestingly, for a number of years, colleagues at the Institute of Criminology in Cambridge. These two treatments are themselves dependent on antecedent political theory considerations derived from political theory. It is not so much the case that these two treatments ignore one another as it is a case of them defining the term 'censure' in radically different ways and employing the term in different theoretical and penological circumstances.

The Ideological Use of Censure

The ideological use of the term 'censure' is allied much more closely to sociological theory than to penology. It asserts the role of social structure, history and ideology, as opposed to the normative value, of the censure. In the ideological version, the censure itself is problematic for it is necessarily the result, to a greater or lesser extent, of ideological determination. The censure tells us more about the power relations that give rise to its application than it does about its necessity in any jurisprudentially determined model. Moreover, it is fundamentally related to traditional issues in Marxist scholarship, those of power and the state. It does not so much take issue with those theorists, such as von Hirsch, who employ a normative treatment of censure, as see that entire enterprise as part of a liberal jurisprudence that addresses different questions altogether, and which in the overall scheme of things serves the *status quo*.

Colin Sumner has addressed censure in books and articles since the early 1980s and is the pre-eminent scholar working in censure theory on the progressive left. After early work on ideology and deviancy theory, Sumner focused his attention on the concept of censure, culminating in 1990 with the influential collection of essays *Censure, Politics and Criminal Justice*.[2] This collection conceived criminology not in terms of a sociology of deviance but in terms of the enforcement of dominant social censures by understanding the criminal justice system as being ideologically and politically constructed by dominant capitalist forces. It was an overtly Marxist work which sought not only to critique the discipline of Criminology by developing a rigorous theory of censure drawing upon both historical and sociological research, but also to change the entire thrust of criminological research, which it saw as inadequate.[3]

The sociology of censure grew out of a frustration with existing criminological explanation. As Sumner rather pithily stated:

> Whether we take their abstract, discursive definitions or their practical definitions in the course of law enforcement or moral stigmatization, it is clear that the definitions of deviant behaviour, even within a single society, exclude what should be included, include what should be excluded, and generally fail to attain unambiguous, consistent and settled social meanings. To this we add massive cross-cultural differences in the meaning, enforcement and even existence of categories of deviance, and endless instances of resistance to them involving alternative categories. Clearly, they are highly acculturated terms of moral and political judgement.[4]

In other words, since there is no possibility of using the normal categories of crime and deviance in a scientific, or even consistent, fashion, it is right to analyse them as moral and political discourses. Crime categories should be understood as negatively conceived ideological categories. Moreover, it views crime categories in terms of their institutional forms and practices, i.e. how and why they arise in certain places, at certain times, in relation to certain groups. In Marxist terms, crime categories should also be understood as the hegemonic function they have in signifying, denouncing and regulating individuals and groups. Policing and other functions of the criminal justice system, Sumner argued, reflect capitalist social, economic and political relations. The criminal justice system is in place to uphold the interests of the capitalist class. Accordingly, censures may be said not to reflect a *truth* about the extent of crime, but rather 'a world-view which had not come to terms with its repressed unconscious – the fear of women, blacks, radicals, the working class and the colonized'.[5]

Following Marxist theory on class, Sumner argued that in any society dominant groups, i.e. in terms of class, gender and race, will inevitably seek to maintain their control through the 'capacity to assert its censures in the legal and moral discourses of the day'.[6] He argues that this not only involves the courts and police authorities, but also the mass media. A process is set in motion which supports the discourses and practices of the state over against any dissenting voices. Sumner has frequently been said to be developing the symbolic interactionist's perspective in his work, but this is mistaken since 'labels' involve no reference to hegemonic forces or ideology. Moreover, the labels of the symbolic interactionists derive their philosophical origins from the American School of Pragmatism and philosophers such as Charles Sanders Peirce, John Dewey and William James, rather than from Foucault and Marxian theory. Censures are more than labels and should be seen as 'categories of denunciation or abuse lodged within very complex, historically loaded practical conflicts and moral debates'.[7] Censure theory typically relates social censures to broader issues of power, wealth and meaning, whereas social interactionism rarely attempts this.

In an important article in 1981 Sumner made the point that the Thatcher era was actually an important period in the development of Marxist Criminology.[8] He saw the structuralist Marxism of the 1970s giving way to a form of Marxist writing that was dependant upon cultural analysis. He saw that the 'sociology of deviance' approach was giving way to a broader approach that looked beyond narrow crime categories in order to account for the role of criminal law in the modern world and that related crime to cultural phenomena, though some criminologists have noted a 'romantic and naturalistic' aspect to this analysis.[9] Sumner's theory of social censures is reliant upon earlier criminological and sociological work relating to ideology and cultural studies, notably *Policing the Crisis*.[10] This work suggested that the censure of black mugging, which was expressed in the press and media and supported by the police at the time, had no real evidential basis. Instead, it was the result of the political situation then existing, and the police focus upon blacks in the inner cities. Hall et al. suggested that the censure of blacks was, at root, an ideological phenomenon rather than a criminal justice problem *per se*. Hall et al., as did Sumner, saw the black mugger as a scapegoat for wider social and economic failures. The attention that black mugging received was no more than a deflection away from a crisis in hegemony.

Sumner's work represents a dialogue with contemporary Criminology. Sumner was concerned that criminologists had both taken deviance to be a largely unproblematic term and overlooked the lack of consensus surrounding it. In fact, Sumner argued that deviance was being read off as a *deviation* from a dominant moral code; in other words, deviance was merely a deviation from a social convention. Moreover, he argued that concepts of crime, deviance and difference were not only conflated but were radically subjective terms rather than scientific categories, and not up to the task of criminological analysis.[11] For Sumner, the sociology of deviance was progressive in that it focused attention away from issues of degeneracy and towards concerns around social regulation. He argued that 'crime and deviance cannot be disentangled from the social facts of collective life' and that criminologists ought to realise the sheer complexity of the social world before venturing further in theoretical terms.[12]

Sumner's contribution is immense: he developed his reasoning by suggesting that 'social censures combine with forms of power and economy to provide distinct and important features of practices of domination and regulation'.[13] This line of reasoning has opened up research into crime to encompass areas hitherto outside the domain of criminology, such as the study of the Holocaust.[14] Sumner gave us reasons to question the censures we commonly use and to ask questions about their origin and purpose. He pointed us away from the immediate issues surrounding crime and towards a contextualised analysis of crime and criminalisation, which focused upon the role of censures.

Sumner's analysis is undoubtedly radical. However, while it is easy to see how focusing upon certain groups affects policing and how this, in turn, affects the criminalisation process, it can nevertheless seem overblown. Sumner offers us an overtly political position which often overlooks empirical research and has a tendency to see huge socio-political significance in everyday criminal activity, or to see crime as an epiphenomenon of great historical and economic forces rather than the mundane and straightforward breach of law that it usually is. Moreover, by employing narrowly Marxist terminology, such as *hegemony* and *ideology*, he is forced into an analysis which cannot easily understand censure, and crime, without recourse to a theoretical framework, that can only ever see censure, and crime, as ultimately related to a repressive economic system, i.e. capitalism. If one doubts the Marxist theory upon which Sumner builds, then there is every reason to doubt Sumner's writing in total. His contribution will be either a footnote in criminological theory or nothing less than the development of a whole new social ethics, depending on how one views the role of ideology and economy in contemporary criminological explanation and theory.[15]

The Normative Use of Censure

We have already seen how censure is used to support a theory of punishment. Censure is a concept that has received a great deal of attention from philosophers and criminologists in the past 30 years.[16] However, such treatments tend to see censure operating as an element within a model, such as Just Deserts, in which case censures are always attached to blameworthiness. Censures are addressed to the criminal but also have preventive effects.[17] The actual form of the censure is, though, largely unexamined beyond its role in the normative model. Censure theory, in general, is limited to the view that the political community must punish criminals in proportion to the wrong they have done in order to express proportionate disapproval of criminal behaviour. This view may be located in the Anglo-American liberal philosophical literature and is associated primarily with backward-looking (usually Kantian) justifications of punishment.[18] The importance of censure in Just Deserts theory cannot be understated here. Just Deserts offers a censure theory which holds that punishment is justified because it is the appropriate form of censure for certain crimes. In Just Deserts theory, punishment is structurally aligned with the censure through the elements of desert and proportionality. Proportionality is addressed in *Censure and Sanctions* which states that the argument for proportionality involves:

1. The State's sanctions against proscribed conduct should take a punitive form; that is, visit deprivations in a manner that expresses censure or blame. 2. The severity of a sanction expresses the stringency of the blame. 3. Hence, punitive sanctions should be arrayed according to the degree of blameworthiness (i.e. seriousness) of the conduct.[19]

Moreover, in following this three-part scheme, third parties are addressed. It therefore offers an expanded and educative role for the criminal law. As von Hirsch has written:

The criminal law gives the censure it expresses yet another role: that of addressing third parties, and providing them with reason for desistence. Unlike blame in everyday contexts, the criminal sanction announces in advance that specified categories of conduct are punishable. Because the prescribed sanction is one which expresses blame, this conveys the message that the conduct is reprehensible, and should be eschewed. It is not necessarily a matter of inculcating that the conduct is wrong, for those addressed (or many of them) may well understand that already. Rather, the censure embodied in the prescribed sanction serves to appeal to people's sense of the conduct's wrongfulness, as a reason for desistence.[20]

Zedner has commented on how this multiple function in relation to censure, i.e. addressing not only criminals but also third parties as well as linking it to issues of proportionality and desert, overloads the theory and she raises the question of whether it is 'equal to the task'.[21]

The main idea in Andrew von Hirsch's treatment of censure is that it is justified as the rightful expression of our moral sentiments in relation to crime.[22] Censure is employed in his model of punishment in a proportionate fashion to express differing levels of blameworthiness. It is a moral theory at heart. Censure is seen not only as part of a moral and political conception of persons, which considers them responsible for their actions, but also it is employed to justify the community's condemnation of criminal behaviour. It assumes that criminal behaviour is straightforwardly wrong and largely ignores historical, moral and social considerations of censure and issues concerning the structural relationships between actors. It is not concerned with the socio-political processes which give rise to censures, as Sumner argues.

Censure, in the modern normative formulation, is the process by which the community confronts criminals with the appropriate disapproval of others. Duff has made the point that this appeals to the criminal's own sense of proper action. In treating the criminals as rational actors, censure shows them that their actions were disapproved of and asks them to reconsider their future actions and to display personal restraint. In communicating moral disapproval, we too are exercising our nature as moral and rational agents.[23] In this way censure may be said to provide a disincentive to criminal behaviour. In expressing disapproval of the crime, the state treats the offender as a responsible and moral person. It also affirms the value of the victim through public denouncement. As von Hirsch has argued:

> Censure addresses the victim. He or she has not only been injured, but wronged through someone's culpable act. It thus would not suffice just to acknowledge that the injury has occurred or convey sympathy (as would be appropriate when someone has been hurt by a natural catastrophe). Censure, by directing disapprobation at the person responsible, acknowledges that the victim's hurt occurred through another's fault.[24]

Importantly, censure does not conceive punishment's justification in terms of its future results and this marks a difference from forward-looking justifications, such as deterrence, reform or incapacitation, which tend to be of a utilitarian nature. Censure theory, as a backward-looking account, has a ready-made moral rationale for why only the guilty should be punished. The state punishes and censures only those who have broken the law, regardless of any future considerations. In Just Deserts theory proportionate censure always entails proportionate punishment, and vice versa. The obligation to censure criminal activity entails the obligation to punish it as well – the two elements are entwined.

Criminal sanctions in modern liberal jurisprudence have two essential features: imposing painful consequences and censuring. Censure may be expressed through the imposition of unpleasant consequences, not because they have adverse consequences alone but because they impose public disapproval. The combination of these features is important because the severity of the hard treatment conveys the degree, or extent, of the censure involved. For this reason, even if prevention as well as censure help explain punishment, it is desert that ought to determine the amount of punishment for any criminal offences. The censure expressed by the penalty reflects how blameworthy and serious criminal behaviour is.[25] Employing censure in criminal cases maintains the disapproval of criminal activity in society and this also functions to maintain that general political principle of the general justifying aim of punishment.[26]

Censure is said to be an expressive theory of deserved punishment. It offers a plausible account as to why punishments should be commensurate with the gravity of the offence. However, it is important to point out that the norms governing expression are conventional ones. In equating expression (the act of expressing) and communication (the imparting of information), censure theory often fails to emphasise that definitions necessarily involve conventional representations when transmitting information. It is easy to see how censure theory relates to our everyday moral notions about crime and punishment, and accordingly there ought to be a rational and straightforward relationship between the degree of punishment and criminal conduct. However, our notions about crime are largely a matter of convention and therefore are not necessarily the proper basis for criminal sentencing; for example the punishment of homosexuals prior to the law reforms of the 1960s and 1970s (notably the Sexual Offences Act 1967) may be said to reflect the prevailing conventions of the time, rather than the *rightful* response to private activity.[27] In Joel Feinberg's words:

> Punishment is a conventional device for the expression of attitudes of resentment and indignation, and of judgments of disapproval and reprobation. ... To say that the very physical treatment itself expresses condemnation is to say simply that certain forms of hard treatment have become the conventional symbols of public reproba-tion. This is neither more nor less paradoxical than to say that certain words have become conventional vehicles in our language for the expression of certain attitudes, or that champagne is the alcoholic beverage traditionally used in celebration of great events, or that black is the colour of mourning.[28]

Problems associated with the existence of power relations

The main issue facing those who advocate a normative approach to censure is that of relating it to the broader social and political considerations that exist in the world, notably how power structures social relations and how such broader considerations frame censures. Writers using the normative version of censure, in particular von Hirsch, have cited Kant and Rawls as influences upon their work. It is right to take a closer look at the issue of power in these writers, since this issue is relevant to the institution of punishment and the application of censures. The way power structures the political and social world is surely cru-cial to issues of censure, desert and justice. Just Deserts is a neo-Kantian position and not a fully fledged political liberal theory *per se*. It relies upon a pre-existing liberal framework of jurisprudence and political theory. However, liberal moral, political and social theory, primarily of a neo-Kantian kind, always assumes the autonomy in the moral life and the centrality of the person, which are the ele-ments that Sumner attacks in his work. It assumes that people are like-situated and free to act. Rawls is seen as especially important since his justice as fairness idea and his work on the original position can be argued to point towards a rational chooser determining a central role for desert (the rationale for the dis-tribution of censure), since such a rational chooser would want to determine that he should be punished, and to what extent, only in regard to what he or she deserves.[29] Therefore, although Rawls does not advocate desert in the same fashion as Just Deserts, his work can nonetheless be seen as grounding desert through determining conditions for 'fairness'. Rawls is crucial because he showed in *A Theory of Justice* that punishment is an important component in any just social order. Andrew von Hirsch, in *Past or Future Crimes*, argued that sentencing theory needs to afford a 'central role to notions of equity and justice'.[30] Since von Hirsch has argued for the centrality of issues of equity and justice in his work, it is right to criticise his lack of any serious analysis of the role of power, and its potential impact upon censures. The problem for those using a normative model is not to do with the model so much as a deficient account of those in the real-world operation of censuring. Therefore the argument against the normative model is directed not at the model as such, but at the built-in assumptions of the model, namely autonomous moral life. Autonomy and independence cannot be taken for granted in any theory. Rather, it has to be worked for by individuals, given power relations in the real world.

Andrew von Hirsch is a neo-Kantian. Neo-Kantians have always assumed that the autonomy of moral life is the basis of political theory. As the philosopher Bernard Williams has argued: '...the most interesting recent work in moral philosophy has been a basically Kantian inspiration ... specially characterised by its impartiality and its indifference to any particular relations to particular persons'.[31] Williams also states, in the same passage, that this may 'make it very difficult to assign to those other relations and motivations the significance or structural importance in life which some of them are capable of possessing'. The assumption that there is an autonomous moral realm may be challenged given issues such as power, which may unduly impact upon the independence of persons and which may well structure social censures. It is the case that such issues as class, gender, poverty and race structure our world and show themselves in the power relations that obtain in society. Moreover, our moral choices too reflect such issues as class, gender, poverty and race. They shape the world in which choices, and censures, are exercised.

Experience is underplayed in the Kantian scheme, but nonetheless our knowledge is dependent upon our experience. The point Williams makes about structural issues and the persistence of power relationships would, again, seem to run counter to this scheme as both undermine the way the individual experiences the self. One might speculate that if the social world is no more than a space for persons to prove themselves morally, by acting out of a sense of duty, then the baggage of our given historical moral legacy is of no use in determining the correctness or otherwise of our social relationships. If we take the Kantian moral perspective, and implicitly identify the moral and rational with the universal, we are bound to play down the role of social life because it is of little use in affecting our equality and freedom as moral agents.

Given that our world is determined, our choices are never free but are conditioned by desire. Kant states: 'When we think of ourselves as free, we transfer ourselves into the intelligible world as members and recognise the autonomy of the will.'[32] In this way, the issue of autonomy is reserved for the intelligible world as an issue of moral autonomy. Kant therefore makes it difficult to ask questions about how persons might be undermined by social relations. The division of autonomy and dependence are divided into separate spheres. Moral beings are detached from social relationships because persons only choose freely when they are completely unconditioned by the contingencies of circumstance. It is easy to see how this sort of reasoning necessarily overlooks the sort of ideological analysis advocated by Sumner.

The idea of respect for persons is central to liberal moral and political theory, and yet, this is to focus our sense of respect on our capacity to make free choices within an independent moral realm. It also limits our notions of the good to the quest for individual conceptions of happiness. In the Rawlsian scheme, as long as the original position works with the assumption of the veil of ignorance, one can be sure that it abstracts from personal differences between rational beings and from the content of their private ends. This allows him to think that: 'The original position may be viewed, then, as a procedural interpretation of Kant's conception of autonomy and the categorical imperative.'[33] When we act in accordance with the categorical imperative, we are supposedly expressing our nature as free and equal rational persons. He thinks we can always avail our-selves of this way of thinking, regardless of the social relations in which we find ourselves. Rawls is able to sustain what he takes to be the main Kantian insight – '[t]he idea that moral principles are the object of rational choice'[34] – while making clear that the principles of right are not legislated *a priori* by pure reason, but 'may be conceived as principles that would be chosen by rational persons'.[35] This is one of the merits of a social contract conception. If this strengthens Rawls' sense of people as free and equal rational beings, it also tempts him into thinking that we are always free to treat others with equal respect, since it is always possible for us to appreciate that others have ends they wish to be free to pursue. Paradoxically, it is this compromise that Rawls makes with the empirical characteristics of social life that limits his insight. Since we are assumed to have a desire to express our nature, we might put it as Rawls. We act 'as rational and equal members of the intelligible realm with precisely this liberty to choose, that is, as beings who can look at the world in this way and express this perspective in their life as members of society'.[36] One detects here no sense that there are pre-existing interests or social and political arrangements already in place. In other words, censures could be focused upon the preservation of an unjust set of arrangements.

The idea of justice as fairness is that the principles of justice are agreed in an initial situation that is fair. Rawls also realises that society cannot be a voluntary scheme of cooperation and that, in reality, 'each person finds himself [*sic*] placed at birth in some particular position in some particular society, and the nature of this position materially affects his life prospects'.[37] One of the features assumed by Rawls to be common to all human beings, and thereby non-contingent, is his sense that we all desire to choose our own ends. This is partly what defines us as free and equal rational beings and is embodied in the Rawlsian principle of equal liberty. It is this ability to choose our own ends which is threatened in the relationship of power and subordination between rich and poor. For Kant, it was crucial to realise that if someone was dependent for his or her means of livelihood, it would be difficult for him or her to truly choose his or her individual ends. Kant could only save his assumption from the autonomy of morality by assuming that this was a situation that was freely chosen, although Kant recognised that it grew out of an earlier unequal distribution of property, which in turn produced relationships of power. Rawls seems more willing to guarantee our existence as free and equal rational beings by making it an aspect of our nature, which we can choose to display. As Rawls states: 'Men exhibit their freedom, their independence from the contingencies of nature and society, by acting in ways they would acknowledge in the original position.'[38] This would seem at odds with the reality of pre-existing issues of economic, political and social relationships and the determination of persons to maintain a privileged position, including the use of censuring activity in this process.

Sandel has noted that the priority of the right over the good mirrors the priority of the self over its ends and that '[t]o assert the priority of the self whose sovereign agency is assured, it was necessary to identify an essentially "unencumbered" self, conceived as a pure subject of possession, distinct from its contingent aims and attributes, standing always behind them'.[39] This assists in identifying an important weakness in liberal theory, though Sandel's wish to recognise how certain ends are 'constitutive' of our sense of self, rather than voluntarily chosen as an act of will, still poses the issue in terms of an individual's relationship to his ends. It does, however, recognise that Rawls and Dworkin type right-based theories, which seek to defend certain individual claims against utilitarian calculus of social interests, 'both rely on a theory of the subject that has the paradoxical effect of confirming the ultimate frailty, perhaps even incoherence, of the individual whose rights they seek above all to secure'.[40]

Kantian rationalism

In order to understand the political and social theory dimensions of justice, and the conditions for it, we need to engage with the character of Kantian rationalism. There is a profound tension between morality and reason on the one hand and emotions and desires on the other. It is embodied in Rawls' conception of us as free and equal persons. Even though Rawls wants to connect our principles of justice to the empirical conditions of human conduct, he still assumes that the contingent social and natural conditions are morally irrelevant, at least in the sense that they are irrelevant to the determination of what is just. Since he takes himself to be developing a theory of justice that is fair between persons, only those contingencies that differentiate people from each other need to be ruled out. This helps him develop a thin theory of the good, in which we can think of respect and self-respect, say, as primary goods that people will want whatever their individual ends and goals happen to be. Their inclusion does not threaten the basic idea of ourselves as beings that are free to choose our own ends. But of course this is not enough to develop a substantive theory of the person antecedent to social institutions. For Rawls, the worth of persons has to await the creation of social institutions with the power to create legitimate expectations.

A Kantian tradition which stresses the impersonal character of morality and that reasons have to be universally appropriate if they are to be moral, often fails to illuminate the individuality of our moral experience, even though this is supposedly one of its strengths. Kant would never recognise that there would be any moral significance in developing a sort of inner relationship with ourselves, and because of this he failed to substantiate the individualism he wanted to foster. In stressing moral impartiality as disinterested and impersonal, he oversimplifies the very essence of moral experience. The Kantian tradition encourages us to always see individuals as self-sufficient and self-determining, and always free to work out their individual relationships to the moral law. The downside is that this form of theorising can impersonalise experience. Accordingly, in Kant it is only when we act out of a sense of duty that we exercise our autonomy. We are exalted to identify our sense of self with our reason, and that in turn gives us access to what we require. Similarly, within deontological liberalism, our rights are supposedly guaranteed through the independent workings of reason. However, as I have argued, this trades on Kant's notion that it is only in the exercise of our reason that we can express our choice and so our freedom. Rawls wants us to think of our conception of our happiness, goals and ends as a similar exercise of our freedom.

In Kantian theory. We learn to control our feelings through dominating them and work for a time when our emotions and feelings have less and less influence over our lives. This is a process of reformulating our experience and accepting a certain vision of our lives. I have shown the different ways it disorganises crucial features in our moral experience. It limits the respect we can learn to have for ourselves and our sense of the moral experience of others. I have argued that Kant, and the liberal tradition, leaves us with an attenuated conception of the individual, even though this is traditionally taken as a strength of the theory. Kant is unable to substantiate his idea of respect that we should not treat people merely as means but always as ends in themselves. This idea continues to echo and promises crucial insights into the realities of power. However, it is an idea that Kant and those working in the Kantian tradition cannot develop without challenging his basic conception of the autonomy of morality. This is recognised by Rawls when he writes: '... between equality as it is invoked in a connection with the distribution of certain goods, some of which will almost certainly give higher status and prestige to those who are favoured, and equality as it applies to the respect which is owed to persons irrespective of their social position'.[41] It is clear that Rawls sees the second kind as fundamental. Its deeper significance is explained in its basis in such natural duties as that of mutual respect and the fact that it is owed to human beings as moral persons. Rawls wants a theory of justice which, by arranging inequalities for reciprocal advantage and abstracting from the 'contingencies of nature and social circumstances within a framework of equal liberty, persons express their respect for one another in the very constitution of their society'.[42] Rawls is true to Kant in that he tends to see individuals as essentially free to act justly.[43]

Just deserts theory

The foregoing discussion is important to Just Deserts and to the application of a normative theory of censure. Just Deserts theory offers little in the way of any theoretical work on the nature of individuals, or the nature of society. Very telling are the words of Andrew von Hirsch, who wrote:

> Sentencing policy is not a good tool either for reducing criminality or promoting wider social justice. ... If we want a more equitable society, we will have to establish and pay for the requisite programmes of social assistance. That may also help shrink criminogenic conditions in the community, although one cannot be certain how much and when.[44]

Just Deserts is a form of jurisprudential theory. It rests upon two notions. First, the confining of issues of criminal sentencing to the legal sphere and, secondly, the adoption of a conception of wider notions of justice and the person that are rooted in contemporary liberal, more especially neo-Kantian, thinking. It is open to the charge that it ignores the issue of power and takes over an over-simplified account of moral life. While its central insight may be readily under-stood, it nonetheless cries out for a better account of moral life.

Desert theories are tied to claims about personal responsibility. A person must deserve something, in this case a punishment, which is contingent on a minimal level of voluntarism, in terms of an act committed. This backward-looking element is vital for in placing the emphasis on what has been done, rather than on something which will be done, it is clear that the desert basis of censure must be enacted before a person can properly deserve.[45] Punishment and desert (i.e. the level of censure) must relate to the individual's action and not some wider social goal or outcome. Desert is also a social concept because it is based on certain judgements about a person's blameworthiness (applied censure), which are socially and politically constructed. The Just Deserts doctrine is a bold attempt to place the issues of desert, proportional-ity (which implies the level of censure) and justice, in the broadest sense, at the heart of sentencing theory and practice. The focus on the proper basis for treating individ-ual persons is a useful antidote to theories whose basis is the neglect of the individ-ual in the pursuit of the greater utility, or some other measure, for the many.

The nub of the issue

Without doubt the issue of power is a challenge not only to Just Deserts but also to all normative theories of punishment in general. To conclude, one might argue that censures derive from specific norms, values and historical and politi-cal circumstances, and that any cogent theory involving censures needs to reflect that. However, to only see the historical and political circumstance is surely no useful guide as to the level of punishment a criminal 'deserves'.

–––––––––––––––––––––––––– **Main Summary Points** ––––––––––––––––––––––––––

- The ideological use of censure is a theoretical device for allowing us to under-stand the power relations that give rise to the application of a censure. It relates criminal and other censures with concerns about power and the state.
- Colin Sumner, the main proponent of censure theory in Criminology, built on the work of Stuart Hall et al. and the book *Policing the Crisis*. He followed Hall et al. in seeing the black mugger as a scapegoat for the wider social and eco-nomic failures of the 1970s and 1980s. He argued that the censure of black mugging was no more than a deflection away from a crisis in hegemony.
- Sumner's work on censure also represents a critique of academic Criminology. He argued that criminologists typically saw criminal behaviour as a behaviour

from a social convention and that the concepts of crime, deviance and difference used in Criminology are subjective terms, rather than scientific categories, and not up to the task of criminological analysis.

- Andrew von Hirsch saw three main criteria in his Just Deserts view of censure: '1. The State's sanctions against proscribed conduct should take a punitive form; that is, visit deprivations in a manner that expresses censure or blame. 2. The severity of a sanction expresses the stringency of the blame. 3. Hence, punitive sanctions should be arrayed according to the degree of blameworthiness (i.e. seriousness) of the conduct.' (*Censure and Sanctions*, 1993).
- Censure, in the normative model, is said to be an expressive theory of deserved punishment because it offers a plausible account as to why punishments should be commensurate with the gravity of the offence.
- The Just Deserts doctrine is an attempt to place the issues of desert, proportionality (which entails censure) and justice, in the broadest sense, at the heart of sentencing theory and practice.

Questions

1. What are the things that Sumner and von Hirsch agreed upon in relation to censure?
2. In what way is von Hirsch's view of censure a moral one?
3. Is Sumner's theory a criminological or political theory?

Suggested Further Reading

Amatrudo, A. (1997) 'The Nazi Censure of Art: Aesthetics and the Process of Annihilation', in C. S. Sumner (ed.), *Violence, Culture and Censure*, London: Taylor and Francis.
Sumner, C. S. (1994) *The Sociology of Deviance: An Obituary*, Buckingham: Open University Press.
Tabensky, P. A. (ed.) (2006) *Judging and Understanding*, London: Ashgate.
von Hirsch, A. (1993) *Censure and Sanctions*, Oxford: Clarendon Press.
Zedner, L. (2004) *Criminal Justice*, Oxford: Oxford University Press.

Notes

1. Lacey, N. (1988) *State Punishment: Political Principles and Community Values*, London: Routledge. pp. 61–62.
2. Sumner, C. S. (1990) *Censure, Politics and Criminal Justice*, Buckingham: Open University Press. pp. 1–59.
3. Ibid. pp. 23–26.
4. Ibid. p. 26; Sumner, C. S. (ed.) (2004) *The Blackwell Companion to Criminology*. Oxford: Blackwell. pp. 25–27.
5. Sumner, C. S. (1994) *The Sociology of Deviance: An Obituary*, Milton Keynes: Open University Press. p. 310.
6. Sumner, *Censure, Politics and Criminal Justice*. p. 27.
7. Ibid. p. 28.

8. Sumner, C. S. (1981) 'Race, Crime and Hegemony', *Contemporary Crises*, 5 (3): 277–91.
9. Hall, S. and Winlow, S. (2004) 'Barbarians at the Gate', in J. Ferrell et al. (eds), *Cultural Criminology Unleashed*, London: Glasshouse Press. p. 279.
10. Hall, S., Critcher, C., Jefferson, T., Clarke, J. and Roberts, B. (1978) *Policing the Crisis*, London: Macmillan.
11. Sumner, *The Sociology of Deviance*. pp. 309–312.
12. Sumner, *Blackwell Companion to Criminology*. p. 29.
13. Sumner, *Censure, Politics and Criminal Justice*. p. 35.
14. Amatrudo, A. (1997) 'The Nazi Censure of Art: Aesthetics and the Process of Annihilation', in C. S. Sumner (ed.), *Violence, Culture and Censure*, London: Taylor and Francis. pp. 63–84.
15. Sumner, *The Sociology of Deviance*. p. 315.
16. For example, Feinberg, J. (1970) *Doing and Deserving*, Princeton, NJ: Princeton University Press; and von Hirsch, A. (1993) *Censure and Sanctions*, Oxford: Clarendon Press. Both of these books examine censure.
17. von Hirsch, A. (1986) *Past or Future Crimes*, Manchester: Manchester University Press. p. 52.
18. See Duff, R. A. (1986) *Trials and Punishments*, Cambridge: Cambridge University Press, esp. Chapter 9; von Hirsch, *Censure and Sanctions*; Kleinig, J. (1991) 'Punishment and Moral Seriousness', *Israel Law Review*, 25: 401–421.
19. von Hirsch, *Censure and Sanctions*. p. 15.
20. Ibid. pp. 10–11.
21. Zedner, L. (2004) *Criminal Justice*, Oxford: Oxford University Press. p. 72.
22. von Hirsch, *Censure and Sanctions*. pp. 6–19.
23. Duff, R. A. (2001) *Punishment, Communication and Community*, Oxford: Oxford University Press. p. 101.
24. von Hirsch, *Censure and Sanctions*. p. 10.
25. Ibid. pp. 13–14.
26. Lacey, *State Punishment*. p. 200; Duff, *Trials and Punishments*. pp. 151–164.
27. von Hirsch, *Censure and Sanctions*. pp. 8–12.
28. Feinberg, *Doing and Deserving*. p. 59.
29. Rawls, J. (1955) 'Two Concepts of Rules', *The Philosophical Review*, 44: 3–32; Rawls, J. (1973) *A Theory of Justice*, Oxford: Oxford University Press.
30. von Hirsch, *Past or Future Crimes*. p. 9.
31. Williams, B. A. O. (1981) *Moral Luck*, Cambridge: Cambridge University Press. p. 2.
32. Kant, I. (1964) *Groundwork to the Metaphysics of Morals*, New York: Harper & Row. p. 461.
33. Rawls, *Theory of Justice*. p. 256.
34. Ibid. p. 251.
35. Ibid. p. 16.
36. Ibid. p. 255.
37. Ibid. p. 13.
38. Ibid. p. 256.
39. Sandel, M. (1982) *Liberalism and the Limits of Justice*, Cambridge: Cambridge University Press. p. 121.
40. Ibid. p. 138.
41. Rawls, *Theory of Justice*. p. 511.
42. Ibid. p. 178.
43. Ibid. p. 256.
44. von Hirsch, *Censure and Sanctions*. pp. 97–98.
45. Metz, T. (1999) 'Realism and the Censure Theory of Punishment', *Proceedings of the 19th World Congress of the International Association for Philosophy of Law and Social Philosophy*, (IUR) New York, June 24–30. pp. 116–129.

7

DESERT AND PROPORTIONALITY

The idea of moral desert is not questioned. Rather, the thought is that a conception of moral desert as moral worth of character and actions cannot be incorporated into a political conception of justice in view of the fact of reasonable pluralism. Having conflicting conceptions of the good, citizens cannot agree a comprehensive doctrine to specify an idea of moral desert for political purposes.

John Rawls, 2001[1]

Introduction

This chapter will focus on personal desert and proportionality, which are both crucial to a proper understanding of contemporary criminological work on sentencing. Desert, especially personal desert, is vital to the issue of punishment for only when a punishment is deserved, is it proper. As Andrew von Hirsch has noted: 'The central organising principle of sentencing ... is that of commensurate deserts.' Sentences accord to the gravity of the defendant's criminal conduct. The criterion for deciding the quantum of punishment is retrospective: the seriousness of the violation the defendant has committed.'[2]

Most of the writing on punishment usually raises political and philosophical questions regarding its basis, i.e. desert, although this writing is not usually directed to the underlying political and philosophical basis of punishment, but only to questions about the allocation of punishment.[3] The two issues of 'why punish?' and 'how much?' are obviously linked, and recent scholarship on the basis of judicial sentencing has given perhaps the best accounts of how such considerations play out in the real world. Proportionality is important in maintaining that crimes of an equal nature should be treated equally and that there is a proper rank ordering of offences. This chapter is necessarily technical in nature but it concludes with some practical considerations. Nonetheless, these concepts have a very important function in our criminal justice system, not least in the way they may contain the excesses of penal populism when contained in statute or sentencing guidelines.[4]

Clarifying our Language: Personal Desert and Eligibility

When political philosophers discuss personal desert they usually do so in relation to rules, rights and obligations,[5] and when they make judgements about personal desert, the deserts they think of are those of punishments and rewards.[6] They try to show that desert is a natural moral notion and that rewards and punishments are only two things that persons may be said to deserve. It can also be argued that desert may be applied to the interests of a community, over and against the individual. So that when we say that a person deserves something, we are backing our statement with a sense of moral correctness. If he or she deserves it, then he or she should have it: it is that simple. However, this is also true where a person is qualified or entitled to something and has a special claim, or a right, to it.

Let us begin by considering what it is to be eligible for something. Eligibility we may understand as a base or minimal qualification for something: the state of just not being disqualified. Therefore, eligibility is no more than a basis for something else. For example, when we determine whether a person is eligible for a job, we determine first whether he or she has satisfied the basic eligibility criteria. Did he or she have the basic qualifications? Eligibility is only the satisfaction of certain basic preliminary, and necessary, conditions and it is what philosophers call a rule connected qualification.[7] However, eligibility criteria are not the same thing as desert criteria.[8] When we say that a person deserves some form of treatment, this must necessarily be because of either some possessed characteristic or some past activity. This is a crucial point because no person can deserve something unless there is some basis for that desert. Political theorists would say that desert judgements always carry along with them a commitment to give reasons. It is not possible to state that Marianna deserves commending though she has not done anything. If a person states that Marianna does indeed deserve commending, she must then answer the question 'what for?' If the basis of Marianna's desert is not known, then the language of desert is simply not appropriate. It is right to argue that we all ought to treat Marianna properly, but we cannot commend her desert because there is no basis for commending her on desert grounds.

Moreover, when dealing with the grounds for desert, it is important to note that not just any grounds will do. It must always be the case that the basis for a person's desert must be related directly to facts about the person.[9] For example, if a student deserves a high grade, their desert must be related to facts about them personally, in terms of their ability.[10]

Judgements about desert can be invalidated in one of two ways. They can either lack a proper basis altogether or else have a logically inappropriate basis. In other words, either the judgement may lack an appropriate reason or the reason may not be what is technically termed a justifying reason.[11] So we can see that it is necessary that a person's desert has a basis and that the basis itself consists of facts about him or herself, but that neither of these conditions is sufficient.

We surely cannot list all the necessary and sufficient conditions for personal desert in the abstract, for the bases of desert vary along with the mode of deserved treatment. All we can practically do is to outline the key generic properties of desert, which do not vary with context.

A proper political analysis of the concept of desert must pay attention to each of the major kinds of treatment which persons can be said to deserve. If we devise a scheme A deserves X in virtue of B where A is a person, X a mode of treatment and B some notable fact about A, then it is clear that the values of B (the desert bases) are determined in part by the nature of the various Xs in question. So it follows that what makes a person deserving of punishment, for example, is not the same as that which makes him or her deserving of medical treatment. The question always concerns what are the various kinds of treatment that persons may deserve from others? This is what philosophers call 'affective' in character.

Punishment and Reward

The Victorian philosopher Henry Sidgwick famously wrote that reward is 'gratitude universalised' and that punishment is 'resentment universalised'.[12] It can be argued that the services and deprivations which we typically term rewards and punishments are just conventional means of expressing gratitude and resentment, for these attitudes are simply those involved in the desire to punish and reward. Sidgwick's definition of punishment and reward as resentment and gratitude universalised has a psychological element to it because it relates our deepest feelings with our immediate reactions. We might say that our personal resentment and gratitude become social devices for sharing in the resentment and gratitude of all victims and beneficiaries. This seems a reasonable way of understanding our popular views about punishment. We can understand rewards, like Sidgwick, as conventionally recognised means of expressing gratitude for services. Rewards may also be a means of expressing recognition, appreciation or approval of merit or excellence. Punishment may be a vehicle for the expression of our resentment of injury received, but also for the expression of *recognition* and disapproval of wrongdoing.[13] (The word recognition is being used in its technical sense here.)

Our responsive attitudes, typically expressed through rewards and punishments, all have an important characteristic in common. They all have what sociologists term a phenomenological target. In other words, if we resent a person, then we do not merely dislike him or her. It follows that to have a negative feeling towards a person because of something he or she has done is as much a part of the feelings themselves. Feelings are not the sort of things that can have purposes, whereas attitudes have a notion of desert built into them. We do not use such words as resentful and grateful unless there is a proper desert basis to the logically appropriate sort of feeling. We may be very attracted to a someone without any substantial reason, but we cannot be grateful for no apparent reason – that would not make any sense. Similarly, we can feel hostility for no obvious reason, but we do not resent someone without a proper reason. As long ago as 1927 the philosopher Bradley had argued that punishment without desert is not punishment at all.[14]

The theory and practice of legal punishment and official rewards is necessarily related to rules and regulations, offices and functions and duties and obligations. These rules and regulations, offices and functions and duties and obligations are then formalised beyond a straight correlation with the attitudes they typically express in practice. In the case of punishment, it may consist of such treatment as incarcerating a person, fining, and community service, but not resentment as such. Moreover, punishment may only be executed by those with the necessary authority and then only under certain strict conditions specified by law. Therefore, rewards and punishments are like all other modes of deserved treatment: they have qualifying conditions as well as desert bases, and these are always specified by rules and regulations and, in turn, confer rights and duties.

It is reasonably easy to generalise about punishment, i.e. judicial punishment. It must always have the universal qualifying condition of legal guilt. Although legal guilt is a far from straightforward matter, it is always dependent upon a conviction after a fair trial, held in accordance with due process, which is in turn defined by elaborated codes and procedural rules. Yet of all the official treatments for which a person might qualify under proper institutional rules, only punishment seems resistant to the contemporary language of rights. We do not, as a rule, say of a criminal who is qualified for punishment that he or she is entitled to it or that he or she has any special claim or a right to it.[15] It may be argued that a convicted criminal has a legal right to his or her punishment, whether he or she wants it or not, in the same way that a person who qualifies for a reward has a right to it, whether he or she wants it or not. The only substantial difference is simply that a renounced right ceases, sooner or later, to be a right, and the criminal's right, as Lyons has shown.[16]

In the case of compensation for some wrongful action what is known as a polar concept is often employed.[17] Where compensation is received by a victim, it will be given by the offender. In other words, if one person deserves to take, then another deserves to give. However, this is not usually how we typically frame the situation. What we would say is that the wrongdoer deserves to make compensation and deserves to be held liable for the harm he or she has caused. In other words, he or she deserves to be compelled to compensate the victim because the other pole of deserved compensation is deserved liability.

━━━━━━━━━━━━━━━━━━━ **Desert Criteria** ━━━━━━━━━━━━━━━━━━━

In the real world, conflict is not desert against advantage, justice against utility but desert against desert. Instead, we may describe the situation as a conflict between desert and entitlement, or in political theory terms, between rival claims to justice.[18] It is necessary to detail two areas of concern: (1) utilitarianism, and (2) desert treated as moral entitlement.

Utilitarianism

For a utilitarian the best way to determine the merit or otherwise of a given course of action is to analyse it in terms of its overall social utility. In the case of the threat of punishment, the criminal is deterred. In this respect, utility seems to work very well but the problem arises when we think of the issue differently, as the noted economic and political theorist John Harsanyi has shown.[19] To begin with, utility is not a desert basis for any deserved mode of treatment and we must never forget that. A desert statement, such as A deserves X because giving something to them would be in the greater public interest, is simply a misuse of the word 'deserves'. The political philosopher Derek Parfit has commented that any form of utilitarianism that interprets utility as either a universal basis for desert or as a universal qualifying condition is either absurd or self-defeating.[20] The point of all this for punishment, Feinberg has argued, is that punishment might only be deserved by the criminal because it is the customary way of expressing the resentment or reprobation they have coming.[21]

It is also worth noting that Andrew von Hirsch, long ago, linked desert criteria with the issue of deterrence, although deterrence is often considered a utilitarian consideration.[22] The issue might be, then, not that Just Deserts theorists are indifferent to utilitarian criteria, but rather the priority that different theorists give to utilitarian criteria, and when and in what order utilitarian criteria arise, or are prioritised, in a given theory. Kleinig has recently posed this issue in regard to how punishment is enacted in the real world.[23]

Moral Entitlement

There are political philosophers who have a jurisprudential view of morality.[24] They use existing legal institutions as their models.[25] In our case, the distinction between entitlement and desert is obscured by making desert a special case of entitlement, instead of a notion in essential contrast to entitlement. Desert confers rights but not the usual type of right of the sort winners of competitions and claimants of rewards have, for example, but instead moral rights, which in turn are implicitly treated as regulations of a special moral institution. Moreover, nothing is gained by qualifying the alleged entitlements as moral. Deserved, fitting and appropriate, on the one hand, and right, entitlement and rule, on the other, are terms from altogether different parts of our ethical language. They are reflected in such a way that there is no paradox in saying of a person that he or she deserves certain modes of treatment which, nevertheless, he or she cannot claim as his or her due.

Desert: conclusion

The basic moral intuition that desert is prior to any operational system for it is important. We have seen the variety of conflicts that are possible between desert and entitlement. However, if desert and entitlement are not distinct in nature, the question of their relation cannot be difficult or complicated.[26] Then there could only be real or higher entitlement (desert) and lower or inferior entitlement (qualification), and in cases of conflict the higher would always take precedence over the lower. It is important to emphasise, then, that desert is a moral concept in the sense that it is logically prior to and independent of public institutions and their rules.

Retributive theories of punishment always maintain that desert is the only rightful way to punish persons. Cragg has stated: 'Retributive justice stresses impartiality. This is one of its strengths, since it ensures that individuals receive equal treatment at the hands of the court regardless of their station in life.'[27] Moreover, in stressing the role of desert a moral intuition about punishment is underscored, as Andrew von Hirsch has written: 'We feel there is something wrong, not simply counterproductive in the long run, about inflicting punishments that are not fairly commensurate with the gravity of offences.'[28] We have seen how desert coheres with many of our moral notions of what is rightful conduct and is a proper basis on which to organise a sentencing tariff. Perhaps, the philosopher Ted Honderich summed it up best of all when he wrote:

> Desert-claims are to the effect that someone deserves something for something else. In connection with punishment, they are to the effect that someone deserves a particular penalty, or something bound up with a particular penalty, for a particular offence, or something involved in a particular offence. As in the case of all desert-claims, at least as standardly made, these are somehow to the effect that there exists a certain relation, which relation serves or enters into a reason or justification for something, the thing said to be deserved. ... What, more clearly, is the thing for which an offender deserves something? The still inexplicit but correct answer must be culpable action, which by way of initial description, is an action somehow open to moral disapproval. In the ordinary course of things, this will also be an illegal action.[29]

The Concept of Proportionality in Punishment

Contemporary justifications for punishment

Many thinkers, notably utilitarians, have argued that punishment is justified purely in terms of its consequences, in terms of say crime prevention or rehabilitation. Yet both Beccaria and Bentham, the former arguably a utilitarian and the latter certainly a utilitarian, gave us the earliest theory of proportionality based on a graded system of penalties focused upon deterrence and general prevention rather than on an ethical standard *per se*.[30] Mackie has argued that punishment, though derived from basic human emotional roots, is justified in terms of its social utility in reinforcing community bonds;[31] and that punishment has utility because it functions in consequentialist terms.[32] Andrew von Hirsch has objected to this reasoning because it fails adequately to support ethical limits on the distribution of sanctions.[33] Mackie overlooks the distribution of sanctions as this could lead to disproportionate punishments as well as criminal liability without fault. H. L. A. Hart made the point that relying on crime prevention as a general justifying aim leaves room for putting non-utilitarian limits on the distribution of penalties so long as the latter can be independently justified.[34] H. L. A. Hart pointed out that there must be an independent justification for a retributive limit on substantive criminal law; in other words, liability must be confined to the culpability of criminals alone.[35] Punishment must be proportionate to the seriousness of crimes and always be directed solely at offenders.

The notion of censure may offer good grounds for justifying a non-utilitarian account of proportionality consistent with a consequentialist general justifying aim. The censuring of crime is something we often taken for granted, even where punishment is allocated in terms of crime prevention. The sanction of censure is directly related to how blameworthy, or otherwise, the crime is. If proportionality is not adhered to, then criminals are treated unfairly, as von Hirsch has indicated.[36]

The benefits and burdens approach was advanced, in its contemporary form, by Herbert Morris and Jeffrie Murphy and subsequently by John Finnis and Wojciech Sadurski.[37] This is a view of retribution that accounts for why criminals need to suffer. The idea is that the law itself requires every person to refrain from criminal activity and that this, in turn, benefits from the self-restraint of others. Criminals are unfairly benefiting from the self-restraint of others and are obtaining an undeserved advantage because they do not reciprocate self-restraint: you could call them freeriders. It is the proper function of punishment to impose on criminals a disadvantage in order to restore the rightful balance. This view has been attacked vigorously by Andrew von Hirsch in *Doing Justice*, and latterly by Duff.[38] One of the many shortcomings that this position raises is that it seems that restoring a balance of advantages may not be sufficient reason to invoke the state's coercive powers.[39] The benefits and burdens of retributivism may be said to endorse an expansive contractarian theory of the state, as von Hirsch explains in *Past or Future Crimes* (1986).

As we saw in chapter 5, censure in the form of a public morality has been typically used to account for the degree to which criminals are held responsible for their actions. In other words we intuit a strict relationship between the level of censure and the level of seriousness of offences. We noted that this form of reasoning became central to the understanding of our moral lives, and how in the 1970s work by Feinberg and Strawson placed censuring behaviour at the heart of both criminological theory and philosophical explanation.

Censure

Strawson's account does seem plausible as far as it goes. Blaming persons does seem part of holding them responsible for their actions. Censure expresses the message that certain actions are wrong and that actors are blameworthy. Censure always expresses the rights of the individual censured, as Feinberg and Primoratz in the late 1980s have demonstrated.[40] It is because we share certain moral standards that a response is required which recognises both the wrongness of the action and the blameworthiness of the criminal. Indeed, Primoratz argued that censure can be seen as intrinsic and non-consequentialist, rather than a means of preventing crime.[41] Censure may also maintain the disapproval of persons to criminal and reprehensible acts, a point Duff makes.[42] Censure in confronting the criminal with the disapproval of others (the community, society) has a further function that Duff has commented upon, namely the criminal's own sense of proper action. What censure does, in part, is to draw the attention of the criminal to his or her wrong action and persuade him or her to reconsider future actions and maintain greater self-restraint. In censuring, we are confronting the criminal with a judgement that he or she has done wrong and should be blamed for his or her behaviour.[43]

In communicating censure we are exercising our rightful natures as moral and rational agents. It is not sufficient just to change behaviour, for we need to convey certain critical judgements (censures) about certain behaviour that we wish criminals to reflect upon. Censure may be conveyed through imposing unpleasant consequences, not solely because they have adverse material consequences but also because they are inflicted as a mark of disapproval. The intertwining of these features is crucial for the severity of the hard treatment will convey the degree of censure involved. Ashworth and von Hirsch have summed up the case for censure in the following terms: 'The nexus between punishment and blame has deeper roots than the sentencing rules of the particular jurisdiction. Censure is integral to the very concept of punishment.'[43]

Cardinal and ordinal proportionality

We turn now to the technical issue of how one goes about determining the deserved amount of punishment. Andrew von Hirsch best addresses the resolution to this problem in his book *Censure and Sanctions* (1986), and it relates to the distinction between cardinal and ordinal forms of proportionality.

Ordinal proportionality maintains that comparable offences should receive comparably severe punishments. The basic notion in ordinal proportionality is that persons should receive equal punishments where their offences are similar. Ordinal proportionality is easily explained in terms of an expressive theory, which stresses censure: whenever one crime is treated more harshly than another, it reflects the level of seriousness involved, and the level of censure should follow that.

However, cardinal proportionality addresses the overall magnitude and anchoring points of a penalty scale. Cardinal proportionality relates to the comparison of, for example, robbery by comparing the typical seriousness of this crime with the seriousness of other crimes. It is a conventional mechanism, i.e. a penalty scale is devised and it reflects the relative scaling of crimes and any alteration to the scale's magnitude and anchoring represents a change to that convention. Andrew von Hirsch tackles the idea of parsimony within a Just Deserts framework in his 1986 book, *Past or Future Crimes*.[44] This argued in favour of the possibility of affording a useful censure within the broader political and historical context of sentencing and the width of the bounds.

The important point about recent retributive writing is that proportionality is gauged with regard to moral seriousness with more serious crimes being punished more harshly. This principle is not a new one and Bentham wrote: 'The greater the mischief of the offence, the greater the expense, which it may be worthwhile to be at, in the way of punishment.'[45] In retributivist rationales, moral seriousness is ascertained by looking at two factors: (1) the harm done by the offence, and (2) the culpability of the offender.[46]

Thin proportionality is characterised by constructing solely ordinal scales of crime and punishment and by punishing serious offences more harshly relative to less serious ones. In other words, the level of punishment, the amount and the intervals between adjacent offences on the ordinal scale are not considered. Thin proportionality can never determine the amount of punishment. Thick proportionality, on the other hand, goes beyond the construction of ordinal scales and considers that serious crimes should be punished more harshly. This is a stage beyond just ensuring the scale is maintained since an ordinal scale may be entirely moderate in its punishments or unerringly harsh for all offences. As Andrew von Hirsch has argued when discussing proportionality in sentencing: 'It is less concerned with the supposed crime-prevention effect of this or that penalty, and more with the fairness of penalties' distribution.'[47]

The *lex talionis*

As we saw in chapter 5, under the *lex talionis* the criminal receives exactly what he or she has inflicted on another – 'an eye for an eye'. John Kleinig has shown up the shortcomings of the *lex talionis* in his book, *Punishment and Desert*. He makes the point that 'what punishment would you inflict on a rapist, a blackmailer, a forger, a dope peddler, a multiple murderer, a smuggler ...'.[18]

It would appear that the *lex talionis* only works effectively in one case – where a single murder has been committed.[49] The *lex talionis* would appear to be too crude and brutal to be allowed to function in a modern legal code. Reiman has made the point that the *lex talionis*, if enacted, would destroy the civilising progress of modern states.[50]

The shortcomings of the *lex talionis* have only served to make retributivists think through the concept of equivalence, according to which the offender only gets his just deserts when he is deemed to have suffered what is judged equivalent to the degree of suffering caused by his crime. This may appear similar to the utilitarian position in that it reduces both crime and punishment to a common denominator. However, it is different from utilitarian formulations in two important regards: (1) it sees punishment as equalling the crime without regard to the consequences of punishment; and (2) the equivalence between the crime and the punishment restricts the relevant suffering, i.e. the criminal can only be punished with reference to the suffering he or she caused and no more.

Restorative justice and proportionality

In Chapter 5 we examined restorative justice in relation to theories of punishment and saw how it eschewed strict notions of proportionality in the criminal justice system in favour of sentences derived through a mediated process entered into by several parties, including victims and offenders themselves; and how the parties are expected to agree upon an outcome on punishment which is always focused on social reintegration. The central aims in the restorative justice process are always the mending of social relationships and the public acknowledgment of the harm done to victims, offenders and the community.

Those theorists working with a concept of proportionality are often wary of restorative justice because of what von Hirsch, Ashworth and Shearing have called 'the multiple and unclear goals, underspecified means and modalities, lack of clear criteria, loose criteria for evaluation and inadequate limiting principles of restorative justice, in practice'.[51] In other words, whereas there may be value in the restorative justice procedure of dealing with crime through mediation and interaction between offenders and victims, it is often undermined by unclear or unspecified procedural and legal goals. For example, without proportionality constraints there is every reason to be concerned that restorative justice could actually result in inconsistent, unfair and unduly harsh, or lenient, sentences. Indeed, restorative justice theorists themselves have often been at odds with one another in regard to whether or not proportionality constraints have any place at all in a restorative model of justice. Moreover, leading restorative justice theorists, such as John Braithwaite, have shifted their personal positions regarding the importance of proportionality in relation to the main principles of restorative justice.[52]

'The Project of Sentencing Reform'[53]

It will be very useful to set out the main points of Andrew von Hirsch's 2001 chapter 'The Project of Sentencing Reform', which elegantly draws out some of the main issues we are dealing with here. Foremost in von Hirsch's argument is that sentencing, and sentencing reform, must always be guided by principle, and not by intuition. In the case of desert, he argues that: 'Desert sets the limits for the permissible sentence, within which crime prevention goals (including rehabilitation) may be pursued.'[54] He also upholds fairness as a consideration and links it to proportionality:

The sentence should visit a fair and proportionate sanction on the offender. Debate exists about the criteria for proportionality. Notwithstanding such divergence of view, however, there is agreement that proportionality should be an important, not just a marginal, constraint; and that disproportionate sentences should be impermissible – irrespective of their possible crime preventive effects. This concern with the justice of sentences depends on the assumption of convicted offender's having membership in the moral and legal community.[55]

Andrew von Hirsch demonstrates how a political consideration, that of membership of a moral and legal community, is at the heart of sentencing theory and reform. In other words, penal populism or vengeance, or any other objectifying criteria, ought never to lose sight of or override the humane and rational project of ensuring a fair political and legal settlement for citizens, which sentencing should always aim to uphold.[56]

A move away from proportionality and its consequences

In recent times, criminal sentencing policy has been a fairly confused affair in terms of recent legislation. For example, the Crime (Sentences) Act 1997 promoted mandatory sentences without much regard for the lack of empirical support for them, and the Criminal Justice Act 2003, which aimed to modernise the criminal justice system, has promoted the principle of deterrence. Accordingly, it has raised sentences and the prison population, although the UK is not unique in this regard.[57] However, it is at the lower end of the criminal seriousness range, and in the area of youth justice, that we have seen the greatest departures from the principle of proportionality, notably with civil measures such as ASBOs, the final warning procedures now in place and the increased role of 'diversion' in the criminal justice system.[58] The whole thrust of crime and disorder enforcement policy is now largely decided upon by crime and disorder reduction partnerships, as well as a plethora of multi-agency groupings, including community safety partnerships and crime reduction partnerships. This has tended to impact negatively upon proportionality as discretion, local conditions and target priorities have all undermined the overall fairness of ASBO enforcement policy. This had led to enormous discrepancies of enforcement from one part of the country to another, and even from one part of a city to another, for the same types of offence.[59]

Moreover, between the Criminal Justice Act 1991 and the Criminal Justice Act 2003 the whole of the criminal justice system was reoriented from primary considerations of rights and procedures to ones more taken with issues of future risk, and the Criminal Justice Act 2003 accordingly had special measures reserved for 'dangerous' offenders.[60] Under New Labour, the criminal justice system had to be seen to be responding to the general public's concern about crime, especially in relation to youth offending, anti-social behaviour and the treatment of victims. This all had the effect of undermining proportionality to the extent that those objectively less serious crimes were often prioritised over the more serious, in large measure due to the politicisation of the criminal justice system by New Labour. A good example of this is the anti-social behaviour order (ASBO), ushered in by the Crime and Disorder Act of 1998. These have had the effect of undermining the entire criminal process, with its plethora of safeguards, by imposing civil orders that, if breached, are dealt with by criminal proceedings, with the resulting disproportionate penalties, often for trivial matters, not necessarily even the subject of criminal law.[61]

It is worthwhile looking at recent critical research study undertaken by Keightley-Smith and Francis on the role of final warnings in the youth justice system in northern England which raises serious questions concerning the undermining the proportionality of tariffs.[62] Keightley-Smith and Francis have demonstrated how the final warning scheme, though trumpeted as a progressive measure by policy-makers, has actually worked to 'the detriment of young people involved' and failed to promote 'individual self-responsibility', which was the original policy intention.[63] Final warnings were brought in to replace a previous system of cautioning but they have proven unhelpful in four main areas, all of which impact negatively upon proportionality criteria:

(1) Final warnings may be said to be disproportionate because they are far more extensive due to the relationship they have to the Youth Offending Team (YOT). Final warnings involve a period of YOT intervention, unlike the old reprimands, which did not necessarily.

(2) The institution of the final warning scheme has been patchy, partly due to poor investment in it and partly due to variations in local priority setting. This is disproportionate to the extent that final warnings have been instituted in an inconsistent manner. Therefore, similar cases are not being treated similarly.

(3) The final warning scheme has led to increased police discretion, especially since final warnings do not require the young person's consent, or their guardian's consent, which is not the case with adult offenders. Therefore, young people cannot opt for their day in court, and this can have massive consequences for the young person in terms of their future employment and criminal record status, and for justice *per se*. Alastair Gillespie has shown there are also serious concerns that in practical settings young people may feel pressurised into accepting a final warning in a process that does not sufficiently balance their legal rights with the efficient processing of offenders.[64]

(4) Final warnings are also a *de facto* sentence to the extent that they have to be declared and so still negatively impact upon young people's chances of rehabilitating themselves through education or employment. They are held on the Police National Computer (PNC). However, there is little research to determine how employers, training and education establishments and charities, for example, deal with final warning disclosures.

Final warnings show up very clearly the dangers of discretion, inconsistent implementation of policy and the very real diminution of justice that results from cutting out a person's right to a hearing in court. They demonstrate how a move away from strict notions of proportionality can actually undermine the proper operation of justice. They are, as Keightley-Smith and Francis have argued, '[a] total police administrative process [that] defies the principle of due process on a number of counts ... there is no judicial review of final warnings, no direct lines of police accountability and no means of address through the court'.[65]

Proportionality: conclusion

It is important to note the Kantian lineage of many of the retributivist writings of our current age. The notion Kant gave us of a rebounding maxim whereby criminals bring punishment on themselves is, perhaps, even older and versions of it can be found in all the great world religions. The main point we take from Kant is centrality of proportionality. The notion that there ought to be a strict correspondence between the seriousness of offences and the level of punishments rather than any broader social or predictive considerations is something of a shibboleth in neo-Kantian jurisprudence. It is proportionality that ensures fairness and legitimacy to the system of punishments. Moreover, it is this appeal to fairness that implicates the work of John Rawls. It was Rawls who saw the necessity of fairness in any society but who also realised that no society could ever achieve perfect agreement on moral and political matters. Rawls therefore furnished us with an idealised original position that aimed at moral objectivity behind a veil of ignorance. If you did not know what position you would occupy in society then what rules would you devise to ensure fairness in that society? The point for Kant and, subsequently, Rawls is the necessity to treat persons equally and fairly. That is a political objective as much as a legal one.

The distinctiveness of Just Desert theory lies in the way it stresses the criminal's moral desert in the distribution of punishments and the way it conceives the criminal justice system as concentrating on issues of culpability and proportionality, rather than on wider social considerations. It takes inspiration from older versions of retributive writing, notably the writings of Kant, but it is essentially a practical approach which is underpinned by a commitment to a modern liberal political framework, as has been noted by Lacey.[66]

Practical Considerations

Beneath all the complex theoretical language used to explain desert and proportionality are a few, very simple, propositions. All punishments should be deserved, and all punishments should be proportionately in accord with their seriousness. For justice to be fair and proper it must connect with our basic moral intuition that more serious crimes should be treated more seriously than less serious crimes. Of course, our basic moral intuitions can alter. For example, we now no longer think that homosexual acts between consenting adults are crimes and we hold that violence in domestic settings is the subject of our criminal law, which was not always the case. We see, then, that behind our views on punishment are political notions about how we ought to live. We should acknowledge that many of our views on punishment are conventional. The practical point is that there needs to be a coherent and logically defensible justification for punishment: the concepts of desert and proportionality operate in that regard. Punishments can never be arbitrary and the concepts of desert and proportionality address this systemic necessity to uphold a fair and transparent criminal justice system. It is necessary to determine that persons deserve any punishments they may receive, and to what extent. Thus it is necessary to determine how we rank crimes, both between similar offences as well as between different offences. Who could defend overly harsh or overly lenient sentences?

Moreover, the need to justify any system of punishments links to the defence of the state itself. A legitimate political system needs a fair judicial system as well as a rational, fair and transparent sentencing system. If desert criteria and proportionality were set aside and punishments were randomly allocated, or allocated without regard to desert and proportionality, that would jeopardise the state itself. The perceived legitimacy of punishments is a fundamental necessity for democratic government. The legitimacy of punishments supports the state and vice versa. Indeed, one could not imagine the state maintaining popular support if it supported a criminal justice system which did not allow for desert and proportionality to be a major aspect of any system of punishments. Moreover, whenever we think of totalitarian governments we usually also conceive a system of courts meting out undeserved and disproportionate punishments; we have only to think of the Soviet Union, Mao's China or Hitler's Germany.[67] Therefore, desert and proportionality are not only necessary to the proper determination of criminal sentencing, but their proper functioning in the criminal justice system, in terms of the system of punishments, is closely linked to legitimate democratic government.

Main Summary Points

- Proportionality requires that crimes of an equal nature should be treated equally and that there is a proper rank ordering of offences.
- Retributive theories of punishment, such as Just Deserts, always maintain that desert criteria are the only correct basis for criminal sentencing of persons. In stressing the role of desert, they relate a moral intuition about punishment. Andrew von Hirsch has written: 'We feel there is something wrong, not simply counterproductive in the long run, about inflicting punishments that are not fairly commensurate with the gravity of offences' (*Past or Future Crimes*, 1986).
- The legal theorist H. L. A. Hart stated that there must be an independent justification for a retributive limit on substantive criminal law in order that liability is confined to the culpability of the criminal.
- Neo-Kantian theorists, such as Andrew von Hirsch, always stress the criminal's moral desert in the distribution of punishments. Like Kant, recent retributive theorists have emphasised the fairness of punishments in terms of the relationship between the offender and the punishment rather than between the punishment and its consequence for society.

Questions

1. What are desert criteria?
2. Why should sentencers consider proportionality when sentencing in criminal cases?
3. What is the *lex talionis*?

Suggested Further Reading

Baiasu, S. (2007) 'Institutions and the Normativity of Desert', *Contemporary Political Theory*, 6 (2): 175–195.
Hanna, N. (2008) 'Say What? A Critique of Expressive Retributivism', *Law and Philosophy*, 27 (3): 123–150.
Macleod, A. M. (2005) 'Distributive Justice and Desert', *Journal of Social Philosophy*, 36 (4): 421–438.
Klimchuk, D. (2001) 'Retribution, Restitution and Revenge', *Law and Philosophy*, 20 (1): 81–101.
Kristjánsson, K. (2005) 'A Utilitarian Justification of Desert in Distributive Justice', *Journal of Moral Philosophy*, 2 (2): 147–170.

Notes

1. Rawls, J. (2001) *Justice as Fairness: A Restatement*, Cambridge, MA: Harvard University Press. p 73.
2. von Hirsch, A. (1986) *Past or Future Crimes*, Manchester: Manchester University Press. p. 10.
3. For a discussion of this see von Hirsch, A. (1976) *Doing Justice: The Choice of Punishments*, New York: Wang & Hill; and Ashworth, A. (1989) 'Criminal Justice and Deserved Sentences', *Criminal Law Review*, May: 340–355.
4. Freiberg, A. and Gelb, K. (2008) *Penal Populism, Sentencing Councils and Sentencing Policy*, Cullompton: Willan Publishing. pp. 1–15, 224–239.
5. Classically by thinkers such as Benn, S. I. and Peters, R. S. (1959) *Social Principles and the Democratic State*, London: George Allen and Unwin. p. 137: 'Desert is a normative word; its use presupposes a rule...'. Also Raphael, D. D. (1955) *Moral Judgement*, London: George Allen and Unwin. p. 77: 'Our conclusion then is that the concept of desert ... is a way of speaking of the presence of an obligation in special circumstances.'
6. Hospers, J. (1961) *Human Conduct: An Introduction to the Problems of Ethics*, New York: Harcourt, Brace and World. pp. 433–451. There are innumerable examples of this, however.
7. Kadish, M. R. (1983) 'Practice and Paradox: A Comment on Social Choice Theory', *Ethics*, 93 (4): 680–694; Adams, J. N. and Brownsword, R. (1988) 'Law Reform, Law Jobs, and Law Commission No. 160', *The Modern Law Review*, 51 (4): 481–492.
8. Shepsle, K. A. and Weingast , B. R. (1984) 'When Do Rules of Procedure Matter?', *Journal of Politics*, 46 (1): 206–221; Macey, J. R. (1994) 'Judicial Preferences, Public Choice, and the Rules of Procedure', *Journal of Legal Studies*, 23 (1): 627–646.

9. This also holds for non-personal subjects, such as art objects and even bills of legislation.
10. The basis of desert is a complex relational one but nonetheless the subject must always be a party to that relation. The basis of desert can never be separated from the subject. Lamont, J. (1994) 'The Concept of Desert in Distributive Justice', *The Philosophical Quarterly*, 44 (174): 45–64.
11. Gert, J. (2003) 'Internalism and Different Kinds of Reasons', *The Philosophical Forum*, 34 (1): 53–72.
12. Sidgwick, H. (1963) *The Methods of Ethics*, London: Macmillan. Book 3, Chapter 5.
13. Do note a distinction between angry vengeance and righteous retribution. Hart, H. M. (1958) 'The Aims of the Criminal Law', *Law and Contemporary Problems*, 23: 402, 406; and Cohen, M. R. (1950) *Reason and Law*, Glencoe, IL: The Free Press: p. 50.
14. 'Punishment is punishment only where it is deserved.' Bradley, F. H. (1927) *Ethical Studies*, Oxford: Oxford University Press. pp. 26–27.
15. Hanna, N. (2008) 'Say What? A Critique of Expressive Retributivism', *Law and Philosophy*, 27 (3): 123–150.
16. Lyons, D. (1969) 'Rights, Claimants and Beneficiaries', *American Philosophical Quarterly*, 6: 174–175; and Morris, H. (1968) 'Persons and Punishment', *The Monist*, 52: 475–501. The Hegelian position is that punishment is a necessary condition of moral regeneration and thus the moral agent has a right to it. Hegel's position is set out clearly in Matravers, M. D. (1994) 'Justice and Punishment: The Rationale for Coercion', unpublished PhD thesis, London School of Economics, London. pp. 63–103.
17. Mearman, A. (2005) 'Sheila Dow's Concept of Dualism: Clarification, Criticism and Development', *Cambridge Journal of Economics*, 29 (4): 619–634; Bartlett, K. T. (1990) 'Feminist Legal Methods', *Harvard Law Review*, 103 (4): 829–888.
18. Cohen, G. A. (1989) 'On the Currency of Egalitarian Justice', *Ethics*, 99 (4): 906–944; Hampshire, S. (2002) 'Justice is Strife', *Philosophy & Social Criticism*, 28 (6): 635–645.
19. Harsanyi, J. C. (1996) 'Utilities, Preferences, and Substantive Goods', *Social Choice and Welfare*, 14 (1): 129–145; Becker, E. F. (1975) 'Justice, Utility, and Interpersonal Comparisons', *Theory and Decision*, 14 (1): 471–484.
20. Parfit, D. (1984) *Reasons and Persons*, Oxford: Oxford University Press. pp. 3–49.
21. Feinberg, J. (1970) 'The Expressive Function of Punishment', in *Doing and Deserving*, Princeton, NJ: Princeton University Press. pp. 53–69.
22. von Hirsch, *Doing Justice*. pp. 54–55.
23. Kleinig, J. (2008) *Ethics and Criminal Justice*, Cambridge: Cambrdge University Press. pp. 197–206.
24. Macleod, A. M. (2005) 'Distributive Justice and Desert', *Journal of Social Philosophy*, 36 (4): 421–438.
25. Baiasu, S. (2007) 'Institutions and the Normativity of Desert', *Contemporary Political Theory*, 6 (2): 175–195.
26. Kristjánsson, K. (2005) 'A Utilitarian Justification of Desert in Distributive Justice', *Journal of Moral Philosophy*, 2 (2): 147–170.
27. Cragg, W. (2006) *The Practice of Punishment*, London: Routledge. p. 19.
28. von Hirsch, *Past or Future Crimes*. p. 34.
29. Honderich, T. (1988) *The Consequences of Determinism: A Theory of Determinism*, Oxford: Clarendon Press. p. 193.
30. von Hirsch, A. and Ashworth, A. (2005) *Proportionate Sentencing: Exploring the Principles*, Oxford: Oxford University Press. pp. 132–133.
31. Mackie, J. L. (1985) *Persons and Values*, Oxford: Clarendon Press. Chapter 15.

32. Pettit, P. (2000) 'Non-consequentialism and Universalizability', *The Philosophical Quarterly*, 50 (199): 175–190.
33. von Hirsch, A. (1990) 'The Politics of Just Deserts', *Canadian Journal of Criminology*, 397 (32): 407–409.
34. Hart, H. L. A. (1968) *Punishment and Responsibility*, Oxford: Clarendon Press. Chapters 1 and 7.
35. Ibid. p. 112.
36. von Hirsch, *Past or Future Crimes*. pp. 34–36.
37. Morris, H. (1968) 'Persons and Punishment', *The Monist*, 52: 475; Morris, H. (1981) 'A Paternalistic Theory of Punishment', *American Philosophy Quarterly*, 18 (4): 263; Murphy, J. (1985) 'Retributivism, Moral Education and the Liberal State', *Criminal Justice Ethics*, 4: 3–11; Sadurski, W. (1985) *Giving Desert Its Due*, Dordrecht: Lancaster. Chapter 8; Sher, G. (1987) *Desert*, Princeton, NJ: Princeton University Press. Chapter 5; Finnis, J. (1980) *Natural Law and Natural Rights*, Oxford: Clarendon Press, pp. 263–264; Gerwirth, A. (1978) *Reason and Morality*, Chicago: Chicago University Press. pp. 294–298.
38. von Hirsch, *Doing Justice*; Duff, R. A. (1986) *Trials and Punishment*, Cambridge: Cambridge University Press; Duff, R. A. (1986) *Punishment, Communication and Community*, Oxford: Oxford University Press.
39. von Hirsch, *Doing Justice*. pp. 47–48; Duff, *Trials and Punishment*. Chapter 8; Burgh, R. (1982) 'Do the Guilty Deserve Punishment?', *Journal of Philosophy*, 79 (4): 193.
40. Feinberg, J. (1970) *Doing and Deserving*, Princeton University Press: Princeton. Primoratz, I. (1989) 'Punishment as Language', *Philosophy*, 64: 187–205.
41. von Hirsch A. (1993) *Censure and Sanctions*, Oxford: Clarendon Press. pp. 72–75.
42. Duff, R. A. (1988) 'Punishment and Penance: A Reply to Harrison', *Proceedings of the Aristotelian Society* (Supplementary Volume), 62: 153–167.
43. von Hirsch and Ashworth, *Proportionate Sentencing*. p. 135.
44. von Hirsch, *Past or Future Crimes*. pp. 144, 169, 198.
45. Bentham, J. (1982) *An Introduction to the Principles of Morals and Legislation*, ed. J. H. Burns and H. L. A. Hart. London: Methuen. p. 168.
46. Bedau, H. A. (1978) 'Retribution and the Theory of Punishment', *Journal of Philosophy*, 75: 601–620; and von Hirsch, A. (1978) 'Proportionality and Desert: A Reply to Bedau', *Journal of Philosophy*, 75: 622–624.
47. von Hirsch, *Censure and Sanctions*. p. 102.
48. Kleinig, J. (1973) *Punishment and Desert*, The Hague: Martinus Nijhoff.
49. Ibid. pp. 120–121.
50. Reiman, J. (1985) 'Civilisation and the Death Penalty: Answering van den Haag', *Philosophy and Public Affairs*, 14: 115–148.
51. von Hirsch and Ashworth, *Proportionate Sentencing*. pp. 111–112.
52. Pettit, P. and Braithwaite, J. (1993) 'Not Just Deserts Even in Sentencing', *Current Issues in Criminal Justice*, 4: 225–239; Braithwaite, J. (2003) 'Principles of Restorative Justice', in A. von Hirsch, J. V. Roberts, A. E. Bottoms, K. Roach and M. Schiff (eds), *Restorative Justice and Criminal Justice: Competing or Reconcilable Paradigms?* Oxford: Hart Publishing. pp. 1–20; Braithwaite, J. (2003) 'Does Restorative Justice Work?', in G. Johnstone, (ed.), *A Restorative Justice Reader: Texts, Sources, Context*. Cullompton: Willan Publishing. pp. 320–352; Dignan, J. et al. (2007) 'Staging Restorative Justice Encounters against a Criminal Justice Backdrop', *Criminology and Criminal Justice*, 7 (1): 5–32.
53. von Hirsch, A. (2000) 'The Project of Sentencing Reform', in M. Tonry and R.S. Frase (eds), *Sentencing and Sanctions in Western Countries*, Oxford: Oxford University Press. pp. 405–420.
54. Ibid. p. 405.

55. Ibid. p. 406.
56. Ibid. p. 417.
57. Brownlee, I. (2002) 'New Labour – New Penology? Punitive Rhetoric and the Limits of Managerialism in Criminal Justice Policy', *Journal of Law and Society*, 25 (3): 313–335; Cavadino, M. and Dignan, J. (2006) 'Penal Policy and Political Economy', *Criminology and Criminal Justice*, 6 (4): 435–456.
58. Squires, P. and Stephen, D. (2005) *Rougher Justice: Anti-social Behaviour and Young People*, Cullompton: William Publishing. p. 4; Campbell, S. (2002) *A Review of Anti-Social Behaviour Orders*, Home Office Study 236, London: Home Office.
59. Brown, A. (2004) 'Anti-social Behaviour, Crime Control and Social Control', *The Howard Journal*, 43 (2): 203–211; Stone, N. (2004) 'Legal Commentary: Orders in Respect of Anti-social Behaviour: Recent Judicial Developments', *Youth Justice*, 4: 46–54.
60. Ashworth, A. (2004) 'Criminal Justice Reform: Principles, Human Rights and Public Protection', *Criminal Law Review*, 516–532.
61. Burney, E. (2002) 'Talking Tough, Acting Coy: What Happened to the Anti-Social Behaviour Order?', *The Howard Journal of Criminal Justice*, 41 (5): 469–484.
62. Keightley-Smith, L. and Francis, P. (2007) 'Final Warning, Youth Justice and Early Intervention: Reflections on the Findings of a Research Study Carried Out in Northern England', *Web Journal of Current Legal Issues*, http://webjcli.ncl.ac.uk/2007/contents2.html. pp. 1–16.
63. Ibid. p. 1.
64. Gillespie, A. (2005) 'Reprimanding Juveniles and the Right to Due Process', *Modern Law Review*, 68 (6): 1006–1015.
65. Keightley-Smith and Francis, 'Final Warning, Youth Justice and Early Intervention'. p. 11.
66. Lacey, N. in McCoville, S. (ed.) (2003) *The Use of Punishment*, Cullompton: Willan Publishing. p. 181.
67. Miethe, T. D. and Lu. H. (2005) *Punishment: A Comparative Historical Perspective*, Cambridge: Cambridge University Press. pp. 208–213.

8

FAIRNESS

When any number of persons conduct any joint enterprise according to rules, and thus restrict their liberty, those who have submitted to these restrictions when required have a right to similar submission from those who have benefited by their submission.

H. L. A. Hart, 1984[1]

─────────────────────── **Introduction** ───────────────────────

Legal theorists, such as Andrew von Hirsch and Andrew Ashworth, have made a huge impact upon contemporary Criminology, notably around their work on criminal sentencing. The underlying principles they uphold are to a large extent focused on the issue of fairness and this chapter will set out the basic issues, derived from political theory, which inform their work. It will concentrate upon the work of the pre-eminent American political theorist John Rawls, the work of Kant and the basic notions of justice as fairness, as well as outlining the difficulties of appealing to a moral consensus and justifying a non-utilitarian ethical theory. The chapter will show how many of the ideas used in contemporary Criminology are ultimately based upon solid principles of political theory and demonstrate just how indebted to political theory a great deal of criminological work is.

──────── **The Notion of 'Fairness' Derived from John Rawls** ────────

Different theorists understand the notion of 'fairness' differently, and I shall explore these differences later, but there is one element which unites all contemporary theorists, and that is the concept of the rational chooser. In other words, fairness is that state of affairs that would be preferred by a rational chooser. A debt to the political theorist John Rawls should be noted here – to his notion of the rational chooser operating behind a veil of ignorance in an 'original position' where the individual does not know what place he or she will occupy in society and does not know his or her gender, race or other fundamental characteristics.[2] What Rawls has in mind is the notion that if we could dispense with the baggage associated with knowing who we are, then we would, he argues, choose a 'fair' distribution of justice, rather than one based on pre-understood attributes. Rawls', arguments are employed by retributivist and deterrence theorists working in criminological theory. However, retributivist thinkers, in particular Andrew von Hirsch, maintain that this use of Rawls by deterrence theorists is incorrect since it goes against the non-utilitarian thrust of the original position argument (i.e. it is not based on utility but fairness), and that to apply deterrence considerations is to adopt utilitarian criteria (i.e. considerations based on future outcomes) and to abandon Rawls' intended concept of fairness based on an original position. Retributivists, especially Just Desert theorists, maintain that the rational chooser in the original position would never use utilitarian criteria since any policy which could punish disproportionately to just deserts would inevitably be unfair. Moreover, the adoption of the original position criteria, it is argued, dispenses with emotional, religious, cultural, political and prejudiced reasoning.

Just Desert theorists infer from this that the practice of indeterminate judicial sentencing, derived from utilitarian and rehabilitationalist principles, should be abandoned. They argue that no rational chooser would ever agree to such indeterminacy. Andrew von Hirsch has reasoned: '...the potential benefit done to any one offender under a system of massive discretion is more than offset by the harm done to the vast majority of persons through such a normless system'.[3] This may sound utilitarian, but what von Hirsch is actually pointing to is the essential normlessness of discretionary and rehabilitative regimes. Under a system of Just Deserts, rigorous sentencing standards should be set and judicial discretion severely curtailed. Mitigation should be similarly severely curtailed, as Kellogg has argued: 'The use of plea bargaining and deferred prosecution, not to mention the indeterminate sentence, have constituted a *de facto* abrogation of the principle of punishment strictly regulated according to offence.'[4]

The rejection of utilitarian principles is fundamental to Just Deserts and all other retributive theories and, once again, Rawls becomes important as the theorist whose ideas underpin contemporary retributive theories of criminal justice. Interestingly, Rawls himself was once a utilitarian and had developed a form of rule utilitarianism before rejecting utilitarianism entirely in favour of his new theory of fairness, based on the original position.[5] The perceived failure of rehabilitation as a practice, in the 1970s, enabled fairness to gain ground in academic and policy circles and moves were made to ensure uniform standards in sentencing practice. Andrew von Hirsch famously made the point that this could be seen as 'a shift in perspective from a commitment to do good to a commitment to do as little mischief as possible'.[6]

To the uninitiated, a move to curtail judicial discretion might be interpreted as consistent with deterrence theory, which also advocates uniform sentences and the withdrawal of judicial discretion. However, there is a substantial disparity beneath the superficial surface similarity between deterrence and retribution, as Kellogg has noted: 'On the utilitarian premise punishment would be justified if it deterred sufficiently'.[7] This is because of the utilitarian inability, in theoretical terms, to avoid unfair treatment of the individual while also aiming at the benefit of the greatest number.

There then arises the crucial issue of the individualisation of the treatment of offenders. Frederic Kellogg, following Kant, maintains that only desert criteria, i.e. deserved punishment, can respect individuals as ends in themselves and that rehabilitation and deterrence treat offenders as a means to someone else's ends. So, for example, it would be wrong to make an example of an offender by punishing them harshly to deter others if that also meant treating that person differently from other persons in the same position just to make a point in that instance. The basic argument is to treat persons individually in terms of their punishment in relation to what they have done and there is also the requirement to maintain a close relationship between cases of a particular offence in terms of how seriousness is dealt with. In other words, one must treat individual serious cases more harshly than minor cases, even if this conflicts with broader issues of social justice. This issue of whether there are individual excuses for offences or whether every person committing a crime should be treated the same is tackled by Andrew von Hirsch, who conceives the issue thus: 'If two offenders convicted of the same offence receive different sentences, is that disparity? That depends on what other similarities and differences there are between the offenders and how these relate to the aims of punishment.'[8]

Kellogg advocates, instead of absolutely determinate sentences, a form of 'presumptive sentencing' whereby judges might raise or lower the tariff to adjust for the seriousness of any given offence. The view of individualisation left by the positivism would then remain according to many retributive theorists, though for different reasons. Kellogg states that: 'No longer must it rest upon the ephemeral capacity to understand causation or to administer treatment but it is now a matter of principle, of fairness, of desert.'[9] However, it has to be stated that desert always presupposes culpability.

The big question in modern theories of punishment is how one establishes desert criteria. The essential elements here are harm and culpability. No punishment can be deserved if no harm was done: or put another way, if no harm was likely to result from the offender's actions or where no harm was intended. The harm principle in this contemporary formulation of harm done, intended or risked, distinguishes it from its Durkheimian ancestor.[10] The second factor at issue is culpability, which means that the offender must have known what he or she did was wrong, or illegal, and that the offender must have had the power to commit, or not to commit, a given criminal act. As Andrew von Hirsch has shown:

Different crimes may not be readily comparable in harmfulness, because the interests affected are dissimilar. How likely must the risk of harm be? Should it … be a mitigating circumstance that the offender was motivated by a desire to help someone, or that he sincerely believed the law he violated to be wrong? … Whose standards should govern?[11]

Determining the Seriousness of Offences
and Appealing to a Moral Consensus

Determining the seriousness of offences is a crucial matter for criminologists and it is one that bears on morality and moral relativism. One aspect of moral relativism was pointed out by, among others, Northrop in his classic work *The Complexity of Legal and Ethical Experience*, which is how to judge what is right and wrong across cultures.[12] The culture of eighteenth-century England saw nothing morally wrong in slavery, and similarly in other slave-owning cultures, whether of the classical or modern eras. However, today slavery is universally outlawed. One could also invoke such issues as the use of child labour or animal cruelty, where views have radically changed over time. In a modern multicultural climate there is also the issue of religious diversity and the conflicting moral codes that arise, for example in relation to sexuality, the rights of women or attitudes to sexual behaviour. Theorists have examined the question of whether an individual's religious beliefs can be trumped by another's morality. Inevitably there are clashes. People have different moral consciences and yet live in the same socio-political space. Isaiah Berlin observed that what bothers the poor man does not bother the banker[13] and Alexis de Tocqueville pinpointed the 'tyranny of the majority'.[14] In modern multicultural societies, the dangers of mistreating minorities is a constant danger, given all we know about issues of power and access to influence. Political and moral philosophers themselves do not agree about a whole host of issues, such as the status of private property and the proper basis for distributing goods and services in society. The issue for our purposes is simply that there *is* a disagreement on moral issues and no agreed standard of 'wrongness'.

Moreover, there is also the basic political issue of whether people are capable of distinguishing their personal moral beliefs from their personal self-interest. The majority of people disapprove of whatever causes the most harm on simple utilitarian grounds since that is how most of us operate. The perceived wrongness of an action is usually understood in terms of the harm it does. So we need to note an important tension here between basing the measure of an offence on quasi-utilitarian grounds, i.e. the beliefs held by the majority of people, and rejecting utilitarian notions of rehabilitation and deterrence, which also have popular support within the community that gave us the measure of offences in the first instance.

The issue of how to gauge the unpleasantness of penalties is at least as difficult in real-world situations as gauging the seriousness of crimes. In looking at fines, for example, does the rich man or woman pay the same fine as the poor man or woman? Do we treat the habitual offender more severely than the first-time offender, given that both committed the same crime? The tendency to treat defendants unfairly when using their prior offence records as part of the relevant background information for sentencing was dealt with in a classic study by

Farrell and Swigert, where it was found that this did disproportionately affect sentencing far more than may be expected, and subsequent academic studies have confirmed this.[15]

Erickson and Gibbs gave us the classic study of gauging severity of penalties and a host of scholars have followed in their wake.[16] The original Erickson and Gibbs study involved asking people how they would rate the unpleasantness of a given judicial penalty, but they pointed out flaws in this anecdotal methodology themselves. First, it does not overcome the bias likely to arise from the personal perceptions of those interviewed, and secondly, it raises the issue that the people interviewed were entirely without any personal experience of the penalties they graded in terms of their severity. The study did highlight the problem of relying on the perceptions of ordinary people and the discrepancy between the perceptions of justice system professionals, such as police, lawyers, and the general public. Erickson and Gibbs noted vast differences on the issue of probation, for example, between the police, who see it as a severe sanction, and the general public, who see it as a minor sanction. They showed that the issue of determining severity of sanctions depends largely on who is asked. The point being that retributive theories can never solely rely upon individual perceptions of seriousness.

One of the major failings that retributivist theories, such as Just Deserts, face is the variability of opinions on moral questions, which includes punishment. There is little consensus on the crucial issue of whether moral desert should be a criterion at all among theorists, legal practitioners or the general public. Even when people agree, there is often a great confusion about the principles at stake. The death penalty, for example, is advocated on the grounds of deterrence and moral desert.[17] Among those who uphold the desert principle there is confusion and a lack of consistency, as the political philosophers John Braithwaite and Philip Pettit have shown.[18]

The harsher criticism is whether we should take serious notice of the ordinary person's view at all. It is important to be clear on which of the following consensual validation techniques is to be used as the moral basis of any retributivist theory. Surely, we should not follow the moral judgements of the majority, regardless of just how ill-informed they are or how unaware they are of philosophical or moral considerations? Or should we blindly follow the moral judgements of those who are well informed about the empirical facts and the philosophical reasoning employed? It is obvious that Andrew von Hirsch and other new retributivists favour the latter since their position is derived from a Rawlsian concept of 'fairness' and that is in turn derived from a methodology (the original position). To recap, the original position is a hypothetical situation in which abstracted rational calculators choose those principles of social relations under which their principles would do best without knowing what position they would occupy in society and being unaware of their own attributes. Those choices are subject to certain constraints, which embody the specifically moral elements of Rawls' original position. The rational calculators do not know even the basic facts about their principles. This restriction on their reasoning is embodied in Rawls' veil of ignorance, which precludes information about a person's age, gender, race, etc.[19]

Moral Philosophy

The general approach that theorists have taken to justify non-utilitarian ethical beliefs and practices has usually been driven by the deep-rooted problem of the absence of a moral consensus on controversial issues, notably punishment. The old notion that we can derive our ethical knowledge through intuition has been discredited, and the notion of the disinterested observer has become the dominant view. However, it is still useful to say something about the moral intuitionists, notably Bishop Butler.[20] Bishop Butler conceived that the human conscience is the source of all of our intuitions. This view was termed the 'conscience theory' and is now generally rejected as a valid method for determining ethical beliefs. Moreover, there are also good persons who are unduly troubled by their conscience and this would seem to be at odds with the theory too. The issue of being bothered by one's conscience would seem itself to rest upon what the given ethical beliefs of the person were in the first place, and that would appear random, or at least dependent upon a great many contingencies, notably context, age, and sex, to name three. To argue that our consciences determine our beliefs in many ways is to put the issue in the incorrect order. Butler is writing with a belief in the moral consensus of the eighteenth century, which, in turn, was guided by his Anglicanism.

In the twentieth century, the moral theorists David Ross, C. D. Broad and G. E. Moore attempted a far more rigorous intuitionist approach, which rests on the assumption that 'reason', as opposed to conscience, is the source of all our direct intuitions of moral qualities.[21] They held that our personal moral values cannot be pre-defined for us. They also held that anyone who tries to define morality in non-moral terms, such as happiness, ultimately misunderstands the meaning of them. This was the basis of G. E. Moore's criticism of utilitarianism – that by trying to define desirable to mean what people actually do desire, utilitarianism collapses our moral concepts into a form of egoistic hedonism. Moore's argument is that this misses the entire point of ethics, which he understood as showing people that their moral responsibility can conflict with their own personal happiness and self-interest. Moreover, as moral terms cannot be defined in non-moral terms, the only way to understand what they mean is to directly experience, or intuit, the phenomena for which they stand. However, the basic problem with this rationalistic-intuitionist approach is that if its basic point were true (i.e. if every person was actually capable of intuiting moral qualities correctly), then there would be no real moral disagreement among people concerning the fundamental moral principles they should follow, unless, that is, only a select few were equipped with the needed intuitive moral sense. In that case, there would be no way for the rest of us to discover the truth, or to know whose alleged intuitive sense to trust.

Moore argued that only those moral principles that any 'reasonable man' would accept ought to be accepted. The key word here is 'any'. If a substantial number of reasonable men disagree, then the principle should be rejected altogether.[22] Moore maintained that there were examples where all reasonable people would agree on moral decisions. However, even if there is a consensus on a given point, that would not also necessarily equate with a similar consensus on the reasons that lie behind the consensus. Universal agreement, in itself, can never give us adequate evidence of a common morality. Indeed, the existence of reasonable and disinterested people that do disagree should itself be adequate evidence that moral qualities are not directly intuited in specific cases.

All contemporary formulations of a non-utilitarian kind of social policy can be understood as attempts to overcome this problem, and this certainly covers Rawls. In one way or another, political philosophers attempt to demonstrate that any rational and disinterested person must agree with the value judgement in question; they do so by introducing the notion of an ideally objective deliberative context in which rational deliberators could not possibly disagree, because to do so would be demonstrably irrational. Among those who are seriously concerned about the lack of consensus on controversial value issues, such as the purpose of punishment, Rawls has become paradigmatic for this sort of approach. Rawls attempts to show that the one principle that any rational chooser would agree with is 'fairness' – not because there is any special moral sense that would allow us to directly intuit the meaning of fairness, but because it would be irrational for a rational chooser, behind a veil of ignorance, to prefer unfairness. Rawls argues that if you could imagine what opinions you would hold regarding the distribution of benefits without any knowledge of your own interested circumstances (i.e. the original position), then you would know what the rational chooser, behind a veil of ignorance, would prefer. However, Rawls also states that it would be irrational for a person, in the original position, to prefer unfairness in the society which he knows he will live in.[23] Of course, this is because in the original position, and behind a veil of ignorance, nobody knows what place they will occupy in society.

The position that Rawls sets out in *A Theory of Justice* may well be rejected, though, if you remember that not everyone would agree about the degree of inequality to accept in society or how to treat offenders. It has been charged against Rawls that he does not take seriously enough the nature of human desire. Emotions arise out of definite situations, so it is meaningless to discuss what the person in the original position, divorced from concrete reality, would want.[24] A Rawlsian may argue that the person in the original position has knowledge of general human nature and so would know what suffering and emotion are. But this would be a pretty thin form of knowledge. Moreover, it would not begin to address the richness of human emotional life that animates the social and political imagination, notably in relation to issues concerning the criminal justice system. Similarly, it is difficult to imagine what a person in the original position would think of something like poverty without any experience of it. In the context of the criminal justice system, how can a person who has never experienced violent crime make a rational assessment of how much deterrence he or she is willing to sacrifice for the sake of fairness of treatment of offenders?

There is also the huge issue of deciding how much risk-taking behaviour is to be deemed irrational. It is around this point that much recent discussion of Rawls has centred. Rawls' analysis of the kind of decision-making that would be made in the original position is based on game theory.[25] Rawls' application of this principle, in a risk-taking situation, requires that we should begin by determining the worst that can possibly result from each possible decision, and then pick the decision that is the least worst. However, David Kaye has argued that this is far too conservative a rule, and assuming an aversion to risk-taking is highly questionable on Rawls' part.[26] In spite of these very serious objections, Rawls still holds a strong attraction for many criminal justice theorists.

The Idea of 'Justice as Fairness'

The essential idea behind justice as fairness is that the principles of justice are agreed in an initial situation that is fair. Rawls also realises that society cannot be a voluntary scheme of cooperation and that, in reality, 'each person finds himself [sic] placed at birth in some particular position in some particular society, and the nature of this position materially affects his life prospects'.[27] How are people to think about justice in the unequal situations in which they find themselves? Should they compare themselves with the principles of justice as fairness knowing that these are the principles, which free and rational persons would accept in an initial position of equality? Would this help to strengthen people or are there ways in which it serves to undermine them, making it much harder to think clearly about the unequal situations in which they actually find themselves? One of the features assumed by Rawls to be common to all human beings, and thereby non-contingent, is his sense that we all desire to choose our own ends. This is partly what defines us as free and equal rational beings and is embodied in the Rawlsian principle of equal liberty. It is this ability to choose our own ends which is threatened in the relationship of power and subordination between rich and poor, for example. For Kant, it was crucial to realise that if someone was dependent for his or her means of livelihood, it would be difficult for him or her to truly choose his or her individual ends. Kant could only save his assumption from the autonomy of morality by assuming that this was a situation that was freely chosen, though Kant himself recognised that it grew out of an earlier unequal distribution of property, which in turn produced relationships of power and inequality. Rawls is keen to secure our existence as free and equal rational beings by making it an important aspect of our nature. It is useful to note what Rawls states on the matter: 'Men exhibit their freedom, their independence from the contingencies of nature and society, by acting in ways they would acknowledge in the original position.'[28]

Rawls wants to guarantee a situation in which people are equally free to pursue their own ends, within the framework of a society whose basic structure is just or defined by what reasonable persons would rationally derive in the original position. This is the way we show our respect for others. The essence of Kant's moral writing, for Rawls, is not 'a morality of austere command' but 'an ethic of mutual respect and self-esteem'.[29] The notion that we are equally able to live independent and self-sufficient lives was shown to be an implicit assumption of the autonomy of morality: it also remains implicit in Rawls' work on justice as fairness.

When Rawls thinks that the 'essential unity of the self is already provided by the concept of right',[30] he is also confirming the independence of people from each other. We are free to choose our ends and follow our own conception of happiness. It is the autonomy and independence of the person which is guaranteed. However, as the political philosopher Michael Sandel has noted, the priority of the right over the good mirrors the priority of the self over its ends: 'To assert the priority of the self whose sovereign agency is assured, it was necessary to identify an essentially "unencumbered" self, conceived as a pure subject of possession, distinct from its contingent aims and attributes, standing always behind them.'[31] This assists in identifying an important weakness in liberal theory, though Sandel's wish to recognise how certain ends are constitutive of our sense of self, rather than voluntarily chosen as an act of will, still poses the issue in terms of an individual's relationship to his ends.

H. L. A. Hart is surely correct when he states that 'a satisfactory foundation for a theory of rights will [not] be found as long as the search is conducted in the shadow of utilitarianism'.[34] We go astray as long as we separate the right from the good. Kant, the inspiration for Rawls and von Hirsch, left us with a clue in the difficulties he himself faced in giving a more substantial account of respect as not treating others merely as means but as ends in themselves. Criminologists and socio-legal scholars need an account of the ways we, as human beings, hurt and mistreat each other which are not set in utilitarian terms.

The Issue of Respect for Persons and Moral Worth

Kant writes in terms of respect for persons only to prepare us for the recognition that it is only the Moral Law which is due our respect. Rawls states that people having equal liberty to pursue their own ends is a basic principle of justice. Kant thinks that people will naturally pursue their own happiness, but that this is of no moral worth. However, if people learn to act out of a sense of duty, their actions can accumulate moral worth. The focus is upon the moral worth of our individual actions, not, as in Aristotle, on the cultivation of qualities such as honesty, which are considered intrinsically worthwhile in themselves.[35] It is part of the attenuated conception of the person we inherit within a Kantian tradition that we can only attribute moral significance to particular qualities and capacities to the extent that they result in our acting out of a sense of duty. This makes it difficult to investigate the different ways we mistreat and hurt others. Rawls has inherited this difficulty in the priority he gives to right over good and the way he conceives the right as the product of a collective choice in the original position, while conceptions of the good are the products of individual choices in the real world. The fragmentation of the moral universe, which this creates, leaves no room for consideration of intrinsic moral worth or determining want from need. Rather, we are taken in by the idea that different things are good for different people and that it is wrong to make value judgements about the relative value of the ends which individuals are supposedly free to choose for themselves.

We find it difficult to articulate the moral significance of social relationships of power. Rawls is concerned that principles of justice have to be previously derived if we are to be able to guarantee 'the freedom of choice that justice as fairness assures to individuals and groups within the framework of justice'.[36] This depends upon the ideas of independence and self-sufficiency which Kant brought into question in his reflection upon the relations between rich and poor and which, in Rawls, are morally invisible since individuals choose their own ends. Rawls articulates the need of a conception of justice, which will respect persons. This is given in the classic formulation:

> For when society follows these principles, everyone's good is included in a sense of mutual benefit and this public affirmation in institutions of each man's endeavour supports men's self-esteem. The establishment of equal liberty and the operation of the difference principle (in which economic inequalities are allowed only if this improves everyone's situation, including the least advantaged) are bound to have this effect.[37]

In this acknowledgement of the importance of a public recognition of the equal value of the ends people choose for themselves, Rawls is enriching the territorial conception of respect. He recognises the importance of self-respect and he takes this to be one of the primary goods people will value, whatever their individual ends happen to be. Moreover, self-respect is afforded a dual role by Rawls when he writes:

> First of all ... it includes a person's sense of his [sic] own values, his secure conviction that his conception of his good, his plan of life, is worth carrying out. And second, self-respect implies a confidence in one's ability, so far as it is within one's power, to fulfil one's intentions. When we feel that our plans are of little value, we cannot pursue them with pleasure or take delight in their execution.[38]

This is a solid conception but it assumes that individuals can meaningfully abstract themselves from relations of power, whether of a political or economic kind. It marginalises the striving for autonomy. The autonomy and independence that people enjoy in the moral realm is somehow taken to guarantee the independence people have to work out their own conceptions of the good. Unlike Kant, Rawls wants to value this as an exercise of people's freedom and autonomy. He is left without a moral language in which to explore how people can be undermined and their autonomy threatened through the workings of relationships of power. It assumes that autonomy is compatible with persons choosing their own ends, taking account of their position and relations in a society whose basic structure is just. In such a society, power relations would be compatible with justice. This brings the issue of autonomy into sharper focus, since if you take for granted that your happiness will only come in caring for others, it can be frightening to even formulate a notion of individual dual ends.

Rawls enriches political theory by bringing in the need for public institutions of society to express the equal value of all citizens. However, his idea of the way this is expressed, in the recognition that people should have an equal liberty to pursue their own conceptions of the good, is a shibboleth of liberal theory, not a limitation upon it. We are left powerless to theorise a distinction between human needs and wants and so investigate different ways people can be hurt, denied, negated, etc. Even though individuals will differ over how to define a conception of shared human needs, we should not thereby think this is the same as defining our individual ends. This could be no less contingent than the other features, which Rawls takes to be common to all human beings as such. Rawls wanted to restrict the description of the parties in the original position to those characteristics which all human beings share as free and equal rational beings. If Rawls does not want to rely, even implicitly, on the idea of a noumenal realm[39] (i.e. noumena are objects of pure reason, and have no relation to our sense perceptions), then he has to ponder, as Kant did, the assumptions of independence and self-sufficiency which underpin our conception of ourselves as free and equal rational beings.

We should be able to concede easily that things that are good for one person may not be good for another, without thereby thinking we have dissolved the possibility of an investigation into human needs. Rawls acknowledged that in different situations different kinds of agreements are called for. Rawls states that 'individuals find their good in different ways, and many things may be good for one person that would not be good for another. Moreover, there is no urgency to reach a publicly accepted judgement as to what is the good of particular individuals. The reasons that make such an agreement necessary in questions of justice do not obtain for judgements of value.'[40]

Of course, recognising the moral importance of an investigation of human needs is not connected to drawing up a list to which people can agree. This quest has often been misplaced since it has classically conceived needs as being given prior to people's relationships in society. In traditional contract theories, it is usually conceived that we enter society to fulfil pre-given needs.[41] Against this it has been taken as a strength of deontological liberalism that it does not depend upon any particular conception of human nature. Therefore, Rawls can claim that the key assumption of justice as fairness is to involve 'no particular theory of human motivation'.[42] Likewise, the political and legal theorist Ronald Dworkin can say, 'liberalism does not rest on any specific theory of personality'.[43] But as Dworkin makes clear, the force of this is in the idea that liberals can be 'indifferent to the ways of life individuals choose to pursue'.[44] Contemporary versions of political liberalism take pride in the fact that they do not depend upon any particular theory of the person, at least in the traditional sense that they do not attribute a determinate nature to all human beings. For example, Rawls' *A Theory of Justice*, which gives us the archetype of this sort of liberalism, might well be juxtaposed with, for example, Thomist or utilitarian accounts which offer elaborated accounts of the person. However, rather than being a strength, this turns out to be a fatal flaw.

The Disputed Kantian Conception of Justice

Rawls is concerned to develop a viable Kantian conception of justice. This means denying a prior and independent self that is distinct from its values and ends can only be a transcendental or noumenal subject, lacking all empirical foundation. For Rawls, this means detaching the content of Kant's doctrine from its background in transcendental idealism and recasting it within the 'canons of a reasonable empiricism'.[45] It is an essential part of Sandel's argument in *Liberalism and the Limits of Justice* that for justice to be primary we must be independent and distinct from the ends and values we hold. As subjects we must be constituted independently of our ends and desires. He seeks the limits of justice in the partiality of this self-image and argues that 'Rawls' attempt does not succeed, and that deontological liberalism cannot be rescued from the difficulties associated with the Kantian subject'.[46]

Practical Considerations

Fairness in matters of justice is not just an abstract theoretical position: it is a necessary prerequisite to the criminal justice system itself. Nobody could seriously argue for an unfair criminal justice system. Moreover, it underscores the concepts we examined in Chapter 7 – desert and proportionality. We can see that fairness is the foundational element in the criminal justice system. Fairness curtails the excesses of exemplary sentences. It ensures that the police and courts are even-handed. The concept of fairness is the basis of all anti-discrimination legislation and informs the practical workings of equal opportunities policies in the criminal justice system: it is a bulwark against the tyranny of the majority. Irrespective of what qualities individuals bring to the world, fairness ensures their proper treatment and asserts the moral worth of all citizens. Fairness is a primary consideration for those who draft future legislation as well as for those who work in the police, courts, and probation and prison services.

Main Summary Points

- By 'fairness' the political theorist John Rawls had in mind the notion that if we could dispense with the baggage associated with knowing who we are, then we would choose a 'fair' distribution of justice, rather than one based on our pre-understood attributes.
- Just Deserts theorists argue that a rational chooser in the 'original position' would never use utilitarian criteria because any policy that could punish disproportionately to just deserts would inevitably be unfair.
- The idea of 'fairness' is related to the perceived failure of rehabilitation as a practice, in the 1970s, notably in relation to criminal sentencing. Andrew von Hirsch argued that this was 'a shift in perspective from a commitment to do good to a commitment to do as little mischief as possible' (*Doing Justice*, 1976).

Questions

1. What is 'justice as fairness'?
2. In what ways does Andrew von Hirsch use John Rawls' ideas?
3. What is the 'original position'?

Suggested Further Reading

Barry, B. (1995) *Justice as Impartiality*, Oxford: Oxford University Press.
Braithwaite, J. and Pettit, P. (1990) *Not Just Deserts*, Oxford: Oxford University Press.
Dworkin, R. (1977) *Taking Rights Seriously*, London: Duckworth.
Rawls, J. (2001) *Justice as Fairness: A Restatement*, Cambridge, MA: Harvard University Press.
von Hirsch, A. (2002) 'Record-enhanced Sentencing in England and Wales: Reflections on the Halliday Report's Proposed Treatment of Prior Convictions', *Punishment and Society*, 4 (4): 443–457.

Notes

1. Hart, H. L. A. (1984) 'Are There Any Natural Rights', in J. Waldron (ed.), *Theories of Rights*, Oxford: Oxford University Press. p. 85.
2. Rawls, J. (2001) *Justice as Fairness: A Restatement*, Cambridge, MA: Harvard University Press. pp. 14–38, 80–134, 188–189.
3. von Hirsch, A. (1976) *Doing Justice: The Choice of Punishments*, New York: Wang & Hill. p. xxxv.
4. Kellogg, F. (1977) 'From Retribution to Desert', *Criminology*, 15: 179–192.
5. Rawls, J. (1955) 'Two Concepts of Rules', *The Philosophical Review*, 64: 3–32. Rule utilitarianism maintains that something is morally right if the consequences of adopting a particular rule are more favourable than unfavourable to everyone. It differs from act utilitarianism, which weighs the consequences of each particular action.

6. von Hirsch, *Doing Justice*. p. xxxiv.
7. Kellogg, 'From Retribution to Desert'. p. 185.
8. von Hirsch, *Doing Justice*. p. 32.
9. Kellogg, 'From Retribution to Desert'. p. 189.
10. Di Cristina, B. and Gottschalk, M. (2008) 'The Violence of Persuasive Argument: Using Durkheim to Outline a Latent Barrier to a Non-violent Criminology', *Critical Criminology*, 16 (1): 17–38.
11. von Hirsch, *Doing Justice*. p. 81.
12. Northrop, F. S. C. (1959) *The Complexity of Legal and Ethical Experience*, Boston: Little, Brown & Company.
13. Berlin, I. (ed.) (1992) *Two Concepts on Liberty*, Oxford: Oxford University Press. pp. 170–172.
14. Hamilton, Alexander, Jay, John and Madison, James (1968) *The Federalist Papers*, ed. Andrew Hacker, New York: Washington Square Press. Paper No. 10.
15. Farrell, R. and Swigert, V. (1978) 'Prior Offence Record as a Self-fulfilling Prophecy', *Law and Society*, 12: 437–453.
16. Erickson, M. and Gibbs, J. (1970) 'On the Perceived Severity of Legal Penalties', *Journal of Criminal Law and Criminology*, 70: 102–116; see also May, D. C., Wood, P. B., Mooney, J. L. and Minor, K. I. (2005) 'Predicting Offender-generated Exchange Rates: Implications for a Theory of Sentence Severity', *Crime & Delinquency*, 51 (3): 373–399; Apospori, E. and Alpert, G. (1993) 'Research Note: The Role of Differential Experience with the Criminal Justice System in Changes in Perceptions of Severity of Legal Sanctions over Time', *Crime & Delinquency*, 39 (2): 184–194; Drazga Maxfield, L. (2002) 'Prior Dangerous Criminal Behavior and Sentencing under the Federal Sentencing Guidelines', *Iowa Law Review*, 87 (2); O'Neill, M. E., Drazga Maxfield, L. and Harer, M. (2004) 'Past as Prologue: Reconciling Recidivism and Culpability', *Fordham Law Review*, 73: 245; von Hirsch, A. (2002) 'Record-enhanced Sentencing in England and Wales: Reflections on the Halliday Report's Proposed Treatment of Prior Convictions', *Punishment and Society*, 4 (4): 443–457.
17. The classic studies of this are Erskine, H. (1972) 'The Polls: Capital Punishment', *Public Opinion Quarterly*, 34: 107; Bedau, H. A. and Pierce, C. (1975) *Capital Punishment in the United States*, New York: AMS Press.
18. Braithwaite, J. and Pettit, P. (1990) *Not Just Deserts*, Oxford: Oxford University Press. pp. 157–166.
19. Rawls, J. (1973) *A Theory of Justice*, Oxford: Oxford University Press. pp. 136–148.
20. Butler, J. (1950) *Five Sermons*, New York: Liberal Arts.
21. Ross, W. D. (1965) *The Right and the Good*, Oxford: Clarendon Press; Broad, C. D. (1959) *Five Types of Ethical Theory*, Totowa, NY: Littlefield, Adams and Co; Moore, G. E. (1956) *Principia Ethica*, Cambridge: Cambridge University Press.
22. Moore, *Principia Ethica*. p. 67.
23. Rawls, J. (1973) *A Theory of Justice*, Oxford: Oxford University Press. pp. 17–22.
24. There is a wealth of writing on this point. See especially: Machan, T. (1983) 'Social Contract as a Basis of Norms: A Critique', *Journal of Liberal Studies*, 7: 141–146; Sadurski, W. (1983) 'Contractarianism and Intuition: On the Role of Social Contract Arguments in Theories of Justice', *Australasian Journal of Philosophy*, 61: 321–347; Schaefer, D. (1979) *Justice or Tyranny? A Critique of John Rawls' Theory of Justice*, Port Washington, New York: Kennikat Press; Barry, B. (1989) *Theories of Justice*, Hemel Hempstead: Wheatsheaf Press. p. 196; Barry, B. (1995) *Justice as Impartiality*, Oxford: Oxford University Press. pp. 57–61.

25. Game theory is a branch of economic and political theory that studies the ways in which strategic interactions between rational players produce outcomes with respect to the preferences of the players. See Myerson, R. B. (1997) *Game Theory: Analysis of Conflict*, Cambridge, MA: Harvard University Press.
26. A good example is Kaye, D. (1980) 'Playing Games with Justice', *Social Theory and Practice*, 6: 33–52.
27. Rawls, *Theory of Justice*. p. 13.
28. Ibid. p. 256.
29. Ibid. p. 256 and see also p. 178.
30. Ibid. p. 563.
31. Sandel, M. (1982) *Liberalism and the Limits of Justice*, Cambridge: Cambridge University Press. p. 121.
32. Ibid. p. 138.
33. Ibid. p. 138.
34. Hart, H. L. A. (1979) 'Between Utility and Rights', in Alan Ryan (ed.), *The Idea of Freedom*, Oxford: Oxford University Press. p. 98.
35. Aristotle (1985) *Nicomachean Ethics*. London: Penguin §§ 1.7 and 10.6.
36. Rawls, *Theory of Justice*. p. 447.
37. Ibid. p. 178; Shenoy, P. and Martin, R. (1983) 'Two Interpretations of the Difference Principle in Rawls's Theory of Justice', *Theoria*, 49 (3): 113–141.
38. Rawls, *Theory of Justice*. p. 440.
39. Oizerman, T. I. (1981) 'Kant's Doctrine of the "Things in Themselves" and Noumena', *Philosophy and Phenomenological Research*, 41 (3): 333–350.
40. Rawls, *Theory of Justice*. p. 448.
41. Heller, A. (1976) *The Theory of Need in Marx*, London: Allison and Busby.
42. Rawls, *Theory of Justice*. p. 129.
43. Dworkin, R. (1977) *Taking Rights Seriously*, London: Duckworth. p. 142.
44. Ibid. p. 143.
45. Rawls, J. (1977) 'The Basic Structure as Subject', *American Philosophical Quarterly*, 14 (2): 159–165.
46. Sandel, *Liberalism and the Limits of Justice*. p. 14.

9

ETHICS AND OUR MORAL ACTIONS

Justice was once celebrated as a virtue, indeed a cardinal virtue. Although few have shared the heady metaphysical vision that once led Plato to claim that virtue is enough and that good men need no others, many have thought that justice is not simply one virtue among others, that good laws and good character complement one another and that politics and ethics are distinct but complementary spheres of practical reasoning. Accounts of justice – of good laws and institutions – have nearly always been allied with accounts of the virtues – of the characters of good men and women.

O'Neill, 1996[1]

Introduction

Up to the nineteenth century, issues of ethics and morality relating to the principles and practices of how individuals, groups, corporations and the state operate in the world have been the preserve of philosophers, theologians and legal theorists. This has long since changed and criminological explanation increasingly tackles moral and ethical issues head on. This is partly because some of the best contemporary criminological writers are primarily concerned with practical ethical issues, e.g. Stan Cohen (human rights), Andrew von Hirsch (moral issues and punishment), Colin Sumner (censure) and Jock Young (social exclusion), and partly because Criminology, as a discipline, is increasingly thrown up against ethical and moral issues in terms of the topics it researches, e.g. the treatment of young offenders or the limits of recreational drug use. Moreover, we increasingly feel, as a society, that social scientists should comment on the ethical and moral matters – after all it is they who are the *experts*. When we turn on our televisions to watch serious documentaries it is more often the case that social scientists are the ones commenting upon the ethical and moral issues of the day, rather than philosophers and theologians. However, there is nothing new in social scientists commenting on ethical and moral issues. Adolphe Quetelet had been interested in morality. His work showed how some of the poorest regions of France were the ones with the lowest crime rates and that inequalities of wealth between citizens and their likelihood of committing crime were related to issues concerning moral instruction, as well as opportunity. Karl

Marx was motivated by what he saw as an unfair distribution of wealth and the problems that caused.[2] Emile Durkheim was concerned with moral regulation and the functioning of a moral community.[3] Ervin Goffman's work, notably in his book *Asylums*, represents a moral critique of societal intolerance of difference.[4] More recently, Jock Young has, in his *The Exclusive Society*, set out the moral case for a new form of citizenship to combat crime.[5] So, having established that the treatment of ethical and moral matters is both historically part of the script of Criminology, and is in any case unavoidable given the most basic research material of the criminologist concerns rules and their enforcement, this chapter will look at ethics and morals, even though I would argue that all the previous chapters in this book are necessarily shot through with ethical and moral analysis. This chapter aims to raise awareness of some practical moral issues, especially those associated with late modernity, such as the proliferation of law and the lack of a moral consensus.

The Criminal as Freerider

In *A Theory of Justice*, John Rawls set out the issue of freeriders.[6] He did this in relation to distributive justice.

> The sense of justice leads us to promote just schemes and to do our share in them when we believe that others, or sufficiently many of them, will do theirs. But in normal circumstances a reasonable assurance in this regard can only be given if there is a binding rule effectively enforced. Assuming that the public good is to everyone's advantage, and one that all would agree to arrange for, the use of coercion is perfectly rational from each man's point of view. Many of the traditional activities of government, insofar as they can be justified, can be accounted for in this way. The need for enforcement of rules by the state will still exist even when everyone is moved by the same sense of justice. The characteristic features of essential public goods necessitate collective agreements, and firm assurance must be given to all that they will be honored.[7]

The criminal can also be seen as a freerider, and in legal doctrine the criminal is the person who breaches the principles of fairness and trust, in terms of what is acceptable, in any rules-based system.[8]

The legal theorist H. L. A. Hart tackled this problem in view of political obligation and fair play in his essay 'Are there any natural rights?': 'When any number of persons conduct any joint enterprise according to rules, and thus restrict their liberty, those who have submitted to these restrictions when required have a right to similar submission from those who have benefited by their submission.'[9] In other words, we are all morally duty bound to abide by the laws because we benefit from them. If all other members cooperate in order to create a society of mutual benefit and support, as in the Hart case, then no person should fail to do his or her share or undermine the system, which benefits all. The benefits that accrue from a fair legal system only follow from their being upheld. The criminal deserves punishment because they are not obeying the rules they ought to live by and which secure the free and optimal functioning of society. Ronald Dworkin has further developed this line of thinking in relation to what legal theorists call associative obligation. In Dworkin's scenario, in societies which are characterised by equal and substantial policies focused on the well-being of the people, all individuals are obligated to support that system in general terms, and obey its laws. It is the law which secures the general well-being and it has to be defended. In the Dworkin scenario, it should be noted that it specifically outlaws totalitarian political and legal systems, and ones not focused on the general well-being.[10] Seeing the criminal as a freerider may work in a normative legal model as it undoubtedly has a deal of explanatory force. However, it obviously misses out a great deal of sociological and real-world empirical detail. It is also ahistoric and does not raise serious questions about the fair distribution of goods and services in society, even in the case of Dworkin. The freerider view of criminality is obviously indebted to the liberal rights and obligations thinking we discussed earlier in Chapter 3, but it is easy to see how it can lead to a zero-tolerance regime which completely overlooks broader issues of social inequality. As Jock Young stated in *The Exclusive Society*: 'Crime rates relate to the material conditions within a society: the criminal justice system, whether scripted by liberal ideals or by draconian conservative morality.'[11] The freerider formulation cannot address Young's point.

No Consensus on Crime

One of the problems any ethical theory has to grapple with is the issue that there is no complete agreement about what are the nature and scope of crime and its causation, to say nothing of the criminalisation process. This is a seemingly insurmountable problem for any ethical or moral theory. If there is no rigorous answer to the issues of what exactly the nature and scope of crime and its causation are, then how can any ethical or moral theory address the issues of injustice, which are at its core?[12] A great many people today are in prison for things which at other times or in other places would not be criminal at all. The internet makes determination of jurisdiction problematic in such cases as international fraud, pornography or the downloading of movies. Laws change constantly: expressed homosexual behaviour was once a criminal offence and dog-fighting was once legal. As criminologists and legal scholars have noted, the volume of law has grown exponentially, as has its scope, and it now covers activities which we all take part in, such as downloading music, and this has tended to break down the 'them' and 'us' distinction between criminals and everyone else in society.[13] It is a messy picture and getting messier. Even where there is criminal law, for example in relation to marijuana, confusion often reigns on the street and among prosecutors about the exact way to proceed. Laws are routinely enacted in response to media and ginger group pressure. Many laws are systematically overlooked by the police for practical operational reasons and many crimes of a corporate nature, such as pollution, are ignored for political reasons.[14] Then there is the shifting basis of proof in criminal cases, alterations to criminal liability and new, and complex, policing functions which all further add to the uncertainty. This has led Andrew Ashworth to ask 'Is the criminal law a lost cause?'[15]

Some jurisdictions have tried to overcome many of the problems of determining what exactly are the nature and scope of crime and its causation by resorting to technical definitional measures such as 'dangerousness' or 'seriousness' in an attempt to define core, or prioritised, areas of crime, or at least restrict the problem. The Criminal Justice Act 2003 might be understood as such an attempt in that it distinguishes 'dangerous' and 'serious' offences from less 'dangerous' and less 'serious' offences. However, Monahan has shown, conclusively, that this has not worked either.[16] Leaving aside the issues of objectivity and moral panic that may well arise in relation to 'dangerousness' and 'seriousness', the idea that the criminal law can be restricted to its core, or prioritised, elements (especially in relation to 'dangerousness' and 'seriousness') is almost bound to fail. Robinson has shown the mess, and injustice, that such a move has had in relation to increasing the incarceration rates for certain crimes.[17] The truth is that the criminal law has expanded so far that notions of core and non-core crime are, though initially tempting to some liberal theorists, *practically* useless because they do not add anything to the analysis or the bigger problem of legitimating the criminal law in late modernity. Moreover, we already know that murderers are on average more dangerous than marijuana users, so why waste time on this classificatory enterprise, unless to shore up the legitimacy of criminal law?[18]

There is, then, a crisis in the determination of the criminal law. At the most basic theoretical and practical level there is confusion, with obvious consequences for ethical and moral considerations. It is easy to sustain the charges that there are too many laws and too much punishment, and because of confusion about the nature and scope of crime and its causation, to say nothing of the criminalisation process, there is too little moral communication through the criminal justice system. Moreover, this confusion has only added to state power.[19] If the criminal justice system not only fails to do its job, but also fails to communicate what is and what is not acceptable behaviour, it is not surprising that this impacts negatively in terms of a failure to so order things that individuals know what is and what is not ethically and morally acceptable.[20] Moral communication is, at least partly, a key function of the criminal justice system.

Lack of Moral Consensus

In the epilogue to *Censure and Sanctions*, Andrew von Hirsch spends time to deal with the issue of the lack of consensus surrounding morality, especially in relation to punishment. He argues that:

Traditional societies, it is said, have a considerable degree of agreement about what is right and wrong. In matters of dispute, there are authoritative figures to consult. In such a society, there would be little difficulty grading penalties to fit the supposed degree to reprehensibleness of conduct. Our own societies are not so constituted, however. There are contending groups having differing outlooks about how people should behave. The State also carries no particular authority to resolve ethical disputes. How then, the objection runs, can the degree of various acts' wrongfulness be determined, sufficiently to construct a desert-based sentencing scheme?[21]

He admits that there is 'legal and ethical' dissensus (lack of consensus), notably around drugs, and concedes that this makes the use of the criminal law in such areas problematic. However, von Hirsch goes on to argue that there is consensus, or at least a greater degree of consensus, in core areas of the criminal law, such as 'victimising crime', theft and fraud.[22] He advocates a practical solution based upon a measure of harm and relying on two criteria, which address seriousness: (1) the impact upon an individual's living-standard, and (2) a measure of culpability based on the 'degree of purposefulness or carelessness'. However, even getting agreement on these two measures may itself be problematic, and von Hirsch admits that:

> Matters admittedly become more complicated when one leaves the core area of victimizing offences, and goes to crimes (such as drug offences) the wrongfulness of which is in dispute. Here, analysis is impeded by the lack of an adequate theory of criminalization – a theory of when, and under what circumstances, conduct may be deemed sufficiently reprehensible to warrant the blaming response of the criminal sanction. But if assessing the gravity of these crimes is more difficult, that would seem to me to be a strength, not a weakness, of a proportionalist sentencing theory. When it is doubted whether and why the prohibited conduct is wrong, it should come as no surprise that the gravity is hard to gauge.[23]

The lack of a solid agreement about morals and the proper nature and extent of the criminal law has led some theorists to argue for an imposition of morality.

Legal Moralism

The lack of consensus on what should and what should not be criminalised has led some theorists to advocate legal moralism. Legal moralism is now gaining ground and was the subject of the prestigious 2008 Dewey Lecture in Law and Philosophy at the University of Chicago Law School, where the leading political theorist Robert E. Goodin delivered a lecture entitled 'An Epistemic Case for Legal Moralism'.[24] Goodin and other legal moralists have argued not only for the legitimacy of criminalising *immoral* behaviour, but also for an ideal set of rules and values which the law is to enforce. Beyond that they argue that the state should enforce a moral consensus in society, in lieu of agreement about public morals.[25] The archetypal legal moralist text is Lord Devlin's argument that a shared morality is essential to the proper functioning of society:

[I]f men and women try to create a society in which there is no fundamental agreement about good and evil, they will fail; if having based it on common agreement, the agreement goes, the society will disintegrate. For society is not something that is kept together physically; it is held by the invisible bonds of common thought. If the bonds were too far relaxed the members would drift apart. A common morality is part of the bondage. The bondage is part of the price of society; and mankind, which needs society, must pay its price.[26]

Devlin's view is that individuals cannot have a meaningful existence without the help of society and he saw an expanded role for the law in both maintaining a shared morality and, at a deeper level, maintaining society itself.[27] Ronald Dworkin, the leading contemporary legal moralist, has defended an enlightened form of legal moralism on the grounds that it is a requirement of democratic government. He argues that without it, normal civic life is impossible. Dworkin claims to have developed a set of rational standards for determining when a judgement is a proper moral judgement, although this does not determine whether or not a judgement is correct.

However, the ability of the criminal law to convey morality, i.e. to convey the immoral nature of something as a basis for then criminalising it, is nonetheless contested in legal and criminological circles. The classic anti-legal moralist statement was made by John Hospers. Hospers' argument is drawn from Bentham's work in the *Principles of Morals and Legislation* and amounts to an attack upon the implicit tyranny of legal moralism, in that it seems to leave no room for alternative perspectives.[28] Moreover, H. L. A. Hart pointed out that Devlin's argument, and that of other legal moralists, is overstated in that it argues that without a shared morality, the existence of society as a whole is jeopardised. In the area of sexual morality Hart noted that it is ridiculous, for example, to claim that 'deviation from accepted sexual morality, even by adults in private, is something which, like treason, threatens the existence of society'.[29] So while we need to enforce certain norms which are essential to society, society can nonetheless get along very well with a degree of diversity – in the case Hart cites, homosexuality. The main point here is the extent to which moral, and implicitly political, considerations are at the heart of debates about the extent and scope of the criminal law.

Legal Paternalism

Legal paternalism, in the form we typically encounter it, follows John Stuart Mill's notion in *On Liberty* that is permissible to intervene in a person's affairs to prevent them from inflicting harm, in a variety of forms, on themselves.[30] The political and legal theorist Gerald Dworkin has argued that legal interference is a necessary element in the proper running of society, if needs be by coercion to the 'welfare, good, happiness, needs, interests or values of the person being coerced'.[31] For Dworkin the law can be used to promote general welfare by coercion. He has in mind such things as health and education where the law should, if necessary, be employed to coerce something which is a public good. In other words, we should prosecute those who do not send their children to school and, in the last resort, force a person to obtain medical treatment for a contagious disease. Joel Feinberg follows this and argues: 'It is always a good reason in support of a proposed criminal prohibition that it would probably be an effective way of preventing serious offence (as opposed to injury or harm) to persons other than the actor, and that it is probably a necessary means to that end.'[32]

Knowledge of the Law

One very old issue in legal theory is the issue of knowledge of the law and it follows from our previous discussion about moral communication and the massive expansion of the law. From an ethical standpoint, surely, people need to know what constitutes a breach of the criminal law. The legal theorist H. L. A. Hart argued:

> ... laws should ... be brought to the attention of those to whom they apply. The legislator's purpose in making laws would be defeated unless this were generally done, and legal systems often provide, by special rules ... that this be done. But laws may be complete as laws before this is done, and even if it is not done at all. In the absence of special rules to the contrary, laws are validly made even if those affected are left to find out for themselves what laws have been made and who are affected thereby.[33]

In other words, Hart highlights the fact that law as such does not need to be made known to those whom it affects, though he concedes that it is better if it does. The rather dry words Hart wrote were first penned back in 1961 and it would appear much has moved on since then. Rapid changes in the criminal law, the proliferation of rules and regulations, an increasingly multicultural society and the complexities of life in the twenty-first century all seem to call for more public education about the content of the law. To leave it as Hart does is no basis for a proper ethical standard of culpability in terms of the criminal law. Asking individuals to know when they are breaking the law is not a simple matter of finding out for themselves. So whereas we might consider murder, rape and stealing straightforward cases covered by the criminal law, that assumed prior standard of knowledge may well be inappropriate to such things as purchasing some forms of pornography. Moreover, in a world increasingly characterised by the free movement of people, it seems unrealistic to assume that individuals will be aware of all the laws of a country in which they have not grown up, or are new to. Even Jeremy Bentham, writing back in the early nineteenth century, saw an expanded role for education in the laws and customs of his society, but today this aspect of law, its need to be communicated, is becoming less of a priority for government.[34] If the general content of the criminal law is unknown to the community over which it has authority, and prosecutions follow upon Hart's dictum that 'laws are validly made even if those affected are left to find out for themselves what laws have been made and

who are affected thereby', we can expect the law to lose some, or much, of its
ethical legitimacy.

Crime as a Social Construct

Lucia Zedner has put forward a convincing case that we ought to think of crime
less in terms of the well-worn and problematic naturalistic categories of normal
and deviant and adopt an approach that: 'illuminates the artificial way in which
normality and abnormality is defended.'[35] This approach has some common elements with the censure approach of Colin Sumner, which we looked at in
Chapter 6, and which also takes a more constructivist approach.[36] Social constructivism does, however, raise serious issues for any ethical theory. Traditionally,
in religious systems of ethics, the rightness or wrongness of something is related
to either (a) something stipulated in a religious text, such as the Koran or Bible,
or (b) something developed from a religious text by authorities within a designated religious community, as in the case of where it is not tackled directly in a
religious text, e.g. embryo research. Of course, there will be disagreements
within religious communities, but at least there are agreed core texts or ways of
doing things in the first place. Once religious certainties are dispensed with, the
issue of rightness or wrongness is generally decided upon by a community in a
variety of ways, e.g. based upon precedent, common law or through deliberation. Nevertheless, without the anchorage that religion can afford (whether
right or wrong) there is a great deal of latitude for the agreed morality of a community to alter, including issues of crime.[37] If we are aware of an innate social
constructivism to much of our discussions surrounding crime, this is probably a
good thing in that it highlights the essentially sociological and political nature
of much of what we typically call crime. Crime is constructed by communities,
and as those communities alter so do the crime categories. Leaving aside the ideological aspects of crime construction, which we looked at in Chapter 6, it is
easy to see how agreeing what constitutes crime is something that shapes the
world in which we live and how the morality which mirrors crimes is largely a
matter of convention.

The social construction of crime can be directly linked to the way we are governed. Zedner has highlighted the work of Jonathan Simon.[38] Simon has argued
that '[w]e govern through crime to the extent to which crime and punishment
become the occasions and institutional contexts in which we undertake to guide
the conduct of others (and ourselves)'.[39] Simon argues that all sorts of issues,
such as education, housing, poverty, unemployment and much else, are given a
'crime' spin. In this way, local and national government busily reframes these
issues in terms of crime to obtain the special funding that attaches to crime.
Moreover, the fear of crime has completely altered the way we *construct* our lives,
e.g. by living in gated communities and using mobile telephones, the sales pitch
for which is often in terms of crime prevention. Simon has developed his thinking
in his book, *Governing through Crime: How the Criminal Law Transformed American*

Democracy and Created a Culture of Fear.[40] In it, he shows how such things as an increasingly harsh regime of detention and deportation and employee background checks are all part of this process. The everyday moral code we all live by is increasingly built upon a defensive attitude to criminal attack. We now regularly talk of the morality of preventive detention in terrorist cases, the rightness of prying into an employee's life history, and the impropriety of living near poor communities, precisely because crime now orders our lives, even when we are not subjected to it.

――――――――――――――― **Main Summary Points** ―――――――――――――――

- Criminals can be said to be freeriders in as much as they benefit, or try to benefit, from the work of others, while not adding to the general welfare of others.
- The fact that there is no consensus on what crime is directly undermines a key function of the criminal justice system – that of moral communication.
- In the absence of common agreement on moral and ethical matters, including crime, some theorists have argued for a legal moralism in order to maintain civic life.
- Laws are often not communicated properly to people and while ignorance of a law is no defence, this nonetheless undermines the need to communicate law to citizens.
- Crime may be socially constructed, in which case we need to be aware of its political and sociological aspects.

―――――――――――――――――― **Questions** ――――――――――――――――――

1. Are freerider arguments useful in criminological research?
2. If crime is a social construct does that rule out universal explanations of it?
3. Does a lack of consensus about the nature of crime mean that some version of legal moralism is inevitable?

――――――――――――――― **Suggested Further Reading** ―――――――――――――――

Galvin, R. (2008) 'Legal Moralism and the US Supreme Court', *Legal Theory*, 14: 91–111.
Monahan, J. (2004) 'The Future of Violence Risk Management', in M. Tonry (ed.), *The Future of Imprisonment*, New York: Oxford University Press.
Robinson, P. (2001) 'Punishing Dangerousness: Cloaking Preventive Detention as Criminal Justice', *Harvard Law Review*, 114: 1429–1456.
Simester, A. P. and von Hirsch, A. (2002) 'Rethinking the Harm Principle', *Legal Theory*, 8: 269–295.
Stuntz, W. (2001) 'The Pathological Politics of Criminal Justice', *Michigan Law Review*, 100: 505–600.

Notes

1. O'Neill, O. (1996) *Towards Justice and Virtue*, Cambridge: Cambridge University Press. p. 9.
2. Marx, K. (1969) *Theories of Surplus Value*, Vol. 1, London: Lawrence and Wishart. pp. 387–389.
3. Sumner, C. S. (1994) *The Sociology of Deviance: An Obituary*. Milton Keynes: Open University Press. pp. 11–23.
4. Goffman, E. (1968) *Asylums*, Harmondsworth: Penguin. pp. 134–135.
5. Young, J. (2007) *The Exclusive Society*, London: Sage. pp. 190–199.
6. Rawls, J. (1973) *A Theory of Justice*, Oxford: Oxford University Press. pp. 267–270.
7. Ibid. pp. 267–268.
8. de Jasay, A. (1990) *Social Contract, Free Ride*, Oxford: Clarendon Press. pp. 33–34, 134–137.
9. Hart, H. L. A. (1955) 'Are There Any Natural Rights?', *Philosophical Review*, 64: 175–191.
10. Dworkin, R. (1986) *Law's Empire*, London: Fontana Press. pp. 176–216.
11. Young, *Exclusive Society*. p. 140.
12. Lacey, N. (1988) *State Punishment: Political Principles and Community Values*, London: Routledge. pp. 113–117, 144–163, 188–193.
13. Stuntz, W. (2001) 'The Pathological Politics of Criminal Justice', *Michigan Law Review*, 100: 505–600.
14. Wells, C. (2001) *Corporations and Criminal Responsibility*, Oxford: Oxford University Press.
15. Ashworth, A. (2000b) 'Is the Criminal Law a Lost Cause?', *Law Quarterly Review*, 116: 225–256.
16. Monahan, J. (2004) 'The Future of Violence Risk Management', in M. Tonry (ed.), *The Future of Imprisonment*, New York: Oxford University Press.
17. Robinson, P. (2001) 'Punishing Dangerousness: Cloaking Preventive Detention as Criminal Justice', *Harvard Law Review*, 114: 1429–1456.
18. Dubber, M. (2001) 'Policing Possession: The War on Crime and the End of Criminal Law', *Journal of Criminal Law and Criminology*, 91: 829–996.
19. Husak, D. (1995) 'The Nature and Justifiability of Non-consummate Offenses', *Arizona Law Review*, 37: 151–183.
20. Duff, R. A. (1996) 'Penal Communications', in M. Tonry (ed.), *Crime and Justice: A Review of Research*, Chicago: Chicago University Press. pp. 1–97.
21. von Hirsch, A. (1993) *Censure and Sanctions*, Oxford: Clarendon Press. p. 105.
22. Ibid. Chapter 4, pp. 29–35. Here von Hirsch discusses seriousness and severity.
23 Ibid. p. 106.
24. The lecture is available in full at: http://law.anu.edu.au/news/Bob_Goodin.pdf.
25. Galvin, R. (2008) 'Legal Moralism and the US Supreme Court', *Legal Theory*, 14: 91–111; Dworkin, *Law's Empire*. p. 188.
26. Devlin, P. (1965) *The Enforcement of Morals*, Oxford: Oxford University Press. p. 10.
27. Hayry, H. (1991) 'Liberalism and Legal Moralism: The Hart–Devlin Debate and Beyond', *Ratio Juris*, 4 (2): 202–218.
28. Hospers, J. (1980) 'Libertarianism and Legal Paternalism', *The Journal of Libertarian Studies*, 4 (3): 255–265.
29. Hart, H. L. A. (1963) *Law, Liberty and Morality*, Oxford: Clarendon Press. p. 50.
30. Mill, J. S. (1989) *On Liberty*, Cambridge: Cambridge University Press.
31. Dworkin, G. (1972) 'Paternalism', *The Monist*, 56: 64–84. See also Dworkin, G. (2005) 'Moral Paternalism', *Law and Philosophy*, 24 (3): 305–319.

32. Feinberg, J. (1985) *Offense to Others*, Oxford: Oxford University Press. p. 1; see also Simester, A. P. and von Hirsch, A. (2002) 'Rethinking the Harm Principle', *Legal Theory*, 8: 269–295.
33. Hart, H. L. A. (1994) *The Concept of Law*, Oxford: Clarendon Press. p. 22.
34. Bentham, J. (1982) *An Introduction to the Principles of Morals and Legislation*, Oxford: Clarendon Press. pp. 68–69, 294–300.
35. Zedner, L. (2004) *Criminal Justice*, Oxford: Clarendon Press. p. 39.
36. Sumner, *Sociology of Deviance*. p. 309–312.
37. Beauchamp, T. L. (2003) 'A Defense of the Common Morality', *Kennedy Institute of Ethics Journal*, 13 (3): 259–274.
38. Zedner, *Criminal Justice*. p. 46.
39. Simon, J. (1997) 'Governing through Crime', in L. M. Friedman and G. Fisher (eds), *The Crime Conudrum: Essays on Criminal Justice*, Boulder, CO: Westview Press. p. 174.
40. Simon, J. (2007) *Governing through Crime: How the Criminal Law Trasformed American Democracy and Created a Culture of Fear*, Oxford: Oxford University Press.

GLOSSARY

Capitalism   Capitalism is an economic system, both in theory and practice, which is based on private rather than state ownership of businesses and the profit motive. It stresses commercial competition and self-reliance.

Censure   Censure is the rebuke of an individual, group or idea by another person, persons, official body or corporation. It may have a normative role in criminological theory or contain an ideological aspect.

Chicago School   The Chicago School is the name given to a group of sociologists based at the University of Chicago. The Chicago School stressed the importance of ecological and environmental factors in causing and controlling crime. The Chicago School also developed innovative research strategies in both qualitative and quantitative analysis. Although the work of the Chicago School implied a view of political and economic life, it has been criticised for not relating the social processes of the city to deeper factors relating to the role of economic and political conditions beyond, or beneath, the life of the city.

Communitarianism   Communitarianism is a theory of civil society and social cooperation. It attempts to balance the rights of individuals with those of the wider community. It maintains that views of individuals are formed by the culture and values of their community.

Conservative   This is a form of political thought that gives priority to the established tradition. It favours order, stability and existing social customs and institutions.

Control theory   Control theory places a stress upon social conformity. It has often been associated with psychological and psycho-analytical explanation with concepts related to a 'positive self-concept' and 'attachment'. It has tended to concentrate upon the 'juvenile delinquent' and youth crime.

Desert   Desert theory argues that punishments must be fairly deserved and proportionate to the degree of seriousness of the offence.

Deterrence   Deterrence theory is based on the notion that if the consequences of committing a crime outweigh the potential benefits of crime, then the criminal will be deterred from committing the crime. It assumes a high degree of rationality and forethought. In terms of punishments, it may argue for exemplary sentences to deter would-be criminals.

Deviance   This is a sociological concept that was popular within Criminology up to the 1990s. It always measures 'deviance' from the standpoint of the dominant culture. It largely ignores inequality, health and globalisation. It is an approach that came under sustained attack from Colin Sumner in the 1980s and 1990s.

Enlightenment   The political era that saw the rise of liberal and humane thinking. It marked a break with religious thinking and the embracing of ideas relating to objectivity, rationality and social progress.

Equality   The political notion that all persons should be treated the same.

Feminism   This is the movement and political view which advances the case of gender equality and challenges patriarchy.

Freerider   The freerider issue has been developed mainly in Economics, Political Theory and Psychology. Freeriders are those individuals who take/consume more than their fair share or do not share equally in the costs. The freerider problem is the problem of how to limit the negative effects of individuals taking more than they contribute. This rationale has been applied to criminals.

Functionalism   In Criminology this is employed as parts of a structuralist account that sees crime as something that advances, or maintains, the social and political stability of existing state and social relations.

Hegemony   Hegemony is a key concept in theory, notably Marxist theory, that describes and explains the domination of one group, or class, over another. It is typically understood as requiring some consent from the subordinate group and is therefore often linked to cultural domination.

Historical materialism   Historical materialism is a theory first developed by Karl Marx that argues for a materialist conception of history. It posits that human history is the history of economic development and class struggle.

Human rights   Human rights are those basic rights that follow equally, indivisibly and universally from being a member of the human race. They are enshrined in the United Nations Charter and within EU and UK legislation. Within Criminology, Stan Cohen has shown how they relate to victimology as well as the crimes of genocide, hitherto overlooked by criminologists.

Ideology   An ideology is an organised system of ideas that facilitate a comprehensive understanding of the social world. Ideology may be said to be made up of the deepest set of notions at work in every organised set of beliefs. The common set of shared beliefs that a community has may be said to be an ideology. The origin, content and function of ideology are often disputed, notably by Marxists.

Just Deserts   Just Deserts is a theory of punishment which stresses that the criminal sanction should always be commensurate with the seriousness of the offence.

Legal moralism   This view justifies the laws against certain actions on the basis that they are immoral.

Legal paternalism   This is a justification for a law where the welfare of an actor is in question. For example, we may outlaw drug use on the grounds that it harms the user.

Liberalism   This is a view of political and economic life that gives priority to the freedom of the individual to act unhindered by others or by the state.

Marxism   Marxism is the name given to those theories that follow from the writings of Karl Marx. It argues that the struggle between opposing classes is the main influence on political and economic change, leading to an eventual overthrow of capitalist social relations.

Multi-social   This is the idea that the social world is fragmented, complex or functioning on different levels.

Obligations   Obligations are those actions or duties we undertake due to an explicit or implicit reciprocity linked to rights. Obligations can be to individuals, groups, corporations or states.

Patriarchy   This is a social and political system built upon the domination of women by men.

Positivism   Positivism is a position that tends to reduce reality to that which is quantifiable and measurable. It employs natural science methodology to study social relationships. It has been criticised for ignoring political and social relationships, which are not easily quantifiable or are open to various interpretations, or reducing them to measurable categories.

Proportionality   Proportionality is the idea, found in legal theory, that punishments should always be proportionate to the seriousness of the crime.

Rehabilitation   This is the view that it is better for the offender and the wider society for the offender to be helped into a useful role in society rather than simply punished. It stresses education, therapy and development rather than retribution.

Restorative justice Restorative justice (RJ) is a view that tends to see criminality as a violation of an individual, or community, rather than as an act against the state. It therefore emphasises the role of restorative meetings between victims and offenders in an attempt to demonstrate to the offender the harm they have done to an individual or community. Accordingly restitution is often an element in this process.

Retribution This is a view of punishment that maintains that proportionate punishment is the only response to criminal action, regardless of the consequences. In its modern form it is indebted to the work of contemporary neo-Kantians, such as Andrew von Hirsch.

Rights Rights are legal and moral entitlements that derive from specific political circumstances. They usually place a duty of obligation on those who hold them.

Social control A term often used by Marxist criminologists, sometimes in relation to surveillance, that sees the state as preventing those challenging its rule through stopping persons collectively mounting a challenge to capitalist social relations.

Sovereignty Sovereignty is a notion found in political theory and jurisprudence that sets out the degree of political and legal independence a state or body has. Full sovereignty is therefore the exercise of complete, independent and supreme political power.

State of nature The state of nature is a concept drawn from political philosophy and used to advanced social contract theories. It details a hypothetical situation, before the creation of the state, in which there are no rights.

Strain theory Strain theory is a sociological theory that argues that crime is committed when persons cannot meet their acquisitive desires through legitimate means.

Stratified society This is the idea found in Sociology that there is a hierarchical structure to a society in terms of class, caste or other variable.

Utilitarianism This is the view that the worth of an action is determined in terms of its contribution to overall utility alone, i.e. the greater good of all persons. It is a consequentialist theory of action.

BIBLIOGRAPHY

Adams, J. N. and Brownsword, R. (1988) 'Law Reform, Law Jobs, and Law Commission No. 160', *The Modern Law Review*, 51 (4): 481–492.

Alldridge, P. (2002) 'Smuggling, Confiscation and Forfeiture', *Modern Law Review*, 65: 781–791.

Althusser, L. (1969) *For Marx*, Harmondsworth: Penguin.

Amatrudo, A. (1996) 'The Nazi Censure of Art: Aesthetics and the Process of Annihilation', in C. S. Sumner (ed.), *Violence, Culture and Censure*, London: Taylor and Francis.

Amatrudo, A. (2004) 'Crime in the Country', *Criminal Justice Management*, May.

Amatrudo, A. (2009) 'Adolphe Quetelet', in K. Hayward, S. Maruna and J. Mooney (eds), *Key Thinkers in Criminology*, London: Routledge (forthcoming).

Apospori, E. and Alpert, G. (1993) 'Research Note: The Role of Differential Experience with the Criminal Justice System in Changes in Perceptions of Severity of Legal Sanctions over Time', *Crime & Delinquency*, 39 (2): 184–194.

Aquinas, T. (1993) *Summa Theologiae*, Notre Dame, IN: University of Notre Dame Press.

Arendt, H. (1963) *On Revolution*, New York: Viking Press.

Aristotle (1985) *Nicomachean Ethics*, London: Penguin.

Ashworth, A. (1985) 'Punishment and Compensation: Victims, Offenders and the State', *Oxford Journal of Legal Studies*, 6: 86–122.

Ashworth, A. (1989) 'Criminal Justice and Deserved Sentences', *Criminal Law Review*, May: 340–355.

Ashworth, A. (1992) *Sentencing and Criminal Justice*, London: Weidenfeld & Nicolson.

Ashworth, A. (1993) 'Victim Impact Statements and Sentencing', *Criminal Law Review*, 498–509.

Ashworth, A. (2000) 'Victims' Rights, Defendants' Rights and Criminal Procedure', in A. Crawford and J. Goodey (eds), *Integrating a Victim Perspective within Criminal Justice*, Aldershot: Ashgate.

Ashworth, A. (2004) 'Criminal Justice Reform: Principles, Human Rights and Public Protection', *Criminal Law Review*, 516–532.

Augustine, St (1998) *City of God*, Cambridge: Cambridge University Press.

Baiasu, S. (2007) 'Institutions and the Normativity of Desert', *Contemporary Political Theory*, 6 (2): 175–195.

Barry, B. (1989) *Theories of Justice*, Hemel Hempstead: Wheatsheaf Press.

Barry, B. (1995) *Justice as Impartiality*, Oxford: Oxford University Press.

Bartlett, K. T. (1990) 'Feminist Legal Methods', *Harvard Law Review*, 103 (4): 829–888.

Bayley, D. (1988) 'Community Policing: A Report from the Devil's Advocate', in J.R. Greene and S. D. Mastrofski (eds), *Community Policing: Rhetoric or Reality?*, New York: Praeger.

Beattie, J. A. (1990) *Judicial Punishment in England*, London: Faber & Faber.

Beck, U. (1992) *Risk Society: Towards a New Modernity*, London: Sage.

Becker, E. F. (1975) 'Justice, Utility, and Interpersonal Comparisons', *Theory and Decision*, 14 (1): 471–484.

Bedau, H. A. (1978) 'Retribution and the Theory of Punishment', *Journal of Philosophy*, 75: 601–620.

Beirne, P. (1993) 'Adolphe Quetelet and the Origins of Positivist Criminology', *American Journal of Sociology*, 92 (5): 1140–1169.

Benn, S. I. and Peters, R. S. (1959) *Social Principles and the Democratic State*, London: George Allen & Unwin.

Bentham, J. (1838–43) *Principles of Penal Law*, in *The Works of Jeremy Bentham*, 11 vols, ed. J. Bowring, Edinburgh: W. Tait.

Bentham, J. (1948) *Introduction to the Principles of Morals and Legislation*, ed. J. H. Burns and H. L. A. Hart, London: Methuen.

Bentham, J. (1982) *Introduction to the Principles of Morals and Legislation*, London: Methuen.

Bentham, J. (1987) 'Anarchical Fallacies: Being an Examination of the Declaration of Rights Issued during the French Revolution', in J. Waldron (ed.), *Nonsense upon Stilts: Bentham, Burke and Marx on the Rights of Man*, London: Methuen.

Berlin, I. (1992) *Two Concepts on Liberty*, Oxford: Oxford University Press.

Bonger, W. (1916) *Criminality and Economic Conditions*, London: Heinemann.

Bottoms, A. E. and Brownsword, R. (1982) 'The Dangerousness Debate after the Floud Report', *British Journal of Criminology*, 22: 229–254.

Box, S. (1983) *Power, Crime and Mystification*, London: Tavistock.

Box, S. (1987) *Recession, Crime and Punishment*, Basingstoke: Macmillan.

Bradley, F. H. (1927) *Ethical Studies*, Oxford: Oxford University Press.

Braithwaite, J. (1989) *Crime, Shame and Reintegration*, Cambridge: Cambridge University Press.

Braithwaite, J. (1999) 'Restorative Justice: Assessing Optimistic and Pessimistic Accounts', in M. Tonry, (ed.), *Crime and Justice: A Review of Research*, Chicago: Chicago University Press.

Braithwaite, J. (2003a) 'Principles of Restorative Justice', in A. von Hirsch, J. V. Roberts, A. E. Bottoms, K. Roach and M. Schiff (eds), *Restorative Justice and Criminal Justice: Competing or Reconcilable Paradigms?* Oxford: Hart Publishing, pp. 1–20.

Braithwaite, J. (2003b) 'Does Restorative Justice Work?', in G. Johnstone (ed.), *A Restorative Justice Reader: Texts, Sources, Context*. Cullompton: Willan Publishing, pp. 320–352.

Braithwaite, J. and Pettit, P. (1990) *Not Just Deserts*, Oxford: Oxford University Press.

Brandt, T. (1959) *Ethical Theory*, Englewood Cliffs, NJ: Prentice-Hall.

Brandt, T. (1964) 'The Concepts of Obligation and Duty', *Mind*, 73: 364–393.

Broad, C. D. (1959) *Five Types of Ethical Theory*, Totowa, NJ: Littlefield, Adams and Co.

Brotherton, D. and Barrios, L. (2004) *The Almighty Latin King and Queen Nation*, New York: Columbia University Press.

Brown, A. (1986) *Modern Political Philosophy: Theories of the Just Society*, London: Penguin.

Brown, A. (2004) 'Anti-social Behaviour, Crime Control and Social Control', *The Howard Journal*, 43 (2): 203–211.

Brownlee, I. (2002) 'New Labour – New Penology? Punitive Rhetoric and the Limits of Managerialism in Criminal Justice Policy', *Journal of Law and Society*, 25 (3): 313–335.

Burgh, R. (1982) 'Do the Guilty Deserve Punishment?', *Journal of Philosophy*, 79 (4): 193–210.

Burney, E. (2002) 'Talking Tough, Acting Coy: What Happened to the Anti-Social Behaviour Order?', *The Howard Journal of Criminal Justice*, 41 (5): 469–484.

Butler, J. (1950) *Five Sermons*, New York: Liberal Arts.

Campbell, S. (2002) *A Review of Anti-Social Behaviour Orders*, Home Office Study 236, London: Home Office.

Carnoy, M. (1984) *The State and Political Theory*, Princeton, NJ: Princeton University Press.

Carver, T. (1982) *Marx's Social Theory*, Oxford: Oxford University Press.

Cavadino, M. and Dignan, J. (2006) 'Penal Policy and Political Economy', *Criminology and Criminal Justice*, 6 (4): 435–456.

Chambliss, W. J. (1975) 'Toward a Political Economy of Crime', *Theory and Society*, 2 (2): 149–170.

Chomsky, N. (1975) *Reflections on Language*, New York: Pantheon Books.

Choongh, S. (2002) 'Police Investigative Powers', in M. McConville and G. Wilson (eds), *The Handbook of the Criminal Justice Process*, Oxford: Oxford University Press.

Charvet, J. (1995) *The Idea of an Ethical Community*, Ithaca, NY: Cornell University Press.

Chesney-Lind, M. (1997) *The Female Offender: Girls, Women and Crime*, Thousand Oaks, CA: Sage.

Cicero (1913a) *Laws (De Legibus)*, Loeb Classical Library, Cambridge, MA: Harvard University Press.

Cicero (1913b) *On Duties (De Officiis)*, Loeb Classical Library, Cambridge, MA: Harvard University Press.

Cohen, A. (1966) *Deviance and Control*, Englewood Cliffs, NJ: Prentice-Hall.

Cohen, G. A. (1988) *History, Labour and Freedom*, Oxford: Oxford University Press.

Cohen, G. A. (1989) 'On the Currency of Egalitarian Justice', *Ethics*, 99 (4): 906–944.

Cohen, M. R. (1950) *Reason and Law*, Glencoe, IL: The Free Press.

Cohen, S. (2007) 'Human Rights and Crimes of the State: The Culture of Denial', *Australian and New Zealand Journal of Criminology*, 26 (2): 97–115. Reprinted in E. McLaughlin et al. (eds) (2002) *Criminological Perspectives: Essential Readings*, London: Sage.

Coleman, J. (1990) *Against the State*, London: Penguin.

Coleman, J. (2000) 'Crimes and Transactions', *California Law Review*, 88: 921–930.

Cook, D. (2006) *Crime and Social Justice*, London: Sage.

Coole, D. (1994) 'Women, Gender and Contract: Feminist Interpretations', in D. Boucher and P. Kelly (eds), *The Social Contract from Hobbes to Rawls*, London: Routledge.

Cooter, R. and Ulen, T. (2008) *Law and Economics*, London: Pearson.

Cragg, W. (2006) *The Practice of Punishment*, London: Routledge.

Cullen, F. T. and Gilbert, K. E. (1982) 'Reaffirming Rehabilitation', in A. von Hirsch and A. Ashworth (eds), *Principled Sentencing*, Edinburgh: Edinburgh University Press.

Di Cristina, B. and Gottschalk, M. (2008) 'The Violence of Persuasive Argument: Using Durkheim to Outline a Latent Barrier to a Non-violent Criminology', *Critical Criminology*, 16 (7): 17–38.

Dignan, J. et al. (2007) 'Staging Restorative Justice Encounters against a Criminal Justice Backdrop', *Criminology and Criminal Justice*, 7 (1): 5–32.

Dobash, R. E. and Dobash, R. P. (1992) *Women, Violence and Social Change*, London: Routledge.

Downes, D. (1998) 'Toughing It Out: From Labour Opposition to Labour Government', *Policy Studies*, 19 (3–4): 191–198.

Drazga Maxfield, L. (2002) 'Prior Dangerous Criminal Behavior and Sentencing under the Federal Sentencing Guidelines', *Iowa Law Review*, 87 (2).

Draper, H. (1972) 'The Concept of the "lumpenproletariat" in Marx and Engels', *Economic et Societes*, 6 (12): 2285–2312.

Dubeiel, H. (1997) 'Hannah Arendt and the Theory of Democracy: A Critical Reconstruction', in Kielmansegg, P. G., Mewes, H. and Glaser-Schmidt, E. *Hannah Arendt and Leo Strauss: German Emigres and American Political Thought after World War Two*, Cambridge: Cambridge University Press.

Duff, R. A. (1986) *Trials and Punishments*, Cambridge: Cambridge University Press.

Duff, R. A. (1988) 'Punishment and Penance: A Reply to Harrison', *Proceedings of the Aristotelian Society* (Supplementary Volume), 62: 153–167.

Duff, R. A. (2001) *Punishment, Communication and Community*, Oxford: Oxford University Press.

Durkheim, E. (1933) *The Division of Labour in Society*, New York: The Free Press.

Durkheim, E. (1947) *The Division of Labour in Society*, trans. George Simpson, Glencoe, IL: The Free Press.

Durkheim, E. (1970) *Suicide*, London: Routledge.

Dworkin, R. (1977) *Taking Rights Seriously*, Cambridge, MA: Harvard University Press.

Dworkin, R. (1985) *A Matter of Principle*, Cambridge, MA: Harvard University Press.

Eck, J. and Rosenbaum, D. (1994) 'The New Police Order: Effectiveness, Equity and Efficiency', in D. Rosenbaum (ed.), *The Challenge of Community Policing*, Thousand Oaks, CA: Sage.

Erickson, M. and Gibbs, J. (1970) 'On the Perceived Severity of Legal Penalties', *Journal of Criminal Law and Criminology*, 70: 102–116.

Ericson, R. (1994) *The Spirit of Community: The Reinvention of American Society*, New York: Touchstone Books.

Ericson, R. (2007) *Crime in an Insecure World*, London: Polity Press.

Erskine, H. (1972) 'The Polls: Capital Punishment', *Public Opinion Quarterly*, 34: 290–307.

Etzioni, A. (1989) 'Towards an I and We Paradigm', *Contemporary Sociology*, 18 (2): 171–176.

Farrell, R. and Swigert, V. (1978) 'Prior Offence Record as a Self-fulfilling Prophecy', *Law and Society*, 12: 437–453.

Feinberg, J. (1970) *Doing and Deserving*, Princeton, NJ: Princeton University Press.

Ferrell, J. (1997) 'Criminological *Verstehen*: Inside the Immediacy of Crime', *Justice Quarterly*, 14 (1): 3–23.

Fine, B. (1979) *Capitalism and the Rule of Law: From Deviancy Theory to Marxism*, London: Hutchinson.

Fine, B. and Millar, R. (eds) (1985) *Policing the Miners' Strike*, London: Lawrence and Wishart.

Finnis, J. (1980) *Natural Law and Natural Rights*, Oxford: Clarendon Press.

Fisk, M. (1989) *The State and Justice: An Essay in Political Theory*, Cambridge: Cambridge University Press.

Fleischacker, S. (1992) 'Kant's Theory of Punishment', in H. William (ed.), *Essays on Kant's Political Philosophy*, Cardiff: University of Wales Press.

Flew, A. (1954) 'The Justification of Punishment', *Philosophy*, 29: 291–307.

Fogel, D. (1975) *We Are Living Proof: The Justice Model for Corrections*, Cincinnati, OH: W. H. Anderson and Co.

Frankel, M. E. (1973) *Criminal Sentences: Law without Order*, New York: Hill & Wang.

Freiberg, A. and Gelb, K. (2008) *Penal Populism, Sentencing Councils and Sentencing Policy*, Cullompton: Willan Publishing.

Garland, D. (1994) *Punishment and Modern Society: A Study in Social Theory*, Oxford: Clarendon Press.

Garland, D. (1996) 'The Limits of the Sovereign State: Strategies of Crime Control', *British Journal of Criminology*, 36: 445–471.

Garland, D. (2001) *The Culture of Control*, Oxford: Oxford University Press.

Gert, J. (2003) 'Internalism and Different Kinds of Reasons', *The Philosophical Forum*, 34 (1): 53–72.

Gerwirth, A. (1978) *Reason and Morality*, Chicago: Chicago University Press.

Gierke, O. von, (1934) *Natural Law and the Theory of Society*, ed. E. Baker, Cambridge: Cambridge University Press.

Gillespie, A. (2005) 'Reprimanding Juveniles and the Right to Due Process', *Modern Law Review*, 68 (6): 1006–1015.

Gilligan, C. (1982) *In a Different Voice*, Cambridge, MA: Harvard University Press.

Goffman, E. (1968) *Asylums*. Harmondsworth: Penguin.

Gottfredson, M. (1979) 'Treatment Destruction Techniques', *Journal of Research in Crime and Delinquency*, 16 (1): 39–54.

Gramsci, A. (1971) *Selections from the Prison Notebooks*, (ed.) Q. Hoare and G. Nowell-Smith, London: Lawrence and Wishart.

Gutmann, A. (1985) 'Communitarian Critics of Liberalism', *Philosophy and Public Affairs*, 14: 308–327.

Hale, C. (1998) 'Crime and the Business Cycle in Post-war Britain Revisited', *British Journal of Criminology*, 38: 681–698.

Hale, C. (1999) 'The Labour Market and Post-war Crime Trends in England and Wales', in P. Carlen and R. Morgan (eds), *Crime Unlimited*, London: Macmillan.

Hale, C. (2005) 'Economic Marginalization and Social Exclusion', in C. Hale et al. (eds), *Criminology*, Oxford: Oxford University Press.

Hall, N. G. C. (1995) 'Sexual Offender Recidivism Revisited: A Meta-analysis of Recent Treatment Studies', *Journal of Consulting and Clinical Psychology*, 63: 802–809.

Hall, S. (1997) 'Visceral Cultures and Criminal Practices', *Theoretical Criminology*, 1: 453–478.

Hall, S., Critcher, C., Jefferson, T., Clarke, J. and Roberts, B. (1978) *Policing the Crisis*, London: Macmillan.

Hall, S. and Winlow, S. (2004) 'Barbarians at the Gate', in J. Ferrell et al. (eds), *Cultural Criminology Unleashed*, London: Glasshouse Press.

Halliday, J. (2001) *Making Punishments Work: Report of a Review of the Sentencing Framework* (Halliday Report), London: Home Office.

Halpin, A. (1997) *Rights and Law: Analysis and Theory*, Oxford: Hart Publishing.

Hamilton, A., Jay, J. and Madison, J. (1968) *The Federalist Papers*, ed. Andrew Hacker, Paper No. 10, New York: Washington Square Press.

Hampshire, S. (2002) 'Justice is Strife', *Philosophy & Social Criticism*, 28 (6): 635–645.

Hampton, J. (1984) 'The Moral Education Theory of Punishment', *Philosophy and Public Affairs*, 13 (3): 208–238.

Hanna, N. (2008) 'Say What? A Critique of Expressive Retributivism', *Law and Philosophy*, 27 (3): 123–150.

Harel, A. (2005) 'Theories of Rights', in M. P. Golding and W. A. Edmundson (eds), *Philosophy and Legal Theory*, Oxford: Blackwell.

Harsanyi, J. C. (1996) 'Utilities, Preferences, and Substantive Goods', *Social Choice and Welfare*, 14 (1): 129–145.

Hart, H. L. A. (1968) *Punishment and Responsibility*, Oxford: Clarendon Press.

Hart, H. L. A. (1979) 'Between Utility and Rights', in Alan Ryan (ed.), *The Idea of Freedom*, Oxford: Oxford University Press.

Hart, H. L. A. (1982) 'Legal Rights', in H. L. A. Hart, *Essays on Bentham: Jurisprudence and Political Theory*, Oxford: Clarendon Press.

Hart, H. L. A. (1955) 'Are There Any Natural Rights?', *Philosophical Review*.

Hart, H. L. A. (1992) *Punishment and Responsibility*, Oxford: Oxford University Press.

Hart, H. M. (1958) 'The Aims of the Criminal Law', *Law and Contemporary Problems*, 23: 401–441.

Hasluck, C. (1999) 'Employers and the Employment Option of the New Deal for Young Unemployed People: Employment Additionality and its Measurement', University of Warwick, Institute of Employment Research.

Hay, D. (1975) 'Property, Authority and the Criminal Law', in D. Hay, P. Linebaugh and E. P. Thompson (eds), *Albion's Fatal Tree: Crime and Society in Eighteenth-century England*, London: Penguin. pp. 17–63.

Hay, D., Linebaugh, P. and Thompson, E. P. (eds) (1975) *Albion's Fatal Tree: Crime and Society in Eighteenth-century England*, London: Penguin.

Hayward, K. J. (2002) 'The Vilification and Pleasures of Youthful Transgression', in J. Muncie, G. Hughes and E. McLaughlin (eds), *Youth Justice: Critical Readings*, London: Sage.

Hegel, G. W. F. (1952) *The Philosophy of Right*, ed. and trans. T. M. Knox, Oxford: Oxford University Press.

Hegel, G. W. F. (1967) *The Philosophy of Right*, trans. T. M. Knox, London: Oxford University Press.

Heller, A. (1976) *The Theory of Need in Marx*, London: Allison and Busby.

Hill, J. and Wright, G. (2003) 'Youth, Community Safety and the Paradox of Inclusion', *Howard Journal*, 42 (3): 282–297.

Hills, J. and Stewart, K. (2005) *A More Equal Society?* Bristol: Policy Press.

Hirschi, T. (1969) *Causes of Delinquency*, Berkeley, CA: University of California Press.

Hirst, P. Q. (1972) 'Marx and Engels on Law, Crime and Morality', *Economy and Society*, 1 (1): 28–56.

Hobbes, T. (1991) *Leviathan*, ed. Richard Tuck, Cambridge: Cambridge University Press.

Hobbes, T. (1994) *Leviathan*, ed. E. Curley, Cambridge, MA: Hackett.

Honderich, T. (1982) 'On Justifying Protective Punishment', *British Journal of Criminology*, 22: 268–275.

Honderich, T. (1988) *The Consequences of Determinism: A Theory of Determinism*, Oxford: Clarendon Press.

Hood, R. (1989) *The Death Penalty: A World-wide Perspective*, Oxford: Clarendon Press.

Hospers, J. (1961) *Human Conduct: An Introduction to the Problems of Ethics*, New York: Harcourt, Brace & World.

Hudson, B. (2000) 'Punishment, Rights and Difference: Defending Justice in the Risk Society', in K. Stenson and R. Sullivan (eds), *Crime, Risk and Justice*, Cullompton: Willan Publishing.

Hughes, G. (1996) 'Communitarianism and Law and Order', *Critical Social Policy*, 16 (4): 17–41.

Hughes, G. (2002) 'Plotting the Rise of Community Safety: Critical Reflections on Research, Theory and Politics', in G. Hughes and A. Edwards (eds), *Crime Control and Community: The New Politics of Public Safety*, Cullompton: Willan Publishing.

Hughes, G. (2007) *The Politics of Crime and Community*, Basingstoke: Palgrave Macmillan.

Ignatieff, M. (1978) *A Just Measure of Pain: The Penitentiary in the Industrial Revolution*, London: Macmillan.

Kadish, M. R. (1983) 'Practice and Paradox: A Comment on Social Choice Theory', *Ethics*, 93 (4): 680–694.

Kant, I. (1964a) *The Doctrine of Virtue*, Philadelphia, PA: University of Pennsylvania Press.

Kant, I. (1964b) *Groundwork to the Metaphysics of Morals*, New York: Harper & Row.

Kant, I. (1965) *The Metaphysical Elements of Justice*, New York and London: Macmillan.

Kant, I. (1991) *The Metaphysics of Morals*, Cambridge: Cambridge University Press.

Kaye, D. (1980) 'Playing Games with Justice', *Social Theory and Practice*, 6: 33–52.

Keightley-Smith, L. and Francis, P. (2007) 'Final Warning, Youth Justice and Early Intervention: Reflections on the Findings of a Research Study Carried Out in Northern England', *Web Journal of Current Legal Issues*, http://webjcli.ncl.ac.uk/2007/contents2.html.

Kellogg, F. (1977) 'From Retribution to Desert', *Criminology*, 15: 79–192.

Kleinig, J. (1973) *Punishment and Desert*, The Hague: Martinus Nijhoff.

Kleinig, J. (1991) 'Punishment and Moral Seriousness', *Israel Law Review*, 25: 401–421.

Kleinig, J. (2008) *Ethics and Criminal Justice*, Cambridge: Cambridge University Press.

Kolakowski, L. (1990) *Modernity on Endless Trial*, Chicago: Chicago University Press.

Kramer, M. H. (2001) 'Getting Rights Right', in M. H. Kramer (ed.), *Rights and Wrongs and Responsibilities*, Basingstoke: Palgrave.

Kristjánsson, K. (2005) 'A Utilitarian Justification of Desert in Distributive Justice', *Journal of Moral Philosophy*, 2 (2): 147–170.

Kymlicka, W. (1989) *Liberalism, Community and Culture*, Oxford: Clarendon Press.

Lacey, N. (1988) *State Punishment: Political Principles and Community Values*, London: Routledge.

Lacey, N. (2007) 'Space, Time and Function: Intersecting Principles of Responsibility across the Terrain of Criminal Justice', *Criminal Law and Philosophy*, 1: 233–250.

Lamont, J. (1994) 'The Concept of Desert in Distributive Justice', *The Philosophical Quarterly*, 44 (174): 45–64.

Lea, J. and Young, J. (1984) *What Is To Be Done about Law and Order?*, Harmondsworth: Penguin.

Leonard, E. (1982) *Women, Crime and Society: A Critique of Criminological Theory*, New York: Longman.

Lerman, P. (1975) *Community Treatment and Social Control*, Chicago: University of Chicago Press.

Lipton, D., Martinson, R. and Wilks, J. (1975) *The Effectiveness of Correctional Treatment*, New York: Praeger.

Locke, J. (1988) *Two Treatises of Government*, ed. Peter Laslett, Cambridge: Cambridge University Press.

Lyons, D. (1969) 'Rights, Claimants and Beneficiaries', *American Philosophical Quarterly*, 6: 173–185.

Lyons, D. (1992) 'Bentham, Utilitarianism and Distribution', *Utilitas*, 4 (2): 323–8.

Macey, J. R. (1994) 'Judicial Preferences, Public Choice, and the Rules of Procedure', *Journal of Legal Studies*, 23 (1): 627–646.

Machan, T. (1983) 'Social Contract as a Basis of Norms: A Critique', *Journal of Liberal Studies*, 7: 141–146.

MacIntyre, A. (1981) *After Virtue: A Study in Moral Theory*, London: Duckworth.

Mackie, J. L. (1985) *Persons and Values*, Oxford: Clarendon Press.

MacKinnon, C. (1987) *Feminism Unmodified: Discourses on Life and Law*, Cambridge, MA: Harvard University Press.

MacKinnon, C. (1992) 'Feminism, Marxism, Method and the State: An Agenda for Theory', in M. Humm (ed.), *Feminisms: A Reader*, Hemel Hempstead: Harvester.

Macleod, A. M. (2005) 'Distributive Justice and Desert', *Journal of Social Philosophy*, 36 (4): 421–438.

Maitland, F. W. (1911) 'Moral Personality and Legal Personality', in H. A. L. Fisher (ed.), *The Collected Papers of Frederick William Maitland*, Volume 3, Cambridge: Cambridge University Press.

Marshall, T. (1999) *Restorative Justice: An Overview*. London: Home Office.

Marx, K. (1853) 'On Capital Punishment', *New York Daily Tribune*, 28 February.

Marx, K. (1964) *Class Struggles in France*, New York: International Publishers.

Marx, K. (1965) *Capital: a critical analysis of capitalist production*, London: Lawrence and Wishart.

Marx, K. (1968) *Selected Writings*, London: Lawrence and Wishart.

Marx, K. (1973 [1852]) *The Eighteenth Brumaire of Louis Bonaparte*, trans. B. Fowkes, in *Surveys from Exile*, Harmondsworth: Penguin.

Marx, K. (1976a) *The German Ideology*, ed. C. J. Arthur, London: Lawrence and Wishart.

Marx, K. (1976b) 'The Communist Manifesto', in *Marx and Engels Collected Works*, London: Lawrence and Wishart.

Marx, K. (1978) 'The German Ideology', in R. Tucker (ed.), *The Marx–Engels Reader*, New York: W. W. Norton.

Marx, K. (1987) 'On the Jewish Question', in J. Waldron (ed.), *Nonsense upon Stilts: Bentham, Burke and Marx on the Rights of Man*, London: Methuen.

Marx, K. and Engels, F. (1974) *The German Ideology*, ed. C. L. Arthur, London: Lawrence and Wishart.

Matravers, M. D. (1994) 'Justice and Punishment: The Rationale for Coercion', unpublished PhD thesis, London: School of Economics, London.

May, D. C., Wood, P. B., Mooney, J. L. and Minor, K. I. (2005) 'Predicting Offender-generated Exchange Rates: Implications for a Theory of Sentence Severity', *Crime & Delinquency*, 51 (3): 373–399.

McConville, S. (ed.) (2003) *The Use of Punishment*, Cullompton: Willan Publishing.

McLaughlin, E. (2007) *The New Policing*, London: Sage.

McMillan, D. and Chavis, D. (1986) 'Sense of Community: A Definition and Theory', *Journal of Community Psychology*, 83: 6–23.

Mearman, A. (2005) 'Sheila Dow's Concept of Dualism: Clarification, Criticism and Development', *Cambridge Journal of Economics*, 29 (4): 619–634.

Melossi, D. (1980) 'The Penal Question in *Capital*', in T. Platt and P. Takagi (eds), *Punishment and Penal Discipline*, Berkeley, CA: Center for Research on Criminal Justice.

Merton, R. K. (1968) *Social Theory and Social Structure*, New York: The Free Press.

Merton, R. K. (1993) 'Social Structure and Anomie', in C. Lemert (ed.), *Social Theory: The Multicultural Readings*, Boulder, CO: Westview Press.

Messner, S. and Rosenfeld, R. (2001) *Crime and the American Dream*, Belmont, CA: Wadsworth.

Metz, T. (1999) 'Realism and the Censure Theory of Punishment', *Proceedings of the 19th World Congress of the International Association for Philosophy of Law and Social Philosophy*, (IUR) New York, June 24–30, pp. 116–129.

Miethe, T. D. and Lu, H. (2005) *Punishment: A Comparative Historical Perspective*, Cambridge: Cambridge University Press.

Mill, J. S. (1962) 'Essay on Liberty', in *Utilitarianism*, ed. M. Warnock, London: Collins.

Mill, J. S. (1979) *Utilitarianism*, Indianapolis, IN: Hackett Publishing.

Moore, G. E. (1956) *Principia Ethica*, Cambridge: Cambridge University Press.

Morris, H. (1968) 'Persons and Punishment', *The Monist*, 52: 475–501.

Morris, H. (1981) 'A Paternalistic Theory of Punishment', *American Philosophy Quarterly*, 18 (4): 263–271.

Mosselmans, B. (2005) 'Adolphe Quetelet, the Average Man and the Development of Economic Methodology', *European Journal of Economic Thought*, 12 (4): 565–582.

Moyer, I. L. (2001) *Criminological Theories: Traditional and Non-traditional Voices and Themes*, London: Sage.

Murphy, J. (1985) 'Retributivism, Moral Education and the Liberal State', *Criminal Justice Ethics*, 4: 3–11.

Murphy, J. E. (1995) 'Marxism and Retribution', reprinted in Simmons, J., Cohen, M., Cohen, J. and Beitz, C. R., *Punishment: A Philosophy and Public Affairs Reader*. Princeton, NJ: Princeton University Press.

Myerson, R. B. (1997) *Game Theory: Analysis of Conflict*, Cambridge, MA: Harvard University Press.

Newburn, T. (2002) 'Community Safety and Policing: Some Implications of the Crime and Disorder Act 1998', in G. Hughes, E. McLaughlin and J. Muncie (eds), *Crime Prevention and Community Safety: New Directions*, London: Sage.

Northrop, F. S. C. (1959) *The Complexity of Legal and Ethical Experience*, Boston, MA: Little, Brown and Co.

Oakeshott, M. (1991) *Rationalism in Politics*, Indianapolis, IN: Liberty Fund.

Oizerman, T. I. (1981) 'Kant's Doctrine of the "Things in Themselves" and Noumena', *Philosophy and Phenomenological Research*, 41 (3): 333–350.

O'Malley, P. (2004) 'Globalising Risk? Distinguishing Styles of Neoliberal Criminal Justice in Australia and the USA', in T. Newburn and R. Sparks (eds), *Criminal Justice and Political Cultures: National and International Dimensions of Crime Control*, Cullompton: Willan Publishing.

O'Neill, M. E., Drazga Maxfield, L. and Harer, M. (2004) 'Past as Prologue: Reconciling Recidivism and Culpability', *Fordham Law Review*, 73: 245–296.

Parfit, D. (1984) *Reasons and Persons*, Oxford: Oxford University Press.

Pashukanis, E. B. (1978) *Law and Marxism: A General Theory*, London: Academic Press.

Pateman, C. (1988) *The Sexual Contract*, Cambridge: Polity Press.

Pateman, C. (1991) 'God Hath Ordained to Man a Helper: Hobbes, Patriarchy and Conjugal Rights', in M. L. Stanley and C. Pateman (eds), *Feminist Interpretations and Political Theory*, Cambridge: Polity Press.

Pateman, C. (2002) 'Self-ownership and Property in the Person: Democratization and a Tale of Two Concepts', *Journal of Political Philosophy*, 10: 20–53.

Pearson, F. S. and Lipton, D. S. (1999) 'A Meta-analytic Review of the Effectiveness of Corrections-based Treatments for Drug Abuse', *Prison Journal*, 79: 384–410.

Pettit, P. (2000) 'Non-consequentialism and Universalizability', *The Philosophical Quarterly*, 50 (199): 175–190.

Pettit, P. and Braithwaite, J. (1993) 'Not Just Deserts Even in Sentencing', *Current Issues in Criminal Justice*, 4: 225–239.

Phillips, A. (2000) 'Feminism and Republicanism: Is This a Plausible Alliance?', *The Journal of Political Philosophy*, 8: 282–283.

Phillips, D. L. (1993) *Looking Backward: A Critical Appraisal of Communitarian Thought*, Princeton, NJ: Princeton University Press.

Pincoffs, E. A. (1966) *The Rationale of Legal Punishment*, Atlantic Highlands, NJ: Humanities Press.

Plato (1960) *Gorgias*, London: Penguin.

Plato (1970) *Laws*, London: Penguin.

Plato (1974) *The Republic*, London: Penguin.

Plato (1991) *Protagoras*, Oxford: Clarendon Press.

Posner, R. (1985) 'An Economic Theory of Criminal Law', *Columbia Law Review*, 85: 1193–1231.

Posner, R. (1999) *The Problems of Jurisprudence*, Cambridge, MA: Harvard University Press.

Postema, G. J. (1986) *Bentham and the Common Law Tradition*, Oxford: Oxford University Press.

Poulantzas, N. (1973) *Political Power and Social Class*, London: NLB.

Poulantzas, N. (1978) *State Power and Socialism*, London: Verso.

Presdee, M. (2000) *Cultural Criminology and the Carnival of Crime*, London: Routledge.

Primoratz, I. (1989) 'Punishment as Language', *Philosophy*, 64: 187–205.

Raphael, D. D. (1955) *Moral Judgement*, London: George Allen and Unwin.

Rawls, J. (1955) 'Two Concepts of Rules', *The Philosophical Review*, 64 (1): 3–32.

Rawls, J. (1958) 'Justice as Fairness', *Philosophical Review*, 67: 164–194.

Rawls, J. (1973) *A Theory of Justice*, Oxford: Oxford University Press.

Rawls, J. (1977) 'The Basic Structure as Subject', *American Philosophical Quarterly*, 14 (2): 159–165.

Rawls, J. (1993) *Political Liberalism*, New York: Columbia University Press.

Rawls, J. (2001) *Justice as Fairness: A Restatement*, Cambridge, MA: Harvard University Press.

Raz, J. (1979) *The Authority of Law*, Oxford: Clarendon Press.

Raz, J. (1986) *The Morality of Freedom*, Oxford: Clarendon Press.

Raz, J. (1988) *The Morality of Freedom*, Oxford: Clarendon Press.

Reiman, J. (1985) 'Civilisation and the Death Penalty: Answering van den Haag', *Philosophy and Public Affairs*, 14: 115–148.

Reiner, R. (2000) *The Politics of the Police* (3rd edition), Oxford: Oxford University Press.

Reiner, R. (2002) 'Classical Social Theory and Law', in J. Penner, D. Schiff and R. Nobles (eds), *Jurisprudence*, London: Butterworth.

Reiner, R. (2007) 'Political Economy, Crime and Criminal Justice', in M. Maguire et al. (eds), *The Oxford Handbook of Criminology*, Oxford: Oxford University Press.

Richardson, J. (2007) 'Contemporary Feminist Perspectives on Social Contract Theory', *Ratio Juris*, 20 (3): 402–423.

Roshier, B. (1989) *Controlling Crime*, Milton Keynes: Open University Press.

Rosen, A. D. (1993) *Kant's Theory of Justice*, Ithaca, NY: Cornell University Press.

Ross, W. D. (1965) *The Right and the Good*, Oxford: Clarendon Press.

Rowe, C. J. (1984) *Plato*, Brighton: Harvester.

Rusche, G. and Kirchheimer, O. (2003) *Punishment and Social Structure*, New Brunswick, NJ: Transaction.

Sadurski, W. (1983) 'Contractarianism and Intuition: On the Role of Social Contract Arguments in Theories of Justice', *Australasian Journal of Philosophy*, 61: 321–347.

Sadurski, W. (1985) *Giving Desert Its Due*, Dordrecht: Lancaster.

Sandel, M. (1982) *Liberalism and the Limits of Justice*, Cambridge: Cambridge University Press.

Sanders, A. and Young, R. (2007) 'From Suspect to Trial', in M. Maguire et al. (eds), *The Oxford Handbook of Criminology*, Oxford: Oxford University Press.

Schaefer, D. (1979) *Justice or Tyranny? A Critique of John Rawls' Theory of Justice*, Port Washington, New York: Kennikat Press.

Schwarzmantel, J. (1994) *The State in Contemporary Society*, Hemel Hempstead: Harvester Press.

Scruton, R. (1984) *The Meaning of Conservatism* (2nd edition), Basingstoke and London: Macmillan.

Scruton, R. (1991) *Conservative Texts*, New York: St Martin's Press.

Segal, L. (1991) 'Whose Left? Socialism, Feminism and the Future', in R. Blackburn (ed.), *After the Fall*, London: Verso.

Selznick, P. (1994) 'Foundations of Communitarian Liberalism', *The Responsive Community*, 4: 16–28.

Sheerman, B. (1991) 'What Labour Wants', *Policing*, 7 (3): 194–203.

Shenoy, P. and Martin, R. (1983) 'Two Interpretations of the Difference Principle in Rawls's Theory of Justice', *Theoria*, 49 (3): 113–141.

Shepsle, K. A. and Weingast, B. R. (1984) 'When Do Rules of Procedure Matter?', *Journal of Politics*, 46 (1): 206–221.

Sher, G. (1987) *Desert*, Princeton, NJ: Princeton University Press.

Showstack-Sassoon, A. (1987) *Gramsci's Politics*, London: Hutchinson.

Sidgwick, H. (1963) *The Methods of Ethics*, London: Macmillan.

Sivanandan, A. (2006) 'Race, Terror and Civil Society', *Race and Class*, 47 (3): 1–8.

Smith, P. and Natalier, K. (2005) *Understanding Criminal Justice: Sociological Perspectives*, London: Sage.

Squires, P. and Stephen, D. (2005) *Rougher Justice: Anti-social Behaviour and Young People*, Cullompton: Willan Publishing.

Stenson, K. (2002) 'Crime Control, Social Policy and Liberalism', in G. Lewis et al. (eds), *Rethinking Social Policy*, London: Sage.

Stenson, K. and Sullivan, R. (2000) *Crime, Risk and Justice*, Cullompton: Willan Publishing.

Stone, N. (2004) 'Legal Commentary: Orders in Respect of Anti-social Behaviour: Recent Judicial Developments', *Youth Justice*, 4: 46–54.

Strauss, L. (1936) *The Political Philosophy of Hobbes: Its Basis and Its Genesis*, Oxford: Oxford University Press.

Strauss, L. (1950) 'On the Spirit of Hobbes' Political Philosophy', *Revue Internationale de Philosophie*, 4 (14): 30–50.

Strauss, L. (1953) *Natural Right and History*, Chicago: University of Chicago Press.

Strawson, P. F. (1974) *Freedom and Resentment*, London: Methuen.

Sumner, C. S. (1979) *Reading Ideologies*, London: Academic Press.

Sumner, C. S. (1981) 'Race, Crime and Hegemony', *Contemporary Crises*, 5 (3): 277–291.

Sumner, C. S. (1983) 'Law, Legitimation and the Advanced Capitalist State: The Jurisprudence and Social Theory of Jürgen Habermas', in D. Sugarman (ed.), *Legality, Ideology and the State*, London: Academic Press.

Sumner, C. S. (1990) *Censure, Politics and Criminal Justice*, Buckingham: Open University Press.

Sumner, C. S. (1994) *The Sociology of Deviance: An Obituary*, Milton Keynes: Open University Press.

Sumner, C. S. (2004) 'The Social Nature of Crime and Deviance' in C. S. Sumner (ed.), *Blackwell Companion to Criminology*, Oxford: Blackwell.

Taylor, C. (2004) *Modern Social Imaginaries*, Durham, NC: Duke University Press.

Taylor, I., Walton, P. and Young, J. (1973) *The New Criminology*, London: Routledge.

Thornberry, T. and Christensen, R. (1984) 'Unemployment and Criminal Involvement', *American Sociological Review*, 49: 398–411.

Tolstoy, L. N. (2005) *Resurrection*, Kila, MT: Kessinger Publishing.

Tonry, M. (1996) *Sentencing Matters*, New York: Oxford University Press.

Tonry, M. (2004) *Punishment and Politics*, Cullompton: Willan Publishing.

Tonry, M. and Frase, R. S. (eds) (2001) *Sentencing and Sanctions in Western Countries*, Oxford: Oxford University Press.

Trasler, G. (1993) 'Conscience, Opportunity, Rational Choice and Crime', in R. V. Clarke and M. Felson (eds), *Advances in Criminological Theory*, New Brunswick, NJ: Transaction.

Tunnick, M. (1992a) *Hegel's Political Philosophy: Interpreting the Practice of Legal Punishment*. Princeton, NJ: Princeton University Press.

Tunnick, M. (1992b) *Punishment Theory and Practice*, Berkeley, CA: University of California Press.

Vishniac, R. (1983) *A Vanished World*, New York: Noonday Press.

von Hirsch, A. (1976) *Doing Justice: The Choice of Punishments*, New York: Hill & Wang.

von Hirsch, A. (1978) 'Proportionality and Desert: A Reply to Bedau', *Journal of Philosophy*, 75: 622–624.

von Hirsch, A. (1986) *Past or Future Crimes*, Manchester: Manchester University Press.

von Hirsch, A. (1990) 'The Politics of Just Deserts', *Canadian Journal of Criminology*, 397 (32): 397–413.

von Hirsch, A. (1993) *Censure and Sanctions*, Oxford: Clarendon Press.

von Hirsch, A. (2002) 'Record-enhanced Sentencing in England and Wales: Reflections on the Halliday Report's Proposed Treatment of Prior Convictions', *Punishment and Society*, 4 (4): 443–457.

von Hirsch, A. and Ashworth, A. (2005) *Proportionate Sentencing: Exploring the Principles*, Oxford: Oxford University Press.

von Hirsch, A. and Maher, L. (1998) 'Should Penal Rehabilitationism be Revived?', in A. von Hirsch and A. Ashworth (eds), *Principled Sentencing: Readings on Theory and Policy*. Oxford: Hart Publishing.

von Hirsch, A., Bottoms, A. E., Burney, E., Wikstom, P-O. (1999) *Criminal Deterrence and Sentence Severity: An Analysis of Recent Research*, Oxford: Hart Publishing.

Waddington, P., Stenson, K. and Don, D. (2004) 'In Proportion: Race and Police Stop and Search', *British Journal of Criminology*, 44 (6): 889–914.

Waddington, P. A. J. (2006) *Policing Citizens*, London: Routledge.

Walker, N. (1991) *Why Punish?*, Oxford: Oxford University Press.

Walklate, S. (2003) *Understanding Criminology: Current Theoretical Debates*, Buckingham: Open University Press.

Wallach, J. (1987) 'Liberal Communitarianism and the Tasks of Political Theory', *Political Theory*, 15: 581–611.

Walsh, A. (2000) 'Behaviour, Genetics and Anomie/Strain Theory', *Criminology*, 38: 1075–1108.

Webster, C. Simpson, D., MacDonald, R., Abbas, A., Cieslik, M., Shildrick, T. and Simpson, M. (2004) *Poor Transitions: Social Exclusion and Young Adults*, Bristol: Policy Press.

Williams, B. A. O. (1981) *Moral Luck*, Cambridge: Cambridge University Press.

Woolf, H. (1991) *Prison Disturbances, April 1990: A Report of Inquiry*, London: HMSO.

Young, J. (1986) 'The Failure of Criminology: The Need for Radical Realism', in R. Matthews and J. Young (eds), *Confronting Crime*, London: Sage.

Zedner, L. (2004) *Criminal Justice*, Oxford: Oxford University Press.

Zimring, F. E. and Hawkins, G. (1991) *The Scale of Imprisonment*. New York: Oxford University Press.

INDEX

This index is in word-by-word alphabetical order. Glossary entries are indicated by an asterisk (*) after the page number, e.g. censure, 143*.

police/policing *cont.*
  and minority rights, 59
  multi-social, 48
  regulating social relationships
      (Hegel), 52
  senior personnel, distance of, 60
  of terrorism, 59–60
positivism, 48, 75, 145*
Posner, R., 72
Poulantzas, N.
  Political Power and Social Class, 7
  State, Power and Socialism, 7
power relations, 53–4, 61, 126
  and censure, 91–6
  and morality, 92, 126
powers (rights), 33
Presdee, M., 25
prevention orders, 38–9
Primoratz, I., 77, 106
prison and recidivism, 15
prisoners' rights, 31, 39
private property
  basis of social relations, 33, 51
  defended by law, 50–1
  guardianship (Cicero), 50–1
  and punishment, 4–5
probation, 121
'property of the person' (Hobbes), 10
proportionality, 99, 104–11, 145*
  and ASBOs, 109
  cardinal and ordinal, 106–7
  and censure, 77, 89, 105–6
  final warnings, 110–11
  and Just Deserts, 70
  lex talionis, 67, 107–8
  move away from, 109–10
  necessity for, 111–12
  and rehabilitation, 75
  and restorative justice (RJ), 108
  in sentencing, 80, 108–9
  thin and thick, 107
punishment, 65–81
  backward/forward-looking, 66
  censure, 76–8, 81, 85–97, 143*
  consequentialist theory, 71–2
  contemporary justifications for, 104–5
  as a debt (Kant), 34
  deterrence, 71, 72–4, 118–19
  ideological in eighteenth century
      England, 4–5
  incapacitation, 76
  means of enforcing agreed rules, 65–70
  as moral, 66, 69, 70

punishment *cont.*
  paid as debt (Kant), 33
  proportionality, 99, 104–11, 145*
  reflecting prevailing convention, 91
  and rehabilitation, 69–70, 74–5,
      118, 119
  and restorative justice, 78–9, 81
  retributive, 42–3, 67–71, 80, 104
  and reward, 101–2
  and rewards of crime, 25–6
  severity of penalties, 120–1
  therapeutic, 69–70
  utilitarian, 69, 71–2, 80, 118, 119
  see also desert; fairness; Just Deserts;
      sentencing

Quetelet, A., 14–17, 26, 132

rational choice theory, 25–6, 27, 117, 118
Rawls, J.
  criminals as freeriders, 133
  fairness, 68, 91, 111, 117–29, 123
  freedom of action, 93, 94, 95
  Justice as Fairness, 11
  moral desert, 99
  nature of the state, 1, 2
  Political Liberalism, 2
  rights, 32, 33
  Theory of Justice, A, 33, 91, 123, 133
Raz, J., 2, 3, 11, 30
rebellion, 21
Regulation of Investigatory Powers Act
      2000, 38
rehabilitation, 69–70, 74–5, 145*
  criticisms of, 69–70, 75
  and disparities of treatment, 75, 119
  means of social control, 70
  need for infrastucture of professionals, 74
Reiner, R., 25, 27, 47, 53, 59
reparation, 102
resentment, 101, 102
respect for persons, 92–3, 95, 125, 126
restorative justice (RJ), 78–9, 81, 146*
retreatism, 21
retribution, 34, 67–71, 80, 104, 146*
  benefits and burdens, 105
  and class, 42–3
  see also desert
reward, 101–2
Richardson, J., 11
rights, 30–44, 146*
  awareness of, 39–40
  and community, 42, 43